CHRISTIANS IN THE MARKETPLACE SERIES
Biblical Principles and Business: The Practice

Richard C. Chewning, Ph.D., Series Editor

NAVPRESS

A MINISTRY OF THE NAVIGATORS
P.O. BOX 6000, COLORADO SPRINGS, COLORADO 80934

The Navigators is an international Christian organization. Jesus Christ gave His followers the Great Commission to go and make disciples (Matthew 28:19). The aim of The Navigators is to help fulfill that commission by multiplying laborers for Christ in every nation.

NavPress is the publishing ministry of The Navigators. NavPress publications are tools to help Christians grow. Although publications alone cannot make disciples or change lives, they can help believers learn biblical discipleship, and apply what they learn to their lives and ministries.

Scripture quotations in this publication are from several translations: the *King James Version* (KJV); *The Living Bible* (TLB), © 1971 owned by assignment by Illinois Regional Bank N.A. (as trustee), used by permission of Tyndale House Publishers, Wheaton, Illinois, all rights reserved; the *New American Standard Bible* (NASB), © The Lockman Foundation, 1960, 1962, 1963, 1968, 1971, 1972, 1973, 1975, 1977; the *Holy Bible: New International Version* (NIV), copyright © 1973, 1978, 1984, International Bible Society and used by permission of Zondervan Bible Publishers; the *Revised Standard Version Bible* (RSV), copyright 1946, 1952, 1971, by the Division of Christian Education of the National Council of the Churches of Christ in the U.S.A., and used by permission with all rights reserved.

The individual authors of this book have used the following translations unless otherwise noted:
Chewning—NASB; Packer—NIV; Musser—NIV; Rush—NIV; Talarzyk—NASB; Dunkerton—NIV; Harrison—NIV; Haggai—RSV; Hoover—NIV; Mellichamp—NASB; Lavelle—NIV; Potter—NIV; Burkett—NASB; Sparks—NIV.

The Code of Ethics of the American Marketing Association is reprinted by permission of the American Marketing Association, 250 South Wacker Drive, Chicago, Illinois 60606-5819.

Printed in the United States of America

CONTENTS

SERIES EDITOR

Dr. Richard C. Chewning is the Chavanne Professor of Christian Ethics in Business at the Hankamer School of Business of Baylor University in Waco, Texas. He received baccalaureate, master's, and Ph.D. degrees, all in business, from Virginia Polytechnic Institute, the University of Virginia, and the University of Washington, respectively. He began formal academic training in business ethics and corporate social responsibility as a doctoral student and pursued postdoctoral study in comparative ethics at St. Mary's College, the seminary arm of the University of St. Andrews in Scotland.

Dr. Chewning began teaching at the University of Richmond in 1958 where he taught finance, served for some years as a department chairman, and also as an academic dean. In 1979 he was invited by the business faculty to develop and teach courses in the field of business ethics. He moved to Baylor University in 1985. He has published over forty-five essays and articles integrating Scripture with business and economics, and he has authored and coauthored books in the field of ethics and business from a biblical perspective, including *Business Ethics in a Changing Culture* and *Business Through the Eyes of Faith*.

For years Dr. Chewning has been a consultant to government bodies, trade associations, and corporations in matters of both finance and ethics, while maintaining a busy schedule of public lectures and seminar participation. He is the editor of the CHRISTIANS IN THE MARKETPLACE SERIES. Volume 1 is *Biblical Principles & Business: The Foundations* and Volume 2 is *Biblical Principles & Economics: The Foundations*.

ACKNOWLEDGMENTS

Dr. Talarzyk extends special appreciation to Roger Blackwell, Peter Dickson, and Paul Richard for their input to the development of his chapter.

Dr. Mellichamp is indebted to Marcus Brown, Charles Schmidt, and Dorian Yeager, colleagues in information systems and operations research, for sharing their views.

PREFACE

The foundations are laid! Eighteen biblical principles that reveal part of God's thinking about business and economics have been identified by the twenty-four scholars who contributed to the first two volumes in the CHRISTIANS IN THE MARKETPLACE SERIES. Those principles ought to materially shape the most basic assumptions and beliefs Christians have about God's will for them as they form, maintain, and operate business, economic, and political institutions. Biblical principles were defined in an earlier volume as scriptural teachings that are identified through aggregating a number of individual biblical references addressing the same issue, albeit in different contexts (see page 15, Volume 1). For example, Deuteronomy 10:17; 2 Chronicles 19:7; Acts 10:34; Romans 2:11; Galatians 2:6; Ephesians 6:9; and James 2:9 all teach that "God is no respecter of persons," and Matthew 7:22-23; 12:36; Acts 10:42; 17:31; Romans 14:12; and 1 Peter 4:5 tell us that "we shall all give a full accounting to God for our thoughts and actions." These truths, being often repeated, may therefore be legitimately referred to as *biblical principles* and should be applied in life wherever they are pertinent.

In *Biblical Principles and Business: The Foundations*, and its companion volume, *Biblical Principles and Economics: The Foundations*, clear scriptural principles were named that highlight God's revealed will for us as we work and seek to obey Him in the marketplace. Through a greater understanding of God's will, we will be more aware of the constraints and liberties that ought to be incorporated in the very nature of our business and economic institutions. For example, once we recognize the importance God places on our having the ability to make moral choices, and His intentions for us to be stewards (managers) of the created order, it becomes contradictory for us to construct or support

7

economic and political institutions that inhibit responsible personal choices or artificially limit the opportunities for people to own and manage a portion of the natural wealth God has generally made available. Although God has not directed us to establish specific kinds of economic institutions and systems, the ones we form either complement or resist His larger purposes. For this reason, and many others, the biblical principles examined in the first two volumes of this series are extremely important.

1. We are moral creatures—making moral choices with moral repercussions—who are morally responsible for our decisions and actions.
2. God gave His image bearers the freedom to make moral choices, even at the cost of His Son's life, so we are to foster and guard the personal freedoms necessary for individuals to responsibly exercise their God-intended ability to choose in family, work, and worship environments.
3. God created us to work and have dominion over the created order.
4. Humankind is both "fallen" and "capable." This reality explains why humankind can, on the one hand, sink so low as to kill Someone who had never sinned (Christ) and, on the other hand, still accomplish great feats in science, engineering, art, music, and other areas when subduing and ruling the created order.
5. God has a perspective on business and economic practices, and He intends us to have the "mind of Christ" whereby we can acquire a true biblical view of life and the world in order to do His will in every sphere of life, including the marketplace.
6. God created us to both engage in and enjoy the functions and rewards of exchange—economic, social, and intellectual.
7. God created us with motivational characteristics that are externally stimulated by rewards and punishments, and internally moved by our attitudes, desires, and commitments. These are essential for creative and productive lives.
8. We can know those things that make an economic system compatible with God's revealed will and the natural order. For example:
   a. The economy should provide an opportunity for and encourage productivity that enhances the well-being of the general populace. No one who can work should be artificially denied access to work.
   b. Production of goods and services must be for sound moral "ends."
   c. The "ends" for production should include spiritual and temporal purposes.

    d. Resources should be neither wasted nor hoarded, but used efficiently.

    e. The use of all resources should be accompanied by trust in God and thankfulness to Him.

    f. Private ownership of property should be encouraged and protected.

    g. It is not wrong to earn profits by employing other people or by renting one's land and capital resources.

    h. There should be greater rewards for more work and for higher quality work.

    i. There should be rewards for those who cannot work but not for those who will not work.

    j. Individuals should give generously from their surplus to care for the needs of others.

9. Private property is central to the ideas of stewardship and personal moral choice. It is an integral part of biblical history and God's intended will for us as we work to fulfill the creation mandates and carry out the Great Commission.

10. Scripture does not reveal a dichotomy between the "sacred" and the "secular."

11. God calls many Christians to a primary "ministry" of work in the economic arenas of life where He wants them to manifest His character and quality of behavior.

12. Our intentions, thoughts, and actions in the marketplace are of equal importance to God as He works to remake us in Christ's image through the Holy Spirit's use of Scripture in conjunction with life's experiences.

13. Christians are to call for high moral standards in the marketplace. Such appeals are to be made on the grounds of conscience, common experience (loving another as one's self), natural law, moral law, and social mores.

14. There is a parity between and within the teachings of the Old and New Testaments, which means that all of Scripture is to be used in guiding our thoughts and actions in every area, including the marketplace.

15. God's Word contains many truths that seem to compete with one another for our allegiance or focus, but are intended to be received as "both/and" truths rather than as "either/or" propositions. Examples include: We are individuals/we are part of a community; human equality/inequality; law/grace; God's sovereignty/man's

responsibility; stewards/consumers; freedom/control; creation mandates/Great Commission; ruler/servant; and authority/submission.

16. While God's Word is absolute in character and truth, we are nevertheless responsible in our finitude and imperfection to assess situations and make responsible judgments for which we are accountable.

17. Biblically, "individualism" does not stand apart from our concomitant responsibilities toward our neighbors, communities, and those who govern us.

18. Christians are to manifest Christ's love—with their families, in their service to and relationships with other Christians, at play, and *in the marketplace.*

This third book in the CHRISTIANS IN THE MARKETPLACE SERIES shifts its focus from the biblical infrastructure that should undergird business, economic, and public policy programs and institutions and takes a look at the biblical principles that have direct application to the specific functional areas of business—strategic (long-range) management, operational management, marketing, advertising, accounting, organizational behavior, human resources, informational systems, operations research, banking, insurance, personal investment, and business law. These functional areas represent individual aspects of business in the same way that a hand or a foot is a part of a body. No single part is sufficient by itself, or complete without the other parts, but when properly related to one another, they form a functioning whole. In light of this fact it is hoped that this book will persuasively present the case that (1) God is interested in every aspect of business, from the smallest detail to the grandest accomplishment; (2) God's Word is always applicable and relevant to the conduct of business, even for the most mechanically oriented functions and in the most technically sophisticated environments; and (3) business is a God-ordained part of our interdependent social connectiveness—we were created to engage in exchange (social, economic, intellectual)—and is as vital an aspect of life to bring under the lordship of Christ as any other area.

Introducing these chapters, and describing the significance of their content, is a positioning chapter written by Dr. James I. Packer. Dr. Packer was the only theologian participating in this volume, and we were delighted that he would join the effort, for he is eminently capable of describing the larger purpose and hope underlying this particular volume. He has a longstanding and deep interest in the working out of God's call for us to be holy. In addition, he has an abiding commitment to the biblical teaching that personal holiness is to be pervasive and manifested in every dimension of our lives, even in the pressurized environment of the marketplace.

Dr. Packer discusses several basic tenets, such as the Christian's *duty* to accept involvement in the world of business organizations as a part of God's creation mandates; the *certainty* of conflict (provoked by the world and the Devil) as one lives for Christ in the marketplace; the *necessity* of business structures and organizations (we may not evade the task of sanctifying behavior within business structures, as if we could somehow operate without them); and numerous other beliefs commonly held by the authors. These beliefs create a bond between the authors that gives their work the shared purpose of encouraging and helping Christians to be holy in the marketplace.

Dr. Packer also draws attention to common problem posers regularly encountered in business. The chapters, while coming alongside these question-raising subjects, were not designed to address them head-on: the problems of handling *power*, achieving *fairness*, establishing *accountability*, and other similar subjects requiring moral judgment in the marketplace.[1] Dr. Packer concludes by acknowledging that God calls many of His children to serve Him in business, but not without noting that it is a tough calling requiring much support by the Holy Spirit and other Christians.

The twelve functional chapters following Dr. Packer's are of two types. The majority (ten of twelve) are topical; the authors identify specific issues, tasks, and responsibilities related to the business function under discussion (management, marketing, accounting, etc.) and show how specific biblical principles should guide our thinking and actions as we perform the functions. The other two chapters are personal faith testimonies that disclose the individuals' faith in God's integrity (faithfulness in keeping His promises) and His graciousness in honoring their faith as they have lived by it in the marketplace. Both approaches are essential to our understanding and appreciation of God's interaction with us in the business arena.

It is easy for Christians to slip into a mind-set in which God is treated as if He is limited to a particular method of sanctifying His children—too frequently the method experienced by the person speaking. For example, persons who diligently study the Bible and search for an ever-expanding cognitive grasp of God's precepts in order to integrate them in their lives can fall into the error of speaking and acting as if this is the only legitimate way God will lead and mature anyone. God works in this way, but it is not the only way.

Other Christians, though, hold onto specific promises God has impressed on their hearts, waiting for and expecting Him to providentially lead them through difficult situations. And He does! People who live this way often seem to exhibit an uncomplicated childlike faith (highly commended by Christ; see Matt. 18:1-4), and they bear witness to God's faithfulness as He protects and guides them through the labyrinths of the marketplace.

While both groups walk by faith, members of the first one seem to look to God to increase their understanding of His will so they can make decisions and take the actions necessary for them to navigate the shoals of life. The members of the second group seem to wait for and depend more on God's providential intervention in the affairs of their lives. One group appears to be more active and the other more passive, in certain situations. Both are biblical realities, and the following chapters illustrate both.

The material in this book makes no distinctions in regard to applying the biblical principles in a corporate culture or an entrepreneurial environment, in large or small businesses, or in free or regulated economic systems. This fact neither assumes nor implies that there are no differences in the application of biblical principles in the various environments. There are differences. For example, a corporate manager assumes the role of an agent who is stewarding the wealth of others while an entrepreneur is free to treat the assets of his or her business as personal property. The freedom to dispose of assets is not the same in the corporate and entrepreneurial environments. Stewardship responsibilities can and do differ as one moves across particular economic, legal, and structural boundaries. Since this entire series was designed, in part, to increase the awareness of biblical principles, encourage readers to learn how to discover and formulate biblical principles, and illustrate the general application of the biblical principles in the context of specific business functions, the differences in application that can and do arise as a result of the diversity and complexity of the marketplace were simply subordinated to the accomplishment of these broader objectives.

Richard C. Chewning
Chavanne Professor of Christian
Ethics in Business
Hankamer School of Business
Baylor University
Waco, Texas

PART I

RECOVERING RELATIONAL HOLINESS IN THE MARKETPLACE

We do not know if God intends for our generation to be effective leaven in the marketplace, bringing about a resurgence there of the Judeo-Christian ethic, but we do know, without a doubt, that He wants us to be holy as we work in our businesses. We also know that God wants us to be both personally holy and relationally holy—bringing biblical standards to bear on business relationships in a manner that elicits responsible conduct from those exposed to our influence. The Apostle Peter, for example, declares, "Gird your minds for action, keep sober in spirit. . . . Do not be conformed to the former lusts which were yours in your ignorance, but like the Holy One who called you, *be holy yourselves also in all your behavior*; because it is written, 'You shall be holy, for I am holy'" (1 Pet. 1:13-16, emphasis added).

We understand that this is our call, but we do not always understand what is concretely involved in the relational aspects of our call to holiness, especially in the midst of the rough and tumble of business. The difficulty arises, in the editor's opinion, not so much from any intellectual misunderstanding about the fact that we are called to "be holy," to "do justice," or to "act righteously" in the marketplace, but from our failure to ask and flesh out the hard questions that would cause us to focus on the specifics of just what is entailed. Simply being told that we are to "do justice" (Mic. 6:8) does not tell us what it means to do justice toward our competitors or employees, for example. We must dig deep into God's Word and relate it carefully to our daily tasks if an understanding is to be forthcoming and our wills are to be responsive.

This book begins this tough process. There are two distinct approaches by which this fleshing out of God's will can take place. One approach is to examine the common, interdisciplinary *activities* of business—planning, controlling,

13

communicating, exercising authority (power), requiring accountability, and so on—and grapple with them in the light of Scripture. This approach has the advantage of allowing us to think about a particular issue in view of scriptural wisdom (planning, for example; see Prov. 16:9; 19:21; 20:5; Luke 12:54-56; James 4:13-16) and of drawing some general conclusions about how God's principles might be applied to the specific activity.

In a *functional* approach biblical principles that bear on particular business functions, such as accounting, marketing, and management, are identified and applied to our thinking and behavior.

The editor decided to pursue the functional approach for three reasons. First, people generally have a closer *identity* with the functions they perform— accounting, marketing, advertising—than they do with particular activities they engage in, such as communicating, planning, or thinking about accountability. The functional approach has the potential of having a greater impact on those on the firing line of business simply because their identity is much more likely to be associated with the broad functional areas they work in rather than with the specific activities they perform.

Second, the editor believes the functional approach will enable those who are not formally educated in the field of business but who are, for example, educated in engineering, the liberal arts, or the sciences to see more concretely how biblical principles should influence their perceptions and conduct as they carry out their roles in business. Furthermore, this approach will also help those who are in the upper echelons of management, where functional integration is required, to understand how biblical principles apply to the functional areas they work with but were not trained in.

Finally, this approach is new and fresh. Work has been done on integrating Scripture with the commonly encountered *activities* of business, as noted in the Preface, but the *functions* have not been addressed (apart from some substantial efforts in management) because no individual Christian is competent to address, on an in-depth basis and from a biblical perspective, all of the functional areas of business. For this reason, the functional approach has gone begging. The decision to have twelve Christian professionals, each of whom has been called to labor for Christ in a particular functional area of business, write a chapter identifying the biblical principles that most pointedly speak to their discipline, and to integrate the principles with the functions, has provided a significant body of material that should go a long way toward filling this void.

Dr. Packer was willing to join the business scholars, and be the lone theologian in their midst, because he is burdened to see holiness manifested in the lives of all God's people, and this project provided him another opportunity to join in the call for biblical holiness—holiness that produces personal and relational results. He was invited because of his widely recognized ability to do just this. It is his earnest desire, and the fervent hope of the editor, that this pioneering effort will stimulate an ever deeper and wider commitment on the part of those called by God to work in the marketplace to foster relational holiness there. Biblically, it is a contradiction of terms to seek God's face, to delight to know His ways, and to love the sense of His nearness while failing to be relationally holy in the marketplace (see Isa. 58:1-12).

CHAPTER 1

THE CHRISTIAN'S PURPOSE IN BUSINESS

James I. Packer

Educated at Oxford University, J. I. Packer is an Episcopal minister who has spent most of his working life as a teacher of theology. Since 1979 he has been Professor of Historical and Systematic Theology at Regent College, Vancouver, B.C. Among his books are Knowing God, Evangelism and The Sovereignty of God, Fundamentalism and The Word of God, I Want To Be A Christian, God's Words, God Has Spoken, *and* Hot Tub Religion. *He is a Senior Editor of* Christianity Today. *Married, with three adult children, he counts among his other interests music, literature, railroads, English cricket, and silent film comedy.*

SECULARITY AND THE PRIVATIZATION OF RELIGION

A sk where the action is in community life today almost anywhere in the world, and the answer is this: with the businessmen. Ask who are the businessmen, and you find that they fall into two types. In the front line are the manufacturers and distributors, the managers and marketers, the industrialists and entrepreneurs, the developers of real estate and of commercial technology, the traders in raw materials and artifacts. Right behind them stand those who sustain the support structure for the industrial base—bankers, insurers, accountants, advertisers, consultants, construction men, and so on. The captains of industry and the commanders of capital are the focal figures of modern society, for modern society is wealth-conscious and wealth-seeking, and these persons are the creators and conservers of wealth. Politicians may facilitate the creation of wealth and determine to some extent its distribution, but the two sorts of businessmen working in partnership produce it, and in that sense the action is with them rather than with anyone else.

If you had asked where the action was in the world of five centuries ago, you would have gotten a different answer. To start with, there was nothing like so much wealth-creating enterprise in those days as there is now. Economically as well as geographically and demographically, communities were relatively static. Landowners and tenant farmers made some money from the land by herding animals and harvesting crops; merchants with ships imported exotic things for sale at high prices; traders in textiles turned a profit, too. But industry was no more than cottage industry, and such private moneylending as went on had more to do with keeping various sorts of wolves from the door than with moneymaking strategies. Governments concerned themselves with imperial rather than economic power; rulers taxed their subjects to maintain their kingdoms, and that was that. It was quite a different world.

What changed everything was the arrival of manufacturing machines and of large-scale capital-raising facilities (banks and the stock market). Well is this twofold development called the industrial revolution. In terms of mind-set, lifestyle, and social structure, it turned the Western world upside-down. The monetary economy swallowed up the agrarian economy that was there before, and wealth-creating business activity became the mainspring of community life. As a result of the success with which England, parts of Western Europe, and the United States pioneered all this in the nineteenth century, industrialization is now a global goal, and loans to enable younger nations to industrialize have become a major and probably permanent element in the world's financial system. Business as the basis of national life everywhere has come to stay.

The industrial revolution prospered in a world that had only just begun to feel the impact of the anti-Christian rationalism of the French Revolution and the post-Christian philosophies stemming from Descartes, Hume, Kant, and Hegel. Britain and the United States of America were predominantly Protestant, and the historic Protestant concern for truth, honesty, and fair dealing as expressions of neighbor-love kept breaking surface as the industrial establishment grew. The worst inhumanities that cropped up in mines and factories were brought under control, churches and Christian home missions ministered to industrial laborers, workers' rights came to be acknowledged, and Christian philanthropists using money made in business to enrich the less fortunate became familiar figures. A broadly evangelical Christianity presided over the whole nineteenth-century development, and though it was often honored more in the breach than in the observance, and was sometimes used to justify indefensible things like slavery and poverty, there was at least national agreement on the standards by which, and the purposes for which, community development in all its forms should be regulated. Most communities entertained the postmillennial expectation that history under God would end with Heaven on earth—a converted world enjoying universal peace and prosperity—and the wealth-creating potential of the market and the industrial establishment was welcomed and applauded as part of the emerging pattern. The mighty dollar was generally perceived as furthering the Kingdom of the mighty God.

Our century, however, has seen a marginalizing both of evangelical leadership in the churches and of the churches themselves in the larger national communities. In place of evangelical ethics, an outlook compounded of secular humanism, skeptical materialism, and relativistic pragmatism has come to dominate the Western business world, as it has Western education and intellectual culture generally. Frequently it seems that all sense of the need to treat others in a way that affirms their work has been displaced by the idea that profitability legitimizes anything, and the only fault involved in cutting legal corners is to be caught at it. Professedly Christian businessmen make a virtue of living their lives in compartments, not letting religion and business interfere with each other in any way. In business, amorality rules—okay? No; not okay at all. Hence this book.

Business schools today see the problem, and bewail the lack of cogent ethical guidelines to direct their alumni through the thickets of perfidy and swamps of greed with which the fast-changing socioeconomic milieu of the global village surrounds them. Technically, in terms of knowing how the business world functions, these schools have never been so competent, but morally, by their own admission, they have never been so near to bankruptcy. The reality of a moral vacuum in so religious a nation as the United States, where sixty-five percent of the people have a church link and ninety percent believe in God and a future life of happiness or misery, may seem to us strange, but it should not. Secularization has occurred. Secularity as a way of life has become standard, even where secularism as a dogma is denied. The essence of secularity is not the abandoning of religion but the privatizing of it, and privatization means reducing religion to the status of a personal hobby and ruling out all thought of it as a regulative control for community life. No wonder, then, that current business practice easily degenerates into an exploitative war game; no wonder that a moral impetus to dignify business life once more is called for. But it is not clear, within the secular frame, whence such an ethic might come.

Only, it seems, where Christianity has held sway have honesty, equity, and the service of others ever been embraced as ideals in business. In other contexts, whether ancient or modern, greed and power-hunger seem to have won out, and feathering one's nest at others' expense has been the recurring pattern. Nor have Christians who see business as a sphere for expressing godliness by practicing holiness in righteousness ever been more than a minority among businessmen. Nonetheless, consistent discipleship requires this view of business life. Christians are made new in Jesus Christ so that they may henceforth live from entirely new motives by entirely new standards, and thus show the reality of Christ's rule over them in every area of life—business included. By the world's standards, Christians will always be eccentric; there would in fact be something wrong with them if they were not. This principal applies as much in business life as anywhere else.

To consistent Christians, no form of secularization is in the least acceptable; in all lawful activities (and wealth creation through trade, industry, and money management is one such) they know themselves called to please God by serving Christ, and nothing will divert them from that endeavor. In business, therefore, they stand out as seeking to benefit others for their Lord's sake through the wants they supply and the services they render. For them, therefore, the question of moral impetus is resolved, and the only uncertainties remaining for them involve discerning the wise way to plan and manage so that in the process of making an appropriate profit—which they must do, or the business will collapse—they truly fulfill their goal of service. This business ethic, which springs directly from Christian faith, is both noble and viable; it is a pity that secular business schools, by virtue of their required religious pluralism and uncommittedness, cannot avail themselves of it.

SPIRITUALITY IN BUSINESS

To make my formulation of Christian purpose in business clear, I have made it simple in a way that might appear deceptive, or at least thoughtless, by not dwelling on the difficulties of applying it. These are great, particularly when one is not one's own boss. Working for a firm that has no distinctively Christian character, and that expects total loyalty, compliance, and effort from its employees in pursuing its objectives according to its own company code, can present huge problems to one whose prime allegiance is to Jesus Christ and His Church. And keeping one's own business afloat under economic pressure without compromising one's standards of fair dealing with customers and partners and one's work force can become a nightmare. Under such pressures Christian firms may fail and Christians go bankrupt, just as others do; there is no divine guarantee to Christian business venturers that this will not happen. The fact remains, however, that God-given interest and ability lead many to choose entrepreneurial and professional activity as their way of working for a living, serving their neighbor, and glorifying God, and this choice commits them to thinking out the best and most consistent application of the Christian purpose in business that they can envisage. The essays within this volume are the work of Christians seeking to do precisely this.

It is convenient here to spell out some perspectival principles concerning Christian devotion and discipleship that all the following chapters presuppose as they open up for us the practical problems of godly business behavior. All of them emerged as the chapters were discussed in a collective dialogue, with Dr. Chewning as the moderator.

The unity of life under God—This is God's world, a single complex system that each human being shares in managing. Dominion over the earth—in other words, stewarding the environment and using its resources in cultural development—is a privilege and responsibility first given to mankind at creation (See Gen. 1:26-30; Ps. 8), and now extended in a personal and direct way to everyone. ("This means you!") Human individuals must know themselves as creatures made in God's image, which means at least that they are designed for purposive rationality, personal relationships, and practical righteousness, and each must recognize his or her calling to put these capacities to work in every department of life and every interaction with the world.

God's saving grace bestows on us sinners the resources we need for this comprehensive service of God and our neighbor, and Holy Scripture teaches us the goals, values, and states of affairs at which we are to aim. Also, God's many-sided providence works with His servants in "common grace," as Reformed theology calls it, to restrain sin in individuals and to produce in communities a measure of order, cooperation, and constructiveness in cultural tasks going beyond what might have been expected. Nothing in creation is intrinsically evil; everything waits to be harnessed and channeled for the glory of God and the good of man; and all Christ's servants are called to use all their God-given creativity to this end.

This program for living transcends the compartmentalism that views life as so many separate and unrelated fields for performance; its achievement is to integrate all activities together, as aspects of a single devotional and doxological strategy. The unifying goal of the strategy, the goal of honoring God and helping others through all the involvements of communal life that God's work in creation and providence makes possible, provides the frame of reference within which business activity is to be thought out and wrought out by the disciples of Christ.

The necessity of business structures—Under the providence of God, huge complex collectives of industry and trade are now a global fact, with complex managerial and financial arrangements as part of their very being. The temptation to recoil from the supposed soullessness of this vast development and retreat into a sort of Christian culture hippiedom, in which only nonindustrial concerns get noticed, and every interest is local, and every commune is tiny, should be resisted. No doubt some of the existing setups are oversized, and "small is beautiful," and alternative technologies ought to be encouraged. But even the smallest economic unit requires competent management and a sound financial base, so that some business organization remains a necessity; and when the big business of the worldwide industrial establishment has indubitably come to stay, it is simplistic, childish (not childlike), and ultimately unfaithful to God for Christians to ignore it and turn their backs on it instead of seeking to sanctify and humanize it by working within it at all levels and accepting the responsibility of significant executive roles in the structures when such possibilities appear. Large or small, business structures are nowadays necessary, and pretending they are not is unrealistic. And unrealism cannot glorify God!

The duty of accepting involvement in the business world—This principle follows what has been said. The idea that business life is unspiritual must be rejected; no sphere of service to God through service to others is unspiritual. The corollary idea, that the business world is no place for believers, must be rejected, too. Why should the controlling collectives of the modern world—for that is what the multinationals and great finance houses really are—be left entirely to the Devil? We need to see, and say, that business life is as much a calling from God for some Christians as missionary service or pastoral ministry is for others.

The certainty of conflict for Christians in business life—The secularity that marks business practice and company codes today is a pure expression of the secularity that infects Western culture generally, and it creates situation after situation in which strict adherence to Christian principles and values, and observance of the restraints that these impose, can easily look like disloyalty to the firm. It is too much to hope that any Christian working for any firm will be able altogether to evade such tensions, nor should any Christian expect to; after all, the New Testament tells us to expect spiritual warfare. The believer who goes into business should, therefore, look ahead and prepare in mind and heart for the problems that will inevitably arise.

The primacy of righteousness for Christians in business life—

> He has showed you, O man, what is good.
>   And what does the LORD require of you?
> To act justly and to love mercy
>   and to walk humbly with your God. (Mic. 6:8)

This verse applies to all areas of life. Integrity, honesty, trustworthiness, and fair-mindedness before God and men must be seen as matters of top priority all the time—not just in private life but in business, too. (And these are, of course, in any case, the qualities most desired and appreciated by those who have to do with businesspeople.)

The authority of Scripture over Christians in business life—This is not the place to deploy arguments for acknowledging the entire canonical Bible as the true, trustworthy, and authoritative Word of God; such arguments are readily available elsewhere. But this is the place to say that consistent Christians will think of the Bible as coming to us from the hand of our Savior, and will recognize that the Lord Jesus Christ mediates His authority to us through the authority of Scripture over us and that we cannot be Christ's faithful followers without becoming faithful disciples of Holy Writ. To turn a blind eye to biblical teaching and lapse from standards that Scripture sets is often very tempting; at such times Christians need to remember that the Bible is in truth the instruction-book of our heavenly Lord, and we cannot disobey or flout it without being disloyal to Christ Himself.

The difficulty of living by the Bible in business matters—To affirm the authority of Scripture over against Christian opinion, past and present, individual and corporate, is one thing, but to discern how the Bible's ethical teaching should be applied to the modern commercial world and its inhabitants is quite another. Persons who agree on biblical authority still find themselves divided on these questions: How does biblical teaching on morality bear on industrial structures, of which Scripture knows nothing? How far is Jesus' instruction about Christian behavior an ideal that may or may not be practicable? Or a rule of thumb that cannot always be followed slavishly? Or a basis for legislation in the Church and in society? How far, and in what sense, are New Testament Christians set free from the Old Testament law, with its very specific socio-economic teachings for an agricultural way of life? How far will Christian liberty permit tolerance of smaller things that are bad in order to gain, or retain, influence that will enable Christians to achieve great things that are good?

In business, as in other realms of life, Christians are called to the difficult discipline of following conscientiously their own understanding of what Scripture rates permissible and off-limits while respecting the seemingly different understandings and policies of other Christians. This discipline includes hunting for creative ways to express and exalt Christ in awkward circumstances, checking one's ideas as to one's duty by consulting the wisdom of the Christian fellowship, and also being willing to find that another's insight into biblical ethics is superior to one's own. Practicing this discipline is not easy. Finding a scripturally satisfactory way of serving God in one's business will often feel like hacking a path through the jungle. Yet the faithfulness of God guarantees that those who in humility and hope search the Scriptures, study the situation, and keep their conscience clear by declining morally doubtful options will always be shown a way through, even though it may not coincide with the path followed by others.

The vulnerability of disciples to error and failure—Christians live by being forgiven and therefore can afford to fail. This is gospel truth, and nowhere is it likely to bring more encouragement and relief than in the business world, where Christians, like others, take reasonable risks but experience failure again and again. Pride makes the thought of failure abhorrent to everyone, and Christians who have sought the glory of God feel a particular reluctance to admit that they have failed in anything. But God humbles our pride by allowing us to fail, then restores our hearts by His pardoning grace, and repeats this procedure constantly. The proverbial wisdom remains true:

> Trust in the LORD with all your heart
>   and lean not on your own understanding;
> in all your ways acknowledge him,
>   and he will make your paths straight. (Prov. 3:5-6)

Yet businessmen, like other Christians, obey these words and still fail in particular ventures. Has God's promise, then, failed? Has God, after all, proved unfaithful? No; God is not success-oriented and mesmerized by short-term gains in the modern secular manner. He is ripening us for eternity by teaching us to lean on Him as hard as possible, and one way He does this is by taking from us what we would have been leaning on otherwise. Depriving us of an impressive success record may thus at any time be part of His strategy for making our paths straight.

PROBLEMS CHRISTIANS FACE IN BUSINESS

These agreed principles concerning what we may call the spirituality of the business life are assumed as the springboard and vantage point for exploring such specific problems of certain business endeavors and fields of action as those expertly reviewed in this book. It may help to give perspective on the chapters if we note at the outset in a formal and generalizing way the recurring problems running through them all.

There is, first, the problem of properly understanding the structures and processes with which, and within which, one is operating. From one standpoint, it is a problem of professional competence: The blunderings of sanctified amateurism, impervious to the need to get qualified in the area where one hopes to function, are neither good Christianity nor good business. From another standpoint, it is a problem of professional integrity: Christians in business must seek slots in which, on the one hand, the performance required of them matches their ability level and, on the other hand, the gifts of which they are stewards are in full exercise at full stretch in doing their job. The Peter Principle (everyone is offered promotion at least one stage beyond a personal level of competence) points to one way of losing the required integrity—namely, acceptance of what is offered; for this decision, sound judgment, shaped by good advice, is constantly necessary. To settle for becoming a square peg in a round hole, a small-footed person in big shoes, and a human bottleneck cannot either glorify one's Father in Heaven or further the fortunes of the firm one serves on earth.

There is, second, the problem of properly appreciating humanness and the factors that make for others' well-being so that one can tell what activities will genuinely serve and help them, as distinct from exploiting and impoverishing them. The benevolence of authentically Christian love may be defined as a purpose of making the other person great in terms of God's purpose for that person. Much economic theorizing in our day overlooks human values; much economic development is criminally irresponsible in its disregard of the life-threatening environmental pollution that it bids fair to create. The Christian in business must be sharp-sighted as to what brings genuine benefit to consumers and must not treat money in the bank as all that matters.

There is, third, the problem of setting goals for business enterprises and deciding what will constitute success in one's endeavors. It is not always easy in business to know what one is at. Christians in business will think of themselves as trustees for other people's welfare at all times, and will therefore be satisfied only when they can see that the profit they make is correlated appropriately with services rendered, stewardship of gifts and opportunities discharged, and accountability to the public maintained. But in these efforts constant critical assessment of the firm or of oneself as an employee of someone else's firm is mandatory.

There is, fourth, the problem of motivating and activating one's employees, who may or may not fully share one's Christian purposes. How, in any case, does one motivate without being manipulative? How does one evoke enthusiasm for the realization of another party's goals? How does one keep the claim of loyalty from becoming tyrannical? People management of a kind that retains respect for the other party is no easier for Christians than for anyone else, and unwillingness to maximize profit at the expense of others' well-being can cause special difficulties when dealing with one's employees.

There is, fifth, the problem of handling power. As has often been noted, all power tends to corrupt persons holding it—financial and economic power no less than political power. Managing power in such a way that one neither idolizes oneself or one's firm or one's role or one's economic security nor abuses those whom one hires, directs, and fires, but remains a humble steward of the power one has been given, using it responsibly and discerningly for the benefit of others and the glory of God, is difficult, while taking advantage of one's possession of power to play God to those under one is fatally easy.

There is, sixth, the problem of practicing fairness and achieving conditions of justice in all one's business relationships. How, for instance, does one deal equitably with ethnic minorities and women in the work force? Do Christians—whites—blacks—persons with handicapping conditions—have any priority claim on the Christian employer? What constitutes reasonable and humane working conditions?

There is, seventh, the problem of establishing sufficient accountability in administrative structures. The line between business discretion and secretiveness is a fine one, and not easy to walk.

There is, eighth, the problem of overcoming fear—fear that expresses the paranoia marking both the powerful and the powerless. Fear of the new, strange, untried, and unknown produces a defensive inertia, a definite euphoria, and a blind resistance to any suggestion of change. Unrealism takes over; bad news is not allowed to flow, necessary adjustments are not made, and whistling in the dark becomes the firm's official style. In all of this, fear has caused good judgment to fly out the window; in Christian terms, sober faithfulness has been exchanged for irrational foolhardiness. The ideal of being open to all facts that count and constantly ready to make whatever procedural changes they dictate, even when this means letting cherished ways and dreams go, is not easily achieved.

Thus, the business life appears as an extremely demanding vocation, making great claims on the believer's character and calling for a close, humble, faithful, hopeful, and self-distrustful walk with God. Prayer, honest fellowship with other Christians in accountability relationships of full frankness, and constant reflection before God on what is best, according to Bible standards of righteousness, love, and wisdom, are necessities—doubly so if one is in management! Character counts no less than skills and technical knowhow if one is to glorify God in business life. But it can be done . . . and the following chapters offer many precious hints about how to accomplish that goal. This the reader will soon see.

EDITOR'S PERSPECTIVE

Dr. Packer has a deep desire to see relational holiness rekindled in the marketplace. Relational holiness—righteous conduct that elicits a positive response in the conduct of those with whom we live and work—is not holiness distinct from personal holiness but is a reference to the dimension of holiness that spills over from one life to another life in an influential way. We need to think of holiness as going beyond the bounds of personal piety and to conceive of it as also acting like salt, light, and leaven in the world. The dichotomy between personal holiness and relational holiness is a false one, but one that has been fostered and maintained by far too many Christians.

The creation of the dichotomy between personal and relational holiness has its roots in both our fallen nature, which is very defensive and self-protective, and the harsh way in which the world so often presents itself to the sensitive soul, causing it to withdraw in search of peace and rest. The contrast between the values and desires nurtured in the hearts of Christians by the Holy Spirit and the values and demands dumped on us daily by the world can easily cause us to become weary and want to escape from the conflicts we encounter. Thus, a form of private, psychological monasticism is generated that has a subtle appeal to almost every Christian and takes root in far too many.

The biblical exhortations to persevere, overcome, be strong, resist, and be faithful are many, and they are often given in the context of a call to do spiritual battle in the world. We are not to be conformed to the world (see Rom. 12:2), but neither are we to withdraw from the world in our effort to avoid conformity. Christ, in His high priestly prayer at the conclusion of the Last Supper, prayed to the Father, "I have given them Thy Word; and the world has hated them, because they are not of the world, even as I am not of the world. I do not ask

Thee to take them out of the world, but to keep them from the evil one" (John 17:14-15). How to be *in* the world but not *of* the world has troubled Christians for generations.

It is tragic to note, but more than just a few branches of the Church have contributed greatly to the decline in relational holiness in the arenas of business by (1) emphasizing evangelism to the virtual exclusion of any teaching on the creation mandates, especially as they positively relate to work. The Great Commission has often been unintentionally stripped of its full impact by the very group that has wanted to champion it the most. Its commands to "make disciples" and "[teach] them to observe all that I commanded you" (Matt. 28:19-20) really call for discipleship and obedience to take place in our families, in the marketplace, and in the Church. (2) Large segments of the Church have abandoned the Scripture as a cognitively knowable and objective standard of truth that provides sure direction for every area of life. Such churches have substituted the philosophies of existentialism, experientialism, humanism, relativism, materialism, pragmatism, and other subverting partial truths for the truths of Scripture. The false standards they foster have created moral confusion and moral isolationism. (3) Other church groups have diligently taught personal pietism, which they ought to have done, but have failed to expound the scriptures calling for equity and justice in the marketplace.

Yet many Christians are effectively living for Christ in the business community where their relational holiness is having a real impact. Some Christians incorrectly assume that having such an influence can occur only when people are entrepreneurs or well-placed executives. This is not true. While entrepreneurs and officers of corporations do have positions of influence, the very factors that provide them opportunities to be influential are available throughout any organization.

People at all levels in a business hierarchy are very conscious of what their superiors value and reward. Therefore, anybody in a supervisory position can have a positive influence on the conduct of others. Furthermore, integrity, compassionate attitudes, a caring heart, and other positive characteristics always elicit favorable reactions from superiors, peers, and subordinates. Position never precludes individuals from effectively exhibiting relational holiness.

In concluding his chapter, Dr. Packer identifies a family of needs that must be met if relational holiness is to have a meaningful chance of being restored in the marketplace: the need for prayer, the need for genuine fellowship with other Christians in accountability relationships, and the need for reflection, before God and in the light of His Word, on what is *best*—not just legal or workable. A brief word on each of these is in order.

Genuine prayer is a true mark and sign of a healthy relationship between

God and His children. Every great revival, every significant ministry, and the magnificent acts of God's sovereign and providential intervention in history have been preceded and accompanied by much prayer. Prayer as a communication link between man and God is probably not its most vital function, however, for God already knows what we need before we ask Him (see Matt. 6:8), and He knows our every thought before a word is uttered from our lips (see Ps. 139:4). Yes, prayer is a form of communication, but more important, it is evidence of true faith, trust, and love. Within our intimate relationships we share our most important dreams, aspirations, needs, joys, gratitudes, and thanksgiving. God first shared His love for us by giving us a wonderfully created world to live in; sending His only Son to redeem us from our sin; giving us the written Word so we could know His perfect will; and providing us with His own Spirit as a teacher, comforter, and seal of the promise of our eternal adoption. We are invited to pray so we can express our adoration, thanksgiving, desires, and sorrows to Him. Dr. Packer's recognition of the need for prayer is profoundly true; relational holiness must have as its end the glorification of God, and only God can transform our poor works into effectual holy consequences.

Dr. Packer's observation that Christians must be solidly related to one another in accountability relationships before the Christian community can ever hope to establish relational holiness in the marketplace points to a massive void in the modern church in North America. The editor is afraid that the idea of meaningful accountability has all but vanished from our churches, and the idea of businesspeople seeking counsel and help from other Christians in an effort to discern Christ's mind on business matters is so foreign to the world view of most contemporary Christians that even mentioning it seems out of order. We rarely even pay lip service to this truth, but to ignore it is to deny (behaviorally) some clear teachings of Scripture—no Christian is sufficient unto himself or herself with regard to wisdom and discernment; counsel is highly commended throughout Scripture; we provide strength for one another to act righteously when we are bound together in prayer, study, and fellowship; and accountability in the Church is biblical. Christians in business need to join with other Christians in responsible and accountable fellowships that have the mutual goal of appropriating God's Word in the workplace.

Dr. Packer also reminds us that those who desire to bring relational holiness to the marketplace must be willing to constantly reflect, before God, on what is *best* to do (not just meets "minimal standards") as they perform their functions under the light of biblical righteousness, love, and wisdom. It is for this end that the CHRISTIANS IN THE MARKETPLACE SERIES was designed.

PART II

STRATEGIES FOR THE FUTURE

God is a strategic planner, and we are to be strategic planners, too. Yet, there is an implicit tension in this statement, for the plans and purposes of God are not consciously accepted and followed by those who do not love Him (see Luke 7:30; Acts 20:27-30), even though we know that God's ultimate purposes and will cannot be thwarted. Theologians have debated for centuries the tension between Scripture's declaration that God is absolutely sovereign ("Declaring the end from the beginning" [Isa. 46:10]; "Work[ing] all things after the counsel of His will" [Eph. 1:11]; and hundreds of other passages supporting a high view of His sovereignty) and its position that humans are personally responsible for the choices they make in every situation of life ("How often I wanted to gather your children together, the way a hen gathers her chicks . . . and *you were unwilling*" [Matt. 23:37, emphasis added]; "It is not the will of your Father . . . that one of these little ones perish" [Matt. 18:14; 1 Tim. 2:4]; and "Choose for yourselves today whom you will serve" [Josh. 24:15]).

The Lord seems to warn us at times about putting too much confidence in our plans (see Isa. 44:24-25; James 4:13-16), and at other times we are invited to plan and work hard to see our plans fulfilled (see Prov. 16:3; 20:5; Luke 12:54-57). These tensions have led some people to conclude that all planning is presumptuous and a waste of time, for while "the mind of man plans his way . . . the LORD directs his steps" (Prov. 16:9). So why plan at all? Others come to the opposite conclusion and believe that we are capable of forging, shaping, and controlling a large portion of our destiny (see Deut. 30:19; Josh. 24:15). Which position is correct, or how are we to reconcile them into an harmonious whole?

Like all biblical tensions, they are to be understood as being harmonious, and at the same time we are to acknowledge that they transcend our full

29

comprehension of them. They are reconciled only in the perfect understanding and wisdom of God. God has asserted that He is absolutely sovereign, governing every event in history through (1) His active conduct, (2) the natural laws He has created for His own purposes, and (3) the willful choices and activities of all His creatures, which were perfectly known to Him from time eternal (see Ps. 135:6; Isa. 40:8, 13-14, 26, 28; 41:21-23, 26; 44:6-8; 46:5, 8-11; Acts 15:18; Rom. 9:17; Eph. 1:11). In the third category (human choices and activities) our planning takes place under God's watchful eye. He calls us to learn of His will, to set our mind on doing His will, and to construct and commit our plans to Him, knowing that He will help us establish our desires to honor Him as we seek and work to do His will (see Prov. 16:3; 20:5).

While only God knows the future perfectly, we are to prepare and plan for the future in view of what we know of the natural order (see Luke 12:54-56) and of God's revealed will, including His desire for us to serve others as we rule and exercise dominion over His created order. In one sense, all of life is preparation for the future. The ministry of the Church is to prepare us for eternity. The work of nurturing a family is to prepare them for the future. Businesses must also look to the future. This aspect is so widely recognized that an entire function of management, known as *strategic management,* has emerged specifically dedicated to shepherding an organization from the present to ten to twenty years in the future. The function is oriented toward the distant future, not the current operations or near future.

In the following chapter Dr. Steven Musser leads us through a five-step outline that Christian managers can use to steer and position their businesses to successfully encounter the environment of the future, which is certain to be significantly different in several ways. He carefully points to some biblical distinctions that should substantively affect the thinking of a Christian engaged in strategic management. He calls Christians to take discipleship in the market-place seriously with full acknowledgment that there will very likely be some intense short-term pressures exerted by fellow workers to compromise those standards in the name of "higher profits." While it is neither the purpose nor the theme of Dr. Musser's work to relate our obedience to biblical norms with profitability, he observes that biblical standards take the long-run outlook and are much more likely to support long-term profits than are decisions shaped by short-run considerations.

CHAPTER 2

BIBLICAL PRINCIPLES APPLIED TO STRATEGIC MANAGEMENT

Steven J. Musser

Steven J. Musser is Associate Professor of Management at Messiah College. He earned his A.B. from Albright College (1975), and his M.A. and Ph.D. from Temple University (1977, 1984). In addition to teaching, Dr. Musser serves as a consultant to AMP, Inc., Pennsylvania Blue Shield, the Pennsylvania Department of Transportation, and other organizations. He is editor of the Signal, *the newsletter of the International Association for Conflict Management, and is a member of the Academy of Management. Dr. Musser's publications include numerous articles on organizational change, leadership, and conflict management.*

> But the man who looks intently into the perfect law that gives freedom, and continues to do this, not forgetting what he has heard, but doing it— he will be blessed in what he does. (James 1:25)

The advent of the Information Era has brought with it an urgent need for the development of strategies to meet the challenges of an increasingly turbulent environment. Not only are Christian business leaders today confronted with a shrinking world that has stimulated both competition and market opportunities, but perhaps more important, they are also faced with an incredibly expanding technological base.

This technological growth has produced a host of moral and ethical dilemmas for mankind, including genetic engineering, euthanasia, abortion, and artificial intelligence, to name just a few. Unfortunately, our technological advances have raced ahead of our ability to develop carefully thought-out philosophical and legal responses to these dilemmas through traditional social mechanisms. As a result, Christian business leaders have a tremendous responsibility to assure that the moral direction of our world is being influenced by Christian values and principles. This chapter proposes that a primary tool for Christian business leaders to employ in accomplishing this task is the strategic management process.

In his book *The Third Wave*, Alvin Toffler pointed out that one of the most basic changes accompanying the Information Era world of today is a change in social values. As opposed to the Industrial Era values of conformity, such as centralization, standardization, and submission, the Information Era, with its increased power for the individual, has given birth to the values of decentralization, diversity, and individualism. These new values have already affected our world in far-reaching ways. They have produced an incredibly strong emphasis on self, which has led to great ethical concern within the business areas of finance and marketing. These values have also produced a virulent strain of materialism among young and old alike that would have seemed impossible just a decade or so ago. They have created New Age religion, Dial-a-Porn, and terrorism. They have even changed our concepts of marriage and family. Divorce rates are soaring as people express their individuality and desire for variety and choice. Single-parent families are becoming more common, spouses are not living in the same city, and children from different parents are being merged into "aggregate" families as divorced parents remarry.

In the midst of this chaos of change are Christian business leaders. What forces will guide their fundamental decisions with respect to the direction their businesses will pursue to survive in such an environment? Will firms led by Christians seek mere survival by an unquestioned adaptation to the environment and the straightforward pursuit of economically rational choices like everyone else? Or will they, through strategic decision making, seek to alter their environments to reflect their Christian beliefs and values in the adaptation process?

A CHRISTIAN DEFINITION OF STRATEGIC MANAGEMENT

In its most simple form, *strategic management* is defined as a "continuous process of matching the organization to its environment." This matching process is usually accomplished by top management through the completion of five basic steps including (1) determining the organizational mission; (2) analyzing the environment; (3) formulating strategies to exploit environmental opportunities and manage weaknesses; (4) implementing strategies; and (5) monitoring and controlling strategies. Implicit in this model is the clear notion that it is imperative for firms to respond to their environments if they are to avoid the fate of the dinosaur.

A Christian perspective of strategic management should also emphasize the importance of understanding and adapting to the environment. Most Christians have included in their role definitions the need to share the gospel and reflect their Christian values as they "rub shoulders" with the world. Christians have recognized the need to become positive witnesses through victorious daily living before the scrutiny of a lost world (see Heb. 12:14; 1 Pet. 2:9-12).

To reflect our Christian values in a meaningful way, we should endeavor to understand the world in which we live and see to it that the gospel is portrayed as relevant to the needs of this world. For Christian business leaders, this includes making businesses responsive to the array of human needs created by today's world. We should strive to produce goods and services that reflect to the world the depth of our understanding of its needs and our personal commitment to meeting these needs.

We are not, however, to be a part of the world in the sense of participating in its sin. Unlike business leaders who are unbelievers, Christian business leaders must consider additional moral adaptation constraints. Products and practices that either reflect or encourage sinful behavior have no place in Christian leadership, and Christian business leaders must make a continual effort to ensure that such things have not subtly crept into their strategies.

The critical difference between the traditional definition of strategic management and its Christian definition lies in the firm's need to demonstrate Christian values in its decisions and operations. Most writings on traditional strategic management stress the importance of adapting. Little attention is given to the idea that organizations can develop strategies to alter or influence their environments outside discussions on the impact of very large corporations on the environments of oligopolistic industries. Unfortunately, even these discussions are usually limited to noting the influence of large firms on competitive practices within the industry and on government regulatory policies.

For the Christian, the ability for one human being to alter or influence the environment should be quite familiar. The Bible teaches that we are the salt of the earth and that we are to season/preserve our environment with good works. We are to let our lights shine before men to expose our good deeds and bring praise to the Father (see Matt. 5:13-16). Given the scriptural commands on witness through good works, it seems that organizational strategy can and should become an additional vehicle for Christians to influence their environment. A strategy providing purpose and direction for organizational activities is a natural tool for producing good works. In Christian strategic management, therefore, all firms, both large and small, should adapt to circumstances created by the environment in order to be relevant and also consciously seek to alter their environments through the public modeling of behavior consistent with scriptural principles. Such an effort seems crucial to assure that our world is being shaped by Christian values.

Unfortunately, some Christian business leaders try to justify their participation in the production or distribution of a product of highly questionable moral value (e.g., a publication distributor selling pornographic magazines as part of the product line). First, they argue, if they did not provide such a product, their firm would have to exit the industry, and second, by producing the questionable product and thereby remaining in the industry, they have opportunity for influence that would otherwise be lost.

That definition of Christian witness seems very shallow and has no real place in the concept of Christian strategic management developed here. *Christian witness*, which is the focus of this type of strategic management, is defined in this chapter to mean "the production of goods and services and the implementation of business practices reflecting the Person and character of Jesus Christ." This standard, of course, is difficult to attain, but it should at least become a benchmark against which strategic alternatives are evaluated. Only when the strategy approaches congruency with the standards and teachings of Jesus Christ can we become confident that it provides a true Christian witness.

Before moving on to discuss each of the five basic steps in the strategic management process from a Christian perspective, it might be helpful to distinguish between two different types of Christian business leaders and their respective accountability for implementing Christian strategic decision making in their organizations. For the Christian who is the founder/owner of a privately held business, it is absolutely critical that strategic decision making reflect his or her Christian values. As will be discussed later in the section on implementing strategies, the leader of the firm either knowingly or unknowingly constantly influences the culture of the organization. The world will therefore quite naturally look closely at a privately held firm founded or owned by Christians. People will want to see whether Christianity really makes a practical difference. All too many Christian CEOs have caused significant damage to the cause of Christ by not adhering to a Christian definition of strategic management. In many of these cases, Christian CEOs were perceived to possess the same selfish drives and motives as other businesspeople.

The situation for Christian businesspersons who become presidents or CEOs of publicly held firms is quite naturally different. These persons may not be able to form the necessary coalitions and successfully manage the internal and external power systems to fulfill the requirements of Christian strategic management in the short run. They may need time to establish a strong track record of effectiveness to secure the confidence of the power structure before they can fully apply their Christian values to the strategic management process.

Nevertheless, their long-term personal goals in the business setting should also be to produce products and implement business practices reflecting the standards and teachings of Jesus Christ.

DETERMINING THE ORGANIZATIONAL MISSION

Perhaps the most fundamental decision in Christian strategic management is the establishment of an organizational mission stating the purpose for which the organization exists. This purpose then guides the organization's choice process in every area of activity and influences every decision. Just as important, it becomes a dynamic source of motivation that propels organizational members through challenges, crises, and opportunities.

In the strategic management process, organization missions vary widely and reflect the experiences, perceptions, values, and goals of the leadership. The same is true for firms employing Christian strategic management. Each firm should have a unique mission that defines it and distinguishes it from other organizations. Despite the heterogeneity of missions, however, Christian business leaders as a group may do well to consider a more homogeneous, superordinate mission for their firms, that is, to be committed to serving people.

The idea of service is currently popular in the management literature thanks to books like *In Search of Excellence*. The concept of service proposed in this chapter, however, is quite different from the one often defined in the popular management literature. For the Christian, service is to be motivated by nothing less than love. We are not to serve others *just* to experience increased profits, although today a servant attitude in the marketplace is very likely to positively affect the bottom line. Rather, our attitude in business should be the same as that of Christ Jesus who humbled Himself and took on the very nature of a servant (see Phil. 2:5-8). In other words, as Christian business leaders, our personal goal and therefore the superordinate mission of our businesses should be to serve others from a motive of love—nothing more and nothing less.

Three important parts—That mission can be broken down into distinct parts.

Serving consumers—by helping meet the needs of people through the creation and production of goods and services appropriate to Christian values.

The phrase "appropriate to Christian values" is important, although problematic. Few Christians would argue that some products are definitely inappropriate for Christians to produce (e.g., pornography, illicit drugs, etc.). The problem concerns exactly what is "appropriate to Christian values." Because opinions differ, some products may be considered appropriate by one group and inappropriate by another. The intent is not to create a standardized, sanctioned list of Christian products, but to simply assure that the Christian business leader has a clear conscience in producing a particular good or service in the spirit of Romans 14:23—"everything that does not come from faith is sin."

Serving employees—by providing the opportunity for employees to materially support themselves and their families, and by providing the opportunity for satisfying their psychological needs in the workplace.

Scripture affirms that we are responsible to provide for our families (see 1 Tim. 5:8). For Christian business leaders, this teaching would suggest that jobs within their organizations must pay a decent wage enabling the support of a family. To do otherwise is to create a set of circumstances that could foster family breakdown. Of course, Christian business leaders can expect an optimal level of performance in exchange for that wage. Indeed, high performance expectations should be a natural element in the culture of Christian organizations. Pay systems should not, however, be based on offering the lowest wage possible in the local labor market as a way of reducing costs if that wage is not sufficient to support a family. Christian business leaders should never reap additional profits simply because high unemployment has lowered wages in the market. This type of *Grapes of Wrath* profiteering is hardly the type of Christian witness that attracts unbelievers and certainly cannot be what God intended the concept of servanthood to reflect.

We also see in Scripture that God is concerned with the whole person—body, soul, and spirit (see Prov. 20:27; 1 Thess. 5:23). For this reason, Christian business leaders should make a genuine effort to assure that the emotional and psychological needs of employees are met. They should give high priority to job design, morale, job satisfaction, and other human resource management areas.

Serving other stakeholders—by providing a model to the world of the commitment, accountability, and stewardship God would have Christians display toward the total of His creation.

Included in this aspect of serving is the manner in which the firm deals with its environment, particularly the way it treats waste disposal, noise, and other environmental pollutants. Also included is behavior toward competitors, such as predatory pricing and industrial espionage. The firm's relationship with the government in areas of taxation and regulation is another aspect of serving. The firm's approach to these elements of its environment will communicate to the world its degree of respect for both mankind and the planet we share.

The wording of the mission statements of firms led by Christians need not include the specific phrases just discussed. But it should reflect the underlying values of Christianity to the extent that people recognize its Christian character.

This section has emphasized the importance of serving others as a superordinate mission for all Christian business leaders to consider. The concept of servanthood is deeply ingrained in the character of our Savior and in His commandments to us. Thus, for the Christian business leader, this mission takes precedence over the more traditional organizational goals of survival and profit maximization. Other goals are important, but this section has attempted to establish the relative order of priority these goals should hold. Because Scripture always places a higher value on serving than accumulating, and on sacrifice as opposed to gain, it seems only reasonable that this preference should be reflected in the mission statement of the firm as well.

ANALYZING THE ENVIRONMENT

The primary purpose of analyzing the environment is to enhance the organization's success by identifying potential problems *and* potential opportunities. Environment is not a unidimensional concept, however. Philip Thomas has suggested that there are three distinct levels of environment: the general environment, the operating environment, and the internal environment.[1] The general environment includes such elements as the political and legal systems, technological changes, economic growth, and social trends. The operating environment is made up of elements like consumer behavior, the labor market, and competitive pressures. Unlike the general and the operating environments, the internal environment is comprised of elements within the organizational boundaries of the firm, including employee relations, personal values, organizational structure, appraisal systems, and organizational policies.

One issue that merits attention is the selection of criteria to be used in determining whether a situation or an event is an opportunity or a problem. For example, an analysis of the internal environment may reveal that employees are extremely committed to the firm as evidenced by the long hours willingly put into their jobs. While most CEOs would evaluate their extensive commitment as an asset, the Christian business leader may want to explore the issue more deeply. If extremely high commitment to the firm or job is harming workers' relationships with their families or churches, it might be viewed as a problem for the long run. Extreme job commitment that is causing marital/family failure is hardly a constructive situation for workers and their families and is certainly not a positive witness to the community. The firm is often perceived as being insensitive to family members' needs in this situation because it allowed and even rewarded such commitment. Unfortunately, this hypothetical example is becoming a reality for an increasing number of families today.

The internal environment analysis can also indicate the extent to which Christian values have become integrated into the firm. Corporate policies, objectives, employee relations, performance appraisal systems, employee development programs, and incentive systems should all reflect Christian values. The question for the Christian business leader to ponder is, What are the qualitative differences between the internal elements of our firm and those of firms led by unbelievers? If there is no appreciable difference, the Christian business leader may not be as successful as he or she could be in integrating faith with business practice.

Analysis of both external environments also requires the application of Christian principles and values in the development of evaluation criteria. The application of these principles and values is particularly useful in determining opportunities for the firm. For example, the Christian business leader should carefully evaluate whether social trends toward increased materialism and a greater emphasis on self are really market opportunities worthy of exploiting. If these trends are exploited, is the firm, in effect, helping to promote materialism and self-centeredness in our society?

Changes in technology should be carefully examined before they are declared to be opportunities. Unfortunately, value judgments of technological changes are very rare today; technological innovations are perceived as "givens," which either defy or do not require normative evaluation. For Christians, such detachment is unacceptable. We must be willing to test all aspects of our world and determine whether they are pleasing or not to God. In this regard, the Christian business leader who knowingly or not influences the direction of our world in a significant way is particularly responsible. Thus, opportunities are limited for the Christian business leader by the application of normative evaluation criteria based on Christian values and principles.

As was the case for establishing organizational direction, it is very unlikely that Christians will develop a common list of evaluation criteria on which they reach consensus. However, each individual leader should make it a goal to have some set of Christian criteria implemented by his or her firm for evaluating all aspects of the environment. We are to interact with the world but not to be a part of it, to strive to change the world but not to be led by it (see 1 Cor. 10:3-5; 1 John 2:15-17). The implementation of a set of criteria for evaluating the environment as just discussed should enable the Christian business leader to fulfill the firm's superordinate mission by isolating environmental opportunities that provide a positive Christian witness and by identifying areas for improvement to ensure the long-term existence of that witness.

FORMULATING STRATEGIES

Once the manager of a firm has developed the organizational mission and has assessed the internal and the external environments, a strategy to attain the firm's objectives can be formulated. One popular and simple tool for doing that is SWOT (strengths, weaknesses, opportunities, and threats). In this system, the firm's internal strengths and weaknesses are examined in light of opportunities and threats in the external environment. Strategies begin to take form when internal strengths can be matched with environmental opportunities and when internal weaknesses can be matched with threats.

Several criteria can be applied to select among alternative strategies. Some of these criteria typically include the strategy's responsiveness to the external environment, the degree of flexibility it will offer the organization, the appropriateness of the strategy's degree of risk, its consistency with other strategies in the firm, and the extent to which the strategy conforms to the organization's mission and long-term objectives.

When selecting a strategy, Christian business leaders should keep the firm's superordinate Christian mission in the forefront of their thinking. There is likely to be a strong temptation to give priority to strategies holding the promise of maximized short-run profits while only minimally or negatively affecting the firm's Christian mission. Yielding to this temptation seriously compromises the firm's opportunity for public witness and minimizes the distinction between Christian and secular strategic management.

Conservative economists such as Milton Friedman and others have long argued that a firm's strategic manager is to simply maximize profits and hence the rate of return to stockholders. They have asserted that to do anything else is not within the legitimate scope of management behavior. At first glance, the recommendation that Christian business leaders avoid the temptation to select strategies that maximize profits at the expense of the firm's Christian mission may seem to be an example of what conservative economists warn against. If such a practice is indeed unethical, it should not be recommended to Christians. To resolve this apparent dilemma, it is helpful to understand the ethical basis of the conservative economists' viewpoint.

Conservative economists argue that stockholders invest in a firm for the primary purpose of maximizing the financial return of their investment, unless, of course, the owner or owners are believers who are more concerned with the Christian objectives of the firm. Thus, the only charge given to the strategic manager by investors is to maximize their return. The basic question is whether that maximization is to occur in the long or short run.

Because as Christians we believe that the consequences of sin are always destructive in the long run and that righteousness is honored by God, we should be willing to apply this belief, through faith, to every aspect of living, including our practice of business (see Job 15:31; 27:13-23; Ps. 34:21; 37:1-2; Prov. 8:36; 11:3; John 12:26). Indeed, the Old Testament prophets made it very clear that

God was even willing to bring judgment upon Israel at least in part because of their sinful business practices (see Jer. 17:11; 22:13; Ezek. 22:12; Hos. 12:7; Amos 5:11; Mal. 3:5). By the same token, Scripture assures us that God will bless righteous behavior (see Job 36:7; Ps. 34:15; 37:25; 92:12; Prov. 10:22; Isa. 3:10; Luke 18:29-30). Thus, although we cannot assume high profitability in the short run from seeking first to fulfill the firm's superordinate Christian mission, we can trust God to bless our obedience in the long run. We are not assured of higher than average long-run profits, but we will not bring true harm to our firms, or their stockholders, if we run them in ways consistent with biblical principles and values. To state the case as simply as possible, there is probably no better enterprise in which to invest for the long run than one whose leader is being blessed by God for his or her spiritual obedience. Lot found this to be true for Abraham, Potiphar and the Pharaoh for Joseph, Saul for David, and so on.

IMPLEMENTING THE STRATEGIES

After the strategy has been formulated, the next step is to implement it. If a strategy cannot be enacted effectively, its quality is unimportant. For example, a new strategy may require the firm to restructure itself. In many cases the organizational culture also needs to be changed to match strategic requirements.

While the analysis and the modification of organizational structure are often critical for successful strategic implementation, the organization's culture most often requires the immediate attention of the Christian business leader. *Organizational culture* is best defined as "the set of shared values and beliefs within the organization." Because it influences the perceptions and behavior of all organizational members, the culture is a fundamental element to be considered when implementing a strategy.

If the Christian business leader has established a mission statement including the superordinate Christian mission discussed earlier, he or she will necessarily seek to implement an organizational strategy that will reflect Christian values and principles. It is unlikely that such a strategy can be enacted without the preexistence of a compatible organizational culture. Therefore, the Christian business leader will need to become actively involved in building a culture supporting Christian values at the earliest possible opportunity.

According to Edgar Schein, leaders influence organizational cultures through what they pay attention to, measure, and control; their reactions to critical incidents and organizational crises; deliberate role modeling, teaching, and coaching; the criteria they establish to allocate rewards and status; and the criteria they encourage for recruiting, selecting, promoting, and retiring employees.[2] The Christian business leader may want to evaluate his or her managerial behavior relative to how well Christian values and principles are being instilled into the organization's culture through these channels and to devise plans to eliminate any deficiencies.

The personal character of the cultural channels just mentioned points out the futility of attempts by Christian business leaders to build compatible cultures without possessing a close and growing personal relationship with Jesus Christ. In a sense, organizational culture becomes an internal screening mechanism that prevents a hypocritical Christian from successfully leading the organization along the path God desires. If the leader's spiritual life is not what it should be, the organizational culture will ultimately reflect that fact and will hinder the implementation of strategies based on biblical principles and values. Thus, the spiritual requirements placed on Christian business leaders may be no less demanding than those placed on pastors and missionaries. For any organization to bring glory to God, the leaders' spiritual lives must be in order.

MONITORING AND CONTROLLING STRATEGIES

The purpose of strategic control, the last step in the strategic management process, is to render assistance to leaders in achieving the firm's mission by monitoring and evaluating the effectiveness of the organizational strategy. This critical step provides valuable feedback to the firm's leaders, which is used to decide whether to maintain, modify, or eliminate the current strategy. Like most forms of organizational control, strategic assessment involves (1) developing performance standards, (2) measuring organizational performance and comparing it to the standards, and (3) taking corrective action.

Strategic performance standards should be derived directly from the mission statement of the organization. They must reflect the organization's goals as defined by its mission and often include such things as return on investment, market share, productivity, product quality, and employee development and satisfaction. These standards, like any other in the organization, should be quantifiable when at all possible and verifiable at a minimum.

Since the mission statement of a firm headed by a Christian will likely include goals based on biblical values and principles, performance standards should be emphasized that evaluate these goals as well. For example, given the firm's superordinate Christian mission of serving people, strategic performance criteria of employee satisfaction and happiness, community relations, product quality, and the firm's public image and industry reputation should be given higher priority in the Christian leader's firm than in traditional ones. In addition, strategic evaluation criteria unique to organizations led by Christians should be developed. For example, a criterion of "product role" could focus attention on the importance of manufacturing products that continue to foster Christian values and principles. From evaluation criteria like these, more specific performance standards can be developed to assess the firm's Christian impact.

Once strategic standards of performance have been established, the actual performance of the firm can be measured. Where deficiencies are found to exist, corrective action must be taken. Again, the total commitment of the Christian business leader is required to make certain the firm is seeking to fulfill its Christian mission. Motivating organizational members to take corrective action relative to reaching Christian goals can be very difficult when more traditional criteria such as return on investment and market share are at acceptable or above-average levels. That is, in situations of success as well as failure the commitment of leaders to the superordinate Christian mission of the firm will be tested. Also at these times God presents tremendous opportunities for witness. Will Christian business leaders be perceived as people with a real difference in their lives or not? Faith and obedience will determine the outcome.

CONCLUSION

The brief outline of a distinctly Christian approach to strategic management presented in this chapter is a very demanding one. It requires intelligence, risk taking, self-confidence, and most of all, a mature, growing spiritual life. It calls for the committed, persevering application of all of the leader's talents and spiritual gifts. In particular, it demands effective leadership skills to deal with the inevitable internal power coalitions and pockets of power within the organization that may seek to frustrate the infiltration of Christian values into the firm. Interest groups, ambitious executives, and influential board members may attempt to challenge the direction the Christian business leader is pursuing. These potential threats suggest that Christian business leaders are not going to be successful on their own. To implement Christian strategic management in their firms, they must put their trust in the supernatural power of God.

The Christian business leader must rely totally and completely on God for success. He or she must spend whatever time is necessary before God seeking His help and guidance. And churches must regularly spend time in prayer for these individuals as well. We must all pray as faithfully for these individuals as we do for missionaries and pastors. Only when the Body of Christ recognizes the influential role of Christian business leaders in determining the moral direction of our world and prays faithfully for them can we expect to see success. Christian strategic management should be viewed as a heavy responsibility for the Christian business leader, but to whom much is given, much will be required (see Luke 12:48).

EDITOR'S PERSPECTIVE

Dr. Musser's presentation of strategic management is not an effort to call us to be prophetic or to forecast the future in some supernatural way. It is not the Christian's hope that God will give him or her some special insight into future events. It is extrapolative in character. It is the reading of the winds of the time (see Luke 12:54-57). For example, it is not prophetic to say that biotechnology and genetic engineering are *likely* to be massive industries in the future, with proportional social and economic consequences of a magnitude not dissimilar to the current revolution taking place in the field of information technology. The key word in the previous sentence that fixes a vast gulf between our human thinking and God's certain knowledge of every future event is *likely*. That is the hedge and admission of our finitude. Yet it is reasonable to use the example of biotechnology and genetic engineering for many reasons, which we will not take time to enumerate here. The point is simply this: Strategic management is an intelligent effort to prepare oneself, and to position the available resources one oversees, in a way that offers the best discernible hope of being prepared to carry out God's revealed will in the marketplace of the future.

Even as I write this "Perspective," *The Wall Street Journal*'s "Centennial Edition" (June 23, 1989) is before me. Its main message is contained in a front-page editorial entitled "What The Future Holds." It begins with the following three paragraphs:

CONSIDER: Los Angeles as the city of the future . . . and capital of the Third World. Bangladesh as an emerging industrial power. Companies and people you've never heard of, leading business into the next millennium. A world gone digital, with PCs that see and hear. Life in

43

a greenhouse, and American consumers alarmed because they never had it so good.

Welcome, in a word, to our second century.

With this centennial edition, *The Wall Street Journal* is offering readers a glimpse of what life might be like—and what stories might be filling our columns—in the years ahead.

America's most respected and widely read business publication is diligently trying to be relevant and serve its constituency. It is trying to encourage strategic management. It is trying to provide an assessment of what the world *might* look like in a few years, so its readers can take action today to prepare for the future.

When people are moved by God from the ranks of the unregenerate to the family of God, they (1) accept a new mission in life; (2) quickly realize that the old environment of the world can be hostile to their objectives; (3) ask God to teach, lead, protect, and guide them in their daily walk with Him; (4) seek ways to reach the goals God calls them to; and (5) repeatedly assess their progress in fulfilling their mission. This same process is called for in strategic management. If it is incumbent upon us to follow a path similar to the one just outlined as we assess our spiritual life and call on God to enable us to mature and be obedient to His revealed will, surely it is appropriate for us to use this same approach to help us function in the marketplace as we carry out our stewardship responsibilities.

Strategic planning and a sound biblical understanding of stewardship are completely compatible concepts. Good stewardship embodies the wise management of what God has entrusted to us, frequently over extended periods of time, and when we live in a dynamic and rapidly changing environment, we must prudently assess the future if our products or services are to be relevant. This kind of planning is not an effort to control the future but to prepare to successfully encounter it and to be ministers in its midst.

Strategic management is oriented toward the distant future, which is the only context in which fundamental strategies and significant options can be effectively considered and eventually effected. In the short run, managers have very few options to choose from regarding those things that demand immediate attention. Products, marketing strategies, production technology, or other basic and shaping strategies cannot be changed overnight. Most day-to-day management is devoted to addressing decisions that accompany daily operations.

On the other hand, managers can choose from and move toward many options when they look forward one to two decades. The larger an organization, the longer it takes to reposition it. A very small organization may be able to change its product mix or strategies rather quickly, but whether large or small, one is called on to discern the future as well as one can.

Discernment is a critical key to effective strategic management. The discernment of spiritual matters is a gift of God. The discernment of worldly matters is a talent and ability that most of us have to some degree. Seeking discernment is what we are doing when we seek counsel, a frequently commended practice in the Scripture. Success is realized through the careful and reasoned use of counsel (see Prov. 11:14; 15:22; 24:6). God tells us to make our plans through the use of counsel (see Prov. 20:18). Only the proud and arrogant assume they embody in themselves sufficient wisdom and understanding to autonomously plan and decide on appropriate courses of action. We know God wants us to have discernment in spiritual matters (see Deut. 32:28-29). It is no less reasonable to believe He wants us to seek discernment in carrying out His stewardship and cultural mandates. Although we would not expect Him to provide *gifts* to this end, we know He has created us with *talents* that work to this end.

Another incredibly important reason to engage in strategic management in a biblical manner is to do justice in the marketplace. Biblically, doing justice is synonymous with being righteous as we live and work with people. That means we *ought* to seek to enable those with whom we work to grow and develop to their greatest possible potential, and to involve them in the process of strategic management—determining the organization's mission, analyzing the environment, formulating strategies to take advantage of environmental opportunities and manage weaknesses, implementing strategies, and monitoring and adjusting strategies. This is an effective way to encourage their involvement and growth. Without vision and a sense of direction, people lack the motivation for self-constraint, energized involvement, and personal improvement (see Prov. 29:18). Strategic management fosters these and provides a way of developing a sense of purpose, community, and personal worth.

All prophecy reveals that God is a strategic planner and manager. He has perfect foreknowledge and works to fulfill all His purposes. We, on the other hand, are finite and fallen. We have no perfect foreknowledge, apart from what is in biblical revelation, but God, nonetheless, invites us to plan, seek counsel from one another, and work to bring our plans to fruition. We are to do these things in faith, with a servant's heart, and with the goals of a faithful steward in mind.

PART III

MANAGEMENT: A FUNCTION WITH IDENTITY IMPLICATIONS

Being a manager and studying management are two closely related matters, but they are also different in character and substance. Management is a *function* whereby we accept certain responsibilities to accomplish certain goals, assume (if entrepreneurs) or are given positions of authority with the power necessary to achieve the goals, and are held accountable for the discharge of both the responsibility and the authority entrusted to us. A manager, on the other hand, is a *person* with a core of ideas, attitudes, and perceptions on how the management function should be carried out.

The distinction drawn between the manager as a person and management as a function is critical to anyone inquiring into God's interest in the matter of management. No function of management is peculiarly and distinctively biblical or Christian. For example, planning is not limited to a biblical understanding of what is prudent to do in business. Neither is budgeting, marketing, or evaluating responsibilities restricted to a Christian life view. To the contrary. The functions of management are adaptations of natural processes realized by us to be part of our innate abilities, or they are created extensions (information systems, for example) of our inherent capacities, which are in turn applied in problem-solving situations.

God's special revelation is directed to the manager, not the management function. Adam's disobedience and our resulting fall initiated into reality our need for redemption—redemption from sin, to be sure, but also our redemption from the enslaving and controlling attitudes and misperceptions at the core of our old nature. Scripture has a lot to say to the manager about his or her attitudes, motives, identity, desires, drives, and other inner aspects of the heart. God desires to give new life to these inner, shaping aspects of our core nature.

47

Even when the world catches on to the fact that godly behavior has a salutary monetary benefit and therefore encourages new techniques that elicit greater productivity from the workplace, this manifests a depraved mind (see 1 Tim. 6:5). The motives, and even the true ends, have been badly twisted and become dehumanizing in such cases.

The chapter before us goes right to the heart of this matter in a very pointed way. In fact, some of the other scholars felt that Myron Rush's early and heavy focus on *power* as the most significant drive operating in the hearts of worldly managers was a bit restrictive and narrow. The editor would simply point out, however, that if we allow power to have a broader definition than simply "bully force" and include the drives for achievement, status, autonomy, recognition, success, and other popularly recognized needs under the umbrella of power—the energy applied to garner the means to satisfy such needs—we will conclude that Mr. Rush is right on target.

CHAPTER 3

BIBLICAL PRINCIPLES APPLIED TO MANAGEMENT

Myron D. Rush

Myron D. Rush is Founder and President of Management Training Systems, a management consulting firm that has specialized in developing and conducting tailor-made training and consulting services for both secular and religious organizations for more than fifteen years. He has also started several businesses and taught numerous supervisory and management courses at the university level.

Mr. Rush holds a master's degree from Central Missouri State University and has managed and directed educational programs for the University of Alaska and Eastern Montana College. He is the author of the following books, many of which have been published in several foreign languages: Tapping Employee Creativity; Richer Relationships; Management: A Biblical Approach *(a Gold Medallion Award Winner);* Lord of the Marketplace; Burnout; The New Leader; Hope For Hurting Relationships; *and* Developing Your Management Potential.

According to a well-known storyteller, as William Dean Howells and Mark Twain left church one Sunday, Howells turned to Twain and asked, "What do you think of the Bible?" Mark Twain replied, "I think it is the most frequently quoted, poorly understood, and least applied book I have ever read." Unfortunately, there is a great deal of truth in his statement. A lot of individuals give lip service to the Bible, but too few people sincerely work at applying its time-proven principles to their daily lives. The purpose of this chapter is to draw our attention to some of those principles and show how they apply to managing people and organizations.

The Bible is not only the Word of God; it is also the best "textbook" ever written describing how to effectively live life. For example, Solomon wrote the book of Proverbs "to teach his people how to live—how to act in every circumstance" (Prov. 1:2, TLB). According to this verse, the Bible contains principles concerning how we are to act in all of life's situations. Therefore, we can correctly assume it contains principles regarding our daily affairs as managers.

The Bible also warns us not to be deceived or conned into adopting the world's philosophies and standard operating procedures. Paul states, "See to it that no one takes you captive through hollow and deceptive philosophy, which depends on human tradition and the basic principles of this world rather than on Christ" (Col. 2:8).

A BIBLICAL PHILOSOPHY OF MANAGEMENT

The starting point in adopting a biblical approach to management is recognizing the vast difference between the world's philosophy of management and the Bible's philosophy of management. In the Colossians 2:8 passage, Paul warns us to avoid the deceptive philosophies of the world because they are built on human traditions and the self-centered principles of human nature instead of the teachings of Jesus Christ.

As illustrated in Matthew 20:20-28, the world's philosophy of management is diametrically opposed to the philosophy of management taught and practiced by Jesus Christ. The scene opens with the mother of Zebedee's sons (James and John, two of Christ's disciples) approaching Jesus and saying, "Grant that one of these two sons of mine may sit at your right and the other at your left in your kingdom" (Matt. 20:21). She makes an amazing request! She actually asks Jesus to give her sons the two positions directly under Him in His Kingdom.

Let me ask you the same question I have asked many others during my management seminars: "Why did this mother ask Jesus to give her sons the two positions directly under Him in His Kingdom or organization?" Obviously, there could have been many reasons, but the most important one, it seems to me, must have been the desire for power.

The further up the organizational ladder you climb in the world's system of management, the more power and control over others you possess. And that must have been the main reason Zebedee's wife asked Jesus to give her sons the two positions directly under Him. Next to Jesus Christ, she must have wanted her sons to be the most powerful and influential men in God's organization or Kingdom.

Notice the reaction of the other ten disciples when they learned about this request: "When the ten heard about this, they were indignant with the two brothers" (v. 24). And why were they so indignant and upset? Because each man wanted a top position for himself. Each of the disciples wanted to move up the management ladder to obtain more power and the honor and prestige accompanying such a position.

The world's approach to management is to use power to control others. In fact, a traditional definition of *management* is "getting work done through others." This definition, which for decades has appeared in management textbooks around the world, is built around the use of power and control as a means of accomplishing management's plans, goals, and objectives through the rest of the organization's work force.

There is nothing new about this approach to management. It was the popular management philosophy of organizations at the time of Christ's life on earth two thousand years ago, and it has remained the model of management used by most businesses and organizations since then.

Jesus observed how quickly the request of Zebedee's wife created dissension, anger, and quarreling among the disciples. He called them together and said,

> "You know that the rulers of the Gentiles lord it over them, and their high officials exercise authority over them. Not so with you. Instead, whoever wants to become great among you must be your servant, and whoever wants to be first must be your slave—just as the Son of Man did not come to be served, but to serve, and to give his life as a ransom for many." (Matt. 20:25-28)

Jesus clearly illustrated this statement by the vast difference between His and the world's philosophy of management. He began by pointing out that the leaders and managers in the secular world use the power of their position to accomplish through others the things they want done: "You know that the rulers of the Gentiles *lord it over them,* and their high officials *exercise authority over them*" (emphasis added).

And Jesus knew that His disciples were also buying into that same management philosophy. He saw them fighting and quarreling over the top positions in His Kingdom because they were competing for more and more power and authority.

As soon as Jesus recognized that His disciples were accepting the world's approach and philosophy of management, He said, "Not so with you." He emphatically asserted that His disciples were not to adhere to the same management philosophy the world practiced. Then He went on to say, "Instead, whoever wants to become great among you *must* be your servant, and whoever wants to be first *must* be your slave—just as the Son of Man did not come to be served, but to serve, and to give his life as a ransom for many" (vv. 26-28, emphasis added).

First, notice that Jesus was introducing a new philosophy of leadership and management. He was saying that if a person wanted to be a manager in His Kingdom, he must operate as a servant, not use the power of the position to lord it over people the way managers in the rest of society generally do. In fact, He indicated that the further up the organizational ladder a manager climbs, the more he must serve others, and the person at the top must actually serve like a slave. Second, Jesus affirmed that we *must* serve others as leaders and managers. The word *must* does not leave us any options. Jesus was saying, "If you are going to follow *Me*, you will manage this way!" He was saying, "This is not an option. You must use your position to serve the needs of others instead of serving yourselves!" And finally, He suggested there is nothing wrong with wanting to climb the organizational ladder as long as we are willing to use our position to more effectively serve the needs of others.

THE MANAGER AS A SERVANT

Matthew 20:20-28 is the foundation passage on which we build a biblical approach to management. All other biblical principles relating to management simply expand on, or illustrate in action, the principles and philosophy of leadership and management being taught by Jesus Christ in this passage.

I will be the first to admit that this is a very difficult passage to apply from a management perspective. The principles and philosophy of management taught in it are diametrically opposed to our basic fallen nature that is self-seeking and striving to obtain power to fulfill self-centered plans, goals, and objectives. In addition, very few role models effectively demonstrate the type of management philosophy taught by Jesus.

This fact does not free us from our obligation to adopt the management principles and philosophy taught in the Bible, however. As Jesus pointed out to His disciples two thousand years ago, and as He continues to explain to us today through God's Word, if we intend to follow Him, we are expected to adopt His management philosophy. He said we *must* learn to be servants.

Exactly what did Jesus mean when He said, "Whoever wants to become great among you must be your servant, and whoever wants to be first must be your slave" (Matt. 20:26-27)? It seems to me He was redefining the whole purpose and focus of leadership and management. He was stating that the manager was not to be served, but was duty bound to serve.

To effectively apply the principles of leadership and management being taught by Jesus in this passage, we must ask ourselves, "What is a servant?" A servant meets the needs of those he or she serves. Unless we are meeting people's needs, we are not serving them. Therefore, *the biblical approach to management*, based on the principles presented by Jesus in Matthew 20:20-28, can be defined as "serving the needs of others as they work at accomplishing their jobs."

There is a vast difference between the biblical approach to management and the secular approach. Earlier in the chapter, the secular definition of *management* was given as "getting work done through others." The underlying difference between these two philosophies involves the use of power, as illustrated in figure 3.1.

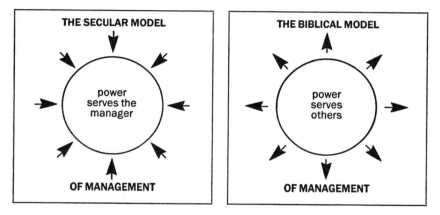

Figure 3.1
POWER MODELS

In the secular model of management, power usually serves the manager. In the biblical model, however, the manager uses his or her power to serve the needs of others.

Power is amoral—neither good nor bad. Power itself is never corrupt. However, people can be corrupted by power and, therefore, misuse the power at their disposal. Figure 3.2 shows how it is used on a daily basis in both the secular and the biblical models of management.

Managers in the secular model tend to use power to promote and serve themselves. That does not mean they never serve the needs of others. It simply means that as a general rule, left to follow their sinful human nature, they will tend to use power to promote their self-interests rather than consider how they can use their power to serve the needs of others.

USE OF POWER IN THE SECULAR MODEL	USE OF POWER IN THE BIBLICAL MODEL
• The manager tends to withhold decision-making power.	• The manager willingly shares decision-making power.
• The manager tends to make the plans and uses subordinates to carry them out.	• The manager eagerly involves subordinates and others in the planning process.
• The manager tends to seek recognition and reward for himself.	• The manager seeks to recognize and reward others.
• The manager tends to promote his own ideas, ignoring all others that conflict with his.	• The manager encourages and promotes his subordinates' ideas and is not threatened when they are better than his.
• The manager tends to view subordinates as a means to an end.	• The manager views subordinates as the organization's most valuable resource.
• The manager tends to be interested in what is best for himself.	• The manager's first concern is what is best for others.

Figure 3.2
USE OF POWER

ACTING ON BIBLICAL PRINCIPLES OF MANAGEMENT

What does it mean to adopt a biblical model of management? Earlier, I pointed out that we have far too few role models sincerely working to apply biblical principles of management as a lifestyle in their organizations. As a result, many managers who are Christians, and who sincerely desire to manage according to biblical principles, wind up being frustrated because they do not know where to start or what to do.

For example, when I was conducting a seminar in Canada recently on applying biblical principles to management, a local Christian businessman, who was unable to attend the seminar, called me during the evening at my hotel room and said, "Myron, I know I should be doing more to integrate the Bible into the way I manage and run my business, but I honestly don't know where to start or what to do." The strain and frustration were evident in his voice as he continued, "I read the Bible, but I need someone to help me take the next step and figure out how to apply it in forming a management perspective."

After hanging up the phone, I recalled my frustration as a manager and business owner when I began to study the Bible and look for its principles applicable to management. I remember that the first time I seriously studied Matthew 20:20-28 from a management perspective, I was unsure about what, how, and where to start applying the principles Jesus was teaching.

I did not know any other managers or businesspeople who were seeking and actively working to apply biblical principles of management on the job. And since many people reading this book may be experiencing some of the same frustrations, I do not want to just draw attention to those passages in the Bible containing principles of management; I also want to share some specific ideas and actions that may be helpful as you develop a biblical model of management for your own work in business. Figure 3.3 illustrates the far-reaching impact of establishing a biblical model of management.

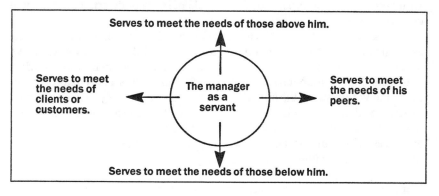

Figure 3.3
WHOM DO YOU SERVE?

Matthew 20:20-28 establishes the manager's purpose and presents a philosophy of management built around the concept that power should be used to serve the needs of others instead of self. Figure 3.3 shows four groups the manager must serve: (1) those below him; (2) those above him; (3) his peers (fellow managers on his level); and (4) his clients or customers.

Let us look at each group individually, and as we do, I will give you a personal assignment that should enable you to put biblical principles of management into action in your work as a manager.

Those below you—As the leader and manager of your subordinates, your primary role is to serve and meet their needs as they work to accomplish their jobs. However, before you can serve them by meeting their needs, you must first know their needs. Therefore, meet with your subordinates individually or in small groups to find out from them how you can more effectively meet their work-related needs. This may be awkward the first time or two you try it, but do not give up. Be sincere and demonstrate your sincerity by honestly working to meet their needs. When you are presented with needs beyond your sphere of control, simply communicate that fact, thank them for making you aware of the needs, and let them know you will do all you can to try to change the interfering conditions so those needs may be met in the future.

Those above you—You must serve and meet the needs of those above you as well. Most managers attend some type of weekly staff meeting to discuss the various issues at hand. However, in addition to that meeting, periodically meet with your immediate supervisor for the sole purpose of determining how you can better meet his or her needs.

Make an honest attempt to meet your supervisor's needs; do not think of it as a time of "buttering up" in order to look better in the boss's eyes. Initiate a discussion of your performance and how and where you can improve it. Most managers complain about not knowing what their boss really expects from them, but very few take the initiative to find out. I can assure you from personal experience that if you will do this, your boss will greatly appreciate it. As you have these discussions, you will be amazed at how you will learn to more effectively do your job and to better serve your supervisor. As Matthew 20:25-28 so clearly illustrates, that is your job!

Your peers—This group is often the most difficult to serve because all too frequently we tend to view our peers as competitors. Besides, it is easy to develop the attitude, "That's not my job!" Serving this group, however, is one of the most effective ways of demonstrating the biblical philosophy of management that Jesus taught. Effectively serving your subordinates and supervisors almost always serves your own needs as well. But you may never benefit personally by serving one of your peers. In fact, he or she may benefit at your expense.

Therefore, talk to your peers on a regular basis, on a one-to-one basis, and find out how you might be of service to them. Let them know that you want to help them meet their work-related needs as much as possible. But never expect anything in return. That is, do not try to meet the needs of your peers so they will owe you a favor in return. Do not refuse their help if it should be offered, though. Let them also learn the value of meeting the needs of others.

Your clients or customers—We need to continually remind ourselves that an organization exists to serve and meet the needs of its members, clients, or customers. It is amazing how frequently managers in organizations (even Christian organizations) seem to forget this fact so fundamental to organizational success.

Remember, your job is to serve people. You cannot serve them if you do not know their needs. Meet with your clients and customers on a regular basis to solicit their input on ways you can more effectively meet their needs. Your clients' needs may change frequently. There is no guarantee that their needs of the past will remain the same in the future. And your ability to meet those needs will be in direct proportion to your willingness and effort to find out these changing needs.

As a nation, we have almost forgotten the meaning of customer service. For example, as a management consultant, I spend a considerable amount of time traveling. Recently when I went to Alaska to conduct a management training program, two boxes of workbooks I shipped with my luggage failed to arrive at the baggage carousel in Juneau. I had used several different airline carriers on my trip there. First, I went to the counter of the airline that had brought me from Seattle to Juneau and tried to find out where my boxes were. I was told that they did not handle missing luggage and that I would have to go to the office that handled such problems.

I went there, but it was closed. I returned to the ticket counter and explained my problem to a different agent, informing her that the luggage office was closed. She explained that luggage was not her department, she only issued tickets, but she finally gave me a toll-free number to call in Seattle.

I called the number and was told that I would have to call a different office. I called that office and was told to check with their people in the luggage department in Juneau. I explained that no one was in that office. I was then given another number to call. I promptly called that number only to get a recorded message saying to call back during working hours the next day.

I gave up and went to my hotel room for the night. The first thing I did the next morning was call the airport and ask about my two boxes. They had not shown up on later flights, so I called the last number I had been given in Seattle the night before. I was informed that I had called the wrong office; they did not deal with missing luggage, either. When I asked who did, I was told, "I don't know. You'll have to check with the ticket counter at the Juneau airport."

By that time I realized I was facing a hopeless situation because the seminar started in less than an hour. Someone had lost my two boxes of workbooks, but no one seemed willing to assume any responsibility for finding out where they might be. When I returned to Colorado Springs a few days later, I learned that the two boxes had arrived at the Juneau airport on a flight two hours earlier than mine, the night before the seminar. They had been put behind a desk in the missing luggage office. The workbooks had been there all the time, but no one was willing to take the time to find them because the attitude was, "It's not my job!"

Do not ever be guilty of telling your clients or customers, "It's not my job!" If they have a need, your job is to do everything in your power to see that the need is met satisfactorily. Remember, service is every manager's and every employee's job.

THE BIBLE'S ROLE IN SHAPING OUR ETHICS

No biblical model of management is complete until biblical principles have been used to shape a set of operating ethics. Several years ago I was asked to write a book on business ethics based on biblical principles. The more I talked to people, however, and researched the subject, the more I discovered how difficult it would be to write such a book.

When they consider the subject of ethics, most businesspeople tend to think in terms of a list of do's and don'ts. As a result, when they attempt to put together a set of biblical ethics, many people look for verses that say, "Thou shalt" or "Thou shalt not." For some people, this may seem like a very simple task. However, even some verses that appear to make a straightforward statement, such as "Remember the Sabbath day by keeping it holy" (Exod. 20:8), are open to numerous interpretations. What does it mean to keep the Sabbath day holy? If you ask ten people, you may get ten different answers. While it may be a little easier to get agreement on the meaning of "You shall not steal" (Exod. 20:15), that verse can present problems in business, too. Therefore, we should use verses that help us establish unambiguous and clear-cut biblical principles.

Two particular passages need to be reviewed in the development of a concept of business ethics. The first one is the foundation on which many other verses pertaining to business ethics rest. It is one of the best-known, most frequently quoted, and least-applied verses in the Bible: "In everything, do to others what you would have them do to you, for this sums up the Law and the Prophets" (Matt. 7:12).

If you *faithfully* apply the principle in this verse, your management decisions, actions, and dealings with others will always be in accordance with what God wants and expects. This verse touches on every act, action, and reaction we experience during each day of our lives. It covers every deed we do and word we say. At all times, in all places, and with all people we are to consistently apply the principle stated in the verse.

And the principle is this: *In any given situation, always treat people just as you would want them to treat you in the same situation.* If we faithfully commit ourselves to applying this principle, we will not have to worry about whether or not the things we do are unethical.

The second passage is found in Matthew 5:39-42 (TLB):

"If you are slapped on one cheek, turn the other too. If you are ordered to court, and your shirt is taken from you, give your coat too. If the military demand that you carry their gear for a mile, carry it two. Give to those who ask, and don't turn away from those who want to borrow."

This passage seems to go against every fiber of our human nature. However, Jesus is teaching some basic principles that apply directly to managers or businesspersons wishing to establish a set of business ethics. That is, we should always be committed to going beyond what people and the law require of us.

I challenge you to study these two passages and use the principles within them to establish your personal set of business ethics.

REASONS TO APPLY BIBLICAL MANAGEMENT PRINCIPLES

As we near the end of this chapter, each of us needs to ask, "Why do I want to apply biblical principles to management?" This question should be answered carefully. What is your motive? Do you want to apply biblical principles to management so that you can manage better than other managers or operate your business better than others in the business community?

For years, my goal was to conduct my business affairs better than any of my competitors. That is why I initially wanted to apply biblical principles to management because I knew that biblical principles worked much better than secular principles and philosophies.

I soon discovered, however, that the Pharisees, who were the religious leaders of their day, also had a "better than" philosophy. They wanted to be better in the practice of their religion than any other group of individuals in their society. They worked harder at fasting—they thought better—than other people. They gave better gifts—they thought—than others. They even prayed better-sounding prayers than others. And yet, some of Christ's strongest criticisms were directed toward the Pharisees. At one point Jesus described the Pharisees by saying, "Everything they do is done for men to see" (Matt. 23:5).

Therefore, I urge you not to apply biblical principles to management simply because you desire to do things better than others. If you do, you are no better than the Pharisees of Christ's day.

There was still another reason I wanted to apply biblical principles to management in my earlier years. My goal was to make money. I knew that biblical principles were the best principles, so it followed that they would help me reach my goal of making money. Paul, however, sharply criticized people "who think that godliness is a means to financial gain" (1 Tim. 6:5). We should not desire to apply biblical principles to management in order to make more money.

Then why should we desire to apply biblical principles to management? James asserts, "Do not merely listen to the word, and so deceive yourselves. Do what it says" (1:22). We should do it because we are commanded to obey God's Word. We should do it out of a love response to Christ's love for us that produces in us a desire to be obedient to what God says in His Word.

Jesus declared, "If you love me, you will obey what I command" (John 14:15). We should want to apply biblical principles to management because of our love for Jesus Christ and His Word, not for any selfish reason.

There is still another reason, though, for applying biblical principles to management. If the friends, peers, and associates we work with every day are to be reached with the gospel, our godly example may pave the way. Jesus said,

> "You are the light of the world. A city on a hill cannot be hidden. Neither do people light a lamp and put it under a bowl. Instead they put it on its stand, and it gives light to everyone in the house. In the same way, let your light shine before men, that they may see your good deeds and praise your Father in heaven." (Matt. 5:14-16)

We should never lose sight of the fact that people are either drawn toward or pushed away from God by our actions. Therefore, what better reason can we have for applying biblical principles to management than to show our love for Christ and to love our neighbors?

EDITOR'S PERSPECTIVE

Myron Rush has drawn our attention to one of Christ's most important messages to managers, which Christ both articulated and modeled: He came to serve; we are called to emulate Him and become servants. The scripture Myron explicated, Matthew 20:20-28, is unambiguous with regard to the contrast between "the rulers of the Gentiles" who "lord it over" their subordinates while "exercis[ing] authority over them" and Christ's statement that "it is not so among you, but whoever *wishes to become great* among you shall be your servant" (emphasis added). Myron's emphasis on power, one aspect of authority, was so forceful that some of the scholars believed he narrowed his focus too much, but it is a legitimate way to call us to contemplate our volitional actions (whether they be active, passive, conscious, or unconscious ones) as we *seek to become great*—great in parenting, work, humility, accomplishments, fruit of the Spirit, character, and so on.

I want to pick up on this theme again shortly and zero in on Christ's use of the phrase "wishes to become great." God knows we all have a deep, inherent need to be significant; He created us to be that way. The Fall, which badly distorted our character and conduct, did not eradicate our need to comprehend and accept our significance.

We are so wonderfully made and carefully created in God's image that we are just "a little lower than God" (Ps. 8:5). In an unregenerate state, though, people have an unsatisfied hunger to be considered of consequence, and they will pervert their knowledge of what is right in an effort to satisfy that inherent need. But they will remain unsatisfied, no matter what they do, until they are reconciled to God. *Biblical Principles and Economics: The Foundations*, the second book of this series, briefly describes our hunger for an authentic human identity:

Fallen people always seek to satisfy their deepest drives and identity needs by relating to people, things, or their own accomplishments in the temporal realm because their identity is of necessity attached to such things when they are alienated from God. For example, they seek acceptance by doing things to please other people, or they strive for wealth, power, success, and other worldly symbols that speak of their personal competency in an effort to bolster their self-esteem. Persons without Christ are self-condemned to a false identity in this life.

Christians, on the other hand, are undergoing an "identity transplant" when their most basic psychological needs are being slowly detached from the world and rooted in God. (Volume 2, Section D, "Editor's Reflections," page 188)

Myron Rush mentioned that he had been asked to think about writing a business ethics book but had come face-to-face with the problem of determining how to present the subject matter in a way that would make it meaningful while avoiding the appearance of its being a book of rules. Everyone who contemplates writing a book on business ethics wrestles with many such problems. Perhaps the greatest temptation is for writers to restrict their discourse on business ethics to the intellectual dimension of people's makeup (the predominant focus in higher education). God's Word gives us the key to understanding ethics in a fuller model that takes into account what the Scripture calls the heart—the core of our intellectual, emotional, and volitional capacities. The biblical model can be diagramed as follows:

A. Intellect
   1. *Beliefs* about why we exist
   2. How we *know* why we exist
   3. Knowledge of *right and wrong*

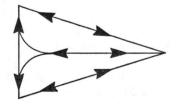

C. Volitional Actions
   1. Principle acts [A=B]
   2. Rationalized acts [A>B] [B>A]
   3. Rebellious acts [A B̸] [B A̸]

B. Core Emotional Needs
   1. Unconditional acceptance
   2. Significance
   3. "Kinship" relationships

Figure 3.4

All three aspects of the heart are integral to an understanding of human behavior in the marketplace. We will look briefly at each one and then interrelate them.

At the core of everybody's intellectual process is a framework of *beliefs* about God, self, other people, and the universe. Being finite, and having been born into an ongoing universe, we are (of necessity) required to walk by *faith*, and the structure of our faith forms the foundation for all other aspects of our reasoning. Every thought we have about our meaning and purpose in life flows from this reality. [See Diagram: A, 1.]

The great hurdle mankind faces, though, is answering the question generated by the faith premise: How do I *know* if my beliefs are true? The unregenerate cannot know if their beliefs are true, for they have suppressed the *true truth*, using Francis Schaeffer's term, in unrighteousness and have substituted their thinking for God's truth (see Rom. 1:18-23). Christians, however, can know that their beliefs are grounded in actuality because God has acted in history and provided us a body of recorded, substantive evidence that undergirds our beliefs (see Heb. 11:1). [See Diagram: A, 2.]

Coupling the truth outlined above with the fact that God's Spirit dwells with His children and convinces them that His unerring truth is plainly revealed in Scripture, the regenerate Christian can know with confidence what is right and wrong. [See Diagram: A, 3.] God's Word, God's Spirit, our mind, and our conscience all bear witness to what is knowable and right. Those who reject God's help (provision of Scripture and offer of His Spirit [see Luke 11:13]) are left to their own experiences and framework of beliefs. [See Diagram: A, 3.]

The intellect, though, is only one-third of what the Bible calls the heart. Another aspect is the emotional dimension. The word *emotional*, however, carries a connotation with it today that is not altogether satisfactory because it misses the depth of the Scripture's meaning. Biblically, emotions transcend feelings; emotions are inherent psychological needs that are an integral part of our makeup. To illustrate, God-created needs in our psyche are not explainable by referring to our intellectual or physiological qualities. As hunger is a created aspect of our physiological nature, not a function of our rational makeup, we also have certain core psychological needs that do not find their genesis in our intellectual or physiological faculties. For example, we all have created needs to be unconditionally loved and accepted. There is no real peace in the heart until we are so loved. [See Diagram: B, 1.]

And there are deep desires in each of us to be great or significant (see Matt. 20:26). This does not mean that everyone aspires to be the chairman of the board, president, or even a manager, but it does mean that everyone needs to be important, have a sense of high self-esteem, be successful, be competent, be powerful, or some other category that reflects his or her perceived worth as a creative contributor to life. [See Diagram: B, 2.]

And finally, we were created as social beings who derive a sense of identity through familial associations. We need to belong; we need to be members of identity-enhancing groups. [See Diagram: B, 3.] When these three core emotional needs are not being met, we perceive ourselves to be rejected or to have failed or to be on the outside looking in. These needs are inextricably attached to our personal identity. Our self-esteem depends on them. When they are not satisfied, as God created them to be, they will nevertheless be attended to in some fashion in the world.

Subconsciously and consciously we are forever monitoring and seeking to balance the intellectual aspects of our personality with our emotional identity needs in an effort to maintain or enhance our self-esteem. This can be understood as the dynamics of what transpires when the elements outlined in parts A and B of the diagram come together, interact, and are then expressed through our volitional actions (outlined in part C of the diagram). In my opinion, business ethics, management behavior, human drives, and the competitive urge—call it what you will—are best understood as an interaction within and between the aspects of our human nature embodied in the three dimensions of the heart just described—the core of our intellect, the core of our emotional (psychological) needs, and the core of our volitional behavior.

When our intellectual knowledge of right and wrong and our core emotional (psychological) needs are in harmony, we can and probably will act in keeping with the moral principles we know, with little inner conflict or strain. [See Diagram: C, 1. where A=B.] If, however, there is conflict between these two seats in the heart, we will begin to rationalize. [See Diagram C, 2. where A>B or B>A.] For the unregenerate, their felt needs for acceptance, significance, and kinship will generally prevail over their intellectual knowledge, unless their identity needs to be self-righteous are extremely strong, in which case their intellect may override their emotional needs.

Healthy regenerate persons, on the other hand, are always going through two kinds of transformations that help them overcome self-centered tendencies to rationalize and follow old volitional drives. Their world and life view is getting a biblical overhaul, which reduces the level of conflict between their intellect and their emotions—their beliefs, values, and knowledge of God's will are being biblically shaped by the Spirit; their core identity needs remain the same, but they begin to satisfy them by accepting Christ's unconditional love, the Holy Spirit's help in their becoming like Christ, and their adoption into the family of God.

But the battle inside some people becomes so intense and distorted that they actually reject a part of their God-given personality and let either their intellect or their psychological (emotional) identity needs totally dominate the other in their behavior. [See Diagram: C, 3.]

Do you wish to be a great Christian as you work as a professional manager? Then grow in Christlikeness and learn to be a servant to those above you, to those beside you, to those below you, and to any others who have an interest or a stake in what you do. Do you acknowledge your need for unconditional acceptance? In the final analysis only Christ can provide that. Only He can forgive our sins and justify us through His finished work. Others can emulate His acceptance—spouse, children, friends—but not our employers. Our relationship with our employers is fundamentally conditional. There we must perform in order to be professionally accepted. That is why the marketplace can offer no lasting remedy for our deepest needs for acceptance. There we must continue to perform repeatedly.

Do you want to be significant and grow in your self-esteem? In the final analysis only the Holy Spirit can re-create in us those qualities of character and interpersonal behavior that can satisfy this inherent need. Accomplishments that are either "position" or "possession" oriented will prove hollow and unrewarding in the long run. If we gain the world but have not loved God, spouse, children, and neighbors, we will experience guilt and emptiness.

Do you want to have true kinship? Only God the Father has the authority to offer us adoption and membership in His family. Being a member of a godly family, or a sound church, can emulate and provide some significant fellowship, but other kinds of memberships are very superficial and limited in their ability to satisfy our core need for kinship.

God wants us to be great! We ought to want to be great, for He created us to be great. But greatness is not achieved through the methods offered by the world. Having a godly character and behaving in a godly manner are the marks of true greatness and are developed in us through living *in* Christ, which fosters dying unto ourselves and living *for* Christ.

PART IV

THE MARKETER IN BIBLICAL PERSPECTIVE

Sheol and Abaddon are never satisfied,
Nor are the eyes of man ever satisfied. (Prov. 27:20)

The eye is not satisfied with seeing,
Nor is the ear filled with hearing. (Eccles. 1:8)

One can never put enough wood on a fire to satisfy it, nor is death ever satisfied with the number of lives it claims (see Hab. 2:5). And so it is with human desires; they are never-ending. Are our desires unending because of the Fall, or did the Fall merely produce a perverted mind-set that has twisted something intrinsically good into something bad? This question has implications for matters of personal stewardship, our selection and support of a particular type of economic system, and the legitimacy of many of our producing and marketing efforts.

The fact that mankind has a never-ending desire to produce and consume an endless array of goods and services is a human reality of God's own design but one perverted by the Fall. Idolatry in its many forms—idol worship, materialism, hedonism—was ushered in by the Fall. The "created" usurped the place of the "Creator" in the minds of fallen men. The assignment of greatest worth to things or persons other than God reflects humanity's alienation, rebellion, and lostness. As self-destructive as this perversion is, however, the capacity and the drive to produce and consume are good inherent characteristics.

God placed everything, except our fellow human beings, under our dominion. Our obligation to rule and exercise dominion and our capacity to carry it out were instituted before the Fall and repeated again after the Fall (see Gen. 1:26-28; 9:1-7). Not only did God give us seemingly unlimited intellectual skills to accomplish His directives (see the end of v. 6 in Gen. 11), He also endowed us with an inquisitive nature, creative drives, and the motivation to fulfill His desires.

If our capacity to desire relationships and things were restricted, we would be limited in our ability to know God and glorify Him by unlocking the wonders in the universe that point directly to His awesome glory, majesty, and splendor. Is this not what was meant when the psalmist declared that the heavens, earth, sea, and everything in them praise God (see Ps. 69:34)? Scripture's declaration that God created us for His own glory (see Isa. 43:7) tells us that when we think and behave according to His intentions, we manifest His glory, for He is the Author of our capacities. In this spirit James says, "Every good thing bestowed and every perfect gift is from above, coming down from the Father" (1:17).

Because the Fall perverted and twisted our motives and perceptions, greed, covetousness, idolatry, and discontentment entered into the lives of men and women. When people's identities are in the world, and not in God, their motives and intentions can only be misdirected and ungodly. That their behavior may serve God's greater purposes is only incidental and accidental from their perspective. God is not the object of either their interests or their desires. Even acknowledging these truths, though, does not make our inherent and seemingly limitless capacity to experience and express desires an ungodly fact.

Our problem is one of the heart. Paul acknowledged that he was made aware of his sin of covetousness through the law and that God used this to convince him of his need for grace, which included the continuing transforming work of the Holy Spirit in his life (see Rom. 7:7; Gal. 3:1-5). Paul also learned to be content with his physical conditions (see Phil. 4:11-12). Our heart's focus and attitudes need changing, not our capacity to desire.

God's stewards who work in marketing are involved in godly activity. They are engaged in carrying out the creation mandates when they, for their part, do their work in a godly manner. Dr. Wayne Talarzyk's chapter is the best comprehensive integration of biblical principles with marketing that I have ever seen. It opens up dozens of ethically sensitive areas where biblical principles apply to marketing, and Dr. Talarzyk relates Scripture to these issues thoroughly and precisely. Christians engaged in marketing would surely profit by taking this material and getting together with other Christians and discussing it so it might permeate their world view on marketing.

CHAPTER 4

BIBLICAL PRINCIPLES APPLIED TO MARKETING

Wayne Talarzyk

Dr. W. Wayne Talarzyk is Professor of Marketing at The Ohio State University, where he was Chairman of the Faculty from 1980 to 1988. His teaching and research interests lie primarily in the areas of managerial marketing, promotional strategies, consumer attitudes and lifestyles, and electronic technologies in marketing. He is the author or coauthor of fifteen college textbooks, three research monographs, and three professional manuals.

Wayne is married and has three children. He and his wife, Rosalie, and others colead a home church, which is part of Xenos Christian Fellowship in Columbus. He is also faculty adviser to Campus Crusade for Christ at Ohio State University.

The Bible tells us that the multitudes were astonished at Jesus Christ's teachings. Likewise today, we can marvel at the relevancy of what the Bible says about Christ, His instructions, and the directions He offers us for every aspect of our lives.

In this chapter we will explore the Scriptures for principles that can lead us into truth and understanding as we attempt to carry out marketing activities within the business arena according to God's will. The underlying perspective for this study is the fact that "all Scripture is inspired by God and profitable for teaching, for reproof, for correction, for training in righteousness; that the man of God may be adequate, equipped for every good work" (2 Tim. 3:16-17). We want to be properly equipped to do God's will as we fulfill our career responsibilities in the field of marketing, along with the other aspects of life.

Since not all readers of this chapter may be familiar with what marketing involves, we will begin with an overview of marketing. The next section focuses on some key issues that can be approached from a scriptural perspective. An ethical framework for integrating the laws of the land along with the ethical standards of the discipline of marketing and organizations that practice marketing are next considered as a floor for examining biblical principles applied to marketing. A list of selective biblical principles related to marketing is next reviewed along with a more in-depth examination of two composite principles with potential significant impact on marketers. A concluding section offers suggestions for adopting a biblical perspective toward the everyday practice of marketing.

OVERVIEW OF MARKETING

At the outset it is appropriate to consider exactly what is involved in this discipline called marketing. Many people, including some working in other areas of business, have only a limited knowledge or awareness of the role that marketing plays or should play in business and society. For example, if you stop people on the street or in shopping malls and ask what is the first word or idea that comes to mind when they hear "marketing," the most common response is "selling." Ask them for a second thought or explanation, and you will likely hear "advertising."

Neither response is totally incorrect. Both selling and advertising are parts of marketing, but they represent only a portion of it. Unfortunately these most visible components are frequently associated with negative thoughts or experiences. The idea of selling conjures up an image of someone trying to convince you to buy something you do not really want. Advertising brings to mind endless streams of messages trying to position the products and organizations they represent as the "best," whatever that means.

So what do practitioners mean when they use the word *marketing*? Perhaps the easiest and most straightforward explanation is "find a need and fill it." The most successful marketers are those who understand their customers and carry out the appropriate marketing activities to satisfy their customers' wants and needs.

This basic description of marketing can be expanded and clarified by a more formal definition, as established by the American Marketing Association: "Marketing is the process of planning and executing the conception, pricing, promotion, and distribution of ideas, goods, and services to create exchanges which satisfy individual and organizational objectives." Marketing, therefore, is much more than selling and advertising. It represents all of the activities necessary in developing and designing products, determining fair prices, getting the product to the right place at the right time, and effectively communicating to the marketplace that the organization has the products to satisfy customers' wants and needs.

Two additional explanations should sharpen the perspective on marketing in today's society. Theodore Levitt, a leading marketing scholar from Harvard, was once asked about the difference between marketing and selling. After reflecting for a few moments, he responded, "With marketing you are trying to make sure you have what you can get rid of, while with selling you are trying to get rid of what you have." His comment may seem like merely a play on words, but it represents a major philosophical difference in approaching the market-place.

Related to this is a second area of explanation, namely, the difference between a marketing orientation and a production orientation in running an organization. With a production orientation, an organization tends to define its business in terms of the characteristics of its products. A marketing-oriented organization, on the other hand, defines its business on the basis of the benefits the customer receives from using its products. For example, one manufacturer of hair shampoos might define its real business as producing shampoos (a production orientation), but another manufacturer might say that it is in the business of satisfying a customer's desire for bright, shiny, easily managed hair (a marketing orientation). Again, this is more than a choice of words. It really reflects a management perspective on how the organization sees the role of marketing.

KEY ISSUES IN MARKETING

With the explanations and perspectives outlined in the previous section, it is now appropriate to discuss a model of marketing that integrates an organization with its environment (see figure 4.1, page 72). Through an understanding of the components of this model and the ways they integrate, some of the key issues in marketing that lend themselves to the application of biblical principles can be identified.

A marketer really operates in two basic environments. The first, the *external environment*, is largely outside the control of the marketer. Marketers may influence their external environments to some extent through their market-ing and lobbying efforts, but by and large they must develop strategies to respond to the dynamics and influences of that environment. The *internal environment*, however, represents those areas where marketers have control. By properly managing the components of their internal environment, marketers attempt to respond to the external environment.

Model components—A marketer keeps in touch with the influences of and changes in the external environment through research. This tool enables the marketer to understand how suppliers and customers are being affected by the external environment. In this context, marketing involves both selling (the influence of customers) and buying (the influence of suppliers). Not all organizations view buying as part of the marketing function, but it makes sense to do so since an organization that trains its sales force to market to its customers should understand how its suppliers are using marketing techniques to try to serve them.

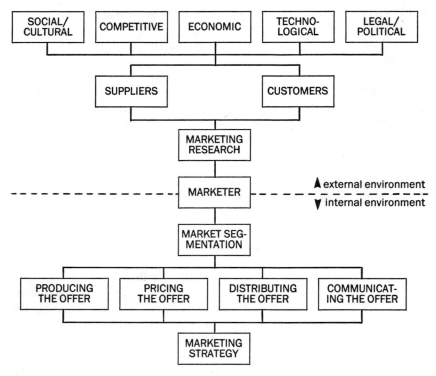

Figure 4.1
A MODEL OF MARKETING

As shown in figure 4.1, marketers need to be aware of how social/cultural, competitive, economic, technological, and legal/political issues and trends affect the goals-objectives and wants-needs of suppliers and customers. Based on an analysis of the external environment as a result of marketing research activities, marketers then determine which market segments they can best serve.

The application of the concept of market segmentation is a key to the success of many organizations. The basic idea is to divide the total market into identifiable, homogeneous subparts with distinct wants and needs and then to develop specialized marketing strategies to fit the needs of one or more of the segments. The logic is that you can more effectively use limited marketing resources by concentrating on a subgroup of customers that one can more efficiently reach and serve. Part of this ties in with the fact that it is difficult to be all things to all people.

Once market segments have been selected, marketers determine what products will be offered to those segments and how the offering will be priced, distributed, and communicated. Obviously decisions in the area of product, pricing, distribution, and communication have to be related to the needs of the chosen market segments along with an understanding of the previously mentioned elements of the external environment, which may constrain the marketing activities of any given organization.

In summary, an organization's marketing strategy is the way it combines the elements of its internal environment to satisfy the needs of various market segments based on marketing research, which helps the marketer better understand and respond to the constraints and opportunities presented by the external environment.

Spiritual topics—Based on this model of marketing, numerous topics can be identified so that marketers can study biblical principles for spiritual insights. In the following sections such topics are listed and briefly described along with a series of questions that need biblical direction.

Environmental issues—This topic deals with major questions addressing the overall external environment in which marketers operate and with some of the broad issues regarding marketing strategy. For example, consider the following questions: To what extent is it appropriate for marketers to try to influence the environmental elements instead of adapting to them? Should marketers try to change social and cultural values of a society to favor their product offerings? What are appropriate levels of interactions between an organization and its suppliers and competitors? Should an organization take an active role in influencing the legal and political environment in which it operates? To what extent is it all right to market products that may not be safe in all operating conditions or products that may cause health problems?

A separate but somewhat related environmental issue concerns whether marketing techniques should be used to "market" political candidates or religious leaders or organizations. Jim Engel, in two of his books (one coauthored with Wil Norton), offers some interesting insights and challenges in using marketing and communications concepts with Christian activities.[1]

Marketing research—Gathering information on customers and the existing business environment can be used to better serve customer needs and better enable the organization to achieve its other goals. A whole series of questions come to light, however, when considering the use of market research and market intelligence. For example, to what extent is it appropriate to disguise a sales presentation as a marketing research study, promise confidentiality in a research project and then not provide it, engage in industrial espionage, invade people's privacy, or gather inappropriate information without an individual's knowledge or approval?

Market segmentation—In deciding which segments to serve, the concerned marketer faces several issues. Should all segments be served in some fashion, even though they might not have the financial resources to justify an adequate return on investment for the marketer? Should marketers focus on what customers want, what they need, or both? Should the needs of certain geographic, ethnic, age, or religious groups of some other market segments receive special treatment or perhaps unequal treatment? Should customers be encouraged to strive for a higher standard of living, seek more possessions, participate in more activities, and so forth? Should larger industrial accounts receive preference compared to smaller accounts?

Product decisions—The marketer who wants to do the "right" thing in designing products must tackle challenging issues: creating planned obsolescence in products; holding a product innovation off the market until current product demand has subsided; adding product features that consumers do not necessarily want but they need (seat belts in automobiles); designing products that are not safe; marketing products that may cause physical harm or are frowned upon by certain segments of society (cigarettes, alcoholic products, three-wheel all-terrain vehicles, and so forth); underdesigning a product to save manufacturing costs; using ingredients or additives that may present a current or future danger to users or society; and changing parts of a product or making product substitutions without properly informing consumers.

Pricing decisions—As with other areas of the marketing mix, a marketer must consider several key areas in designing and implementing pricing strategies. Included in a selected listing are these: charging different prices to different customers for the same product; taking advantage of limited supply to raise prices; establishing prices as a come-on and then attempting to sell the consumer something more expensive (bait-and-switch tactics); implying that this is a "special" price when it is not (confusing people as to the "regular" price); misrepresenting how long the price will be available; and failing to disclose the full price or the financial terms associated with an offer.

Distribution issues—Marketers have to get the right product to the right place at the right time. They make decisions about the physical distribution of products and the channels through which a product is to be marketed. Some of the issues involving distribution include refusing to sell to or through certain middlemen; holding a product off the market somewhat to create an artificial shortage to enhance demand; exerting inappropriate influence over others in the channel; indicating incorrect information about when a product will be available for delivery; filing false claims for shipping problems; showing preferential treatment to certain channel members; and offering or receiving illegal or unethical incentives to do business with various organizations performing the distribution function.

Communication decisions—This area of the marketing mix involves such activities as advertising, sales promotions, packaging, and personal selling. It basically deals with any of the ways in which marketers communicate with their customers. Selected issues involved with marketing communication include implying that a product can perform in a certain fashion when it cannot; unfairly comparing a product against its competition; discussing only the advantages of a product without acknowledging its disadvantages or weaknesses; misrepresenting the terms of a special offer or promotion; exerting some type of pressure to sell a product when it is not needed or is inappropriate for the consumer; convincing a person to buy something that he or she cannot afford; and attempting to create a need for a product when one is not already present.

AN ETHICAL FRAMEWORK

As Richard T. DeGeorge points out in his book *Business Ethics*, much of what has guided the morality of the Western world for centuries and for the United States since its founding has been what is commonly referred to as the traditional Judeo-Christian ethic.[2] The Ten Commandments and the other Hebraic virtues of justice are added to the Christian virtue of charity to form this traditional ethic. In fact, most of the business laws, rules, and regulations in this country can be traced back to this Judeo-Christian ethic.

Businesspeople, both Christian and nonChristian, need to respond to the laws of the land. As shown in figure 4.2, these can be viewed as the floor beneath which we marketers cannot go without the distinct possibility of legal repercussions. Gene Laczniak and Patrick Murphy discuss this idea of the law as a floor in their book *Marketing Ethics*,[3] and Peter Dickson also makes this point in the chapter "Public Policy Analysis" in his book.[4] Many of the laws in this country touching on marketing topics, such as product safety, competitive behavior, truth in packaging and advertising, and so forth, relate to traditional Judeo-Christian directives. As will be seen in the next section, the Bible calls us to obey the laws of the land.

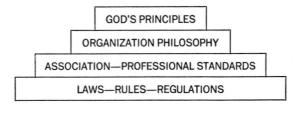

Figure 4.2
AN ETHICAL FRAMEWORK

Marketers, however, should be responsible to a higher standard of behavior than just the law. The idea is to go beyond the letter of the law and concentrate on the spirit of the law, which represents the second layer of figure 4.2. The American Marketing Association (AMA) has devised a comprehensive code of ethics to establish a strong basis for marketing behavior. (This code is presented in figure 4.3 [pages 85-86] and parallels many of the topics raised in the previous sections regarding issues in marketing.) When a given situation comes down to following the higher standard of a professional code of ethics or a lesser standard of a law, the former should prevail. The ideal is that a profession calls its members to a standard equal to or higher than the law. The issue of ethics in marketing has been discussed in the literature for years. Bob Bartels published his article "A Model for Ethics in Marketing" in 1967.[5] Patrick Murphy and Gene Laczniak in a 1981 review article identified over one hundred articles dealing with the topic.[6] In a more recent article, Shelby Hunt and Scott Vitell present a general theory of marketing ethics.[7]

At a third level, the organization an individual works for should have a code of ethics or operating philosophy that is equal to or higher than the profession's code of ethics. The assumption is that an individual would find it difficult to work for an organization holding a lower standard than the individual's professional standards. The next section will remind us that the Bible calls us to be responsible to our employers and those in authority over us. In all probability this responsibility can be extended to the leadings of our professional associations.

In the final analysis we are ultimately responsible to God. The ideal would be to work in an environment where God's principles are the standards, with the organization's goods, the professional association's guidelines, and even the appropriate laws being consistent with those standards. In some instances, however, an individual may have to go against the laws of the land, the standards of a professional association, and even an organization's philosophy if there is a violation of God's principles.

In the case of marketing, fortunately, most of our major activities in recent years have been consistent with the laws governing marketing behavior, the AMA's code of ethics, and even God's principles. It is refreshing to know that much of the traditional Judeo-Christian ethic has been applied in developing the relevant laws and the professional code of ethics, as Geoffrey Lantos points out in his writings.[8]

In several areas, however, it would seem that God's principles call Christian marketers to a higher standard, and as such, we need to carefully consider His directions before engaging in certain types of marketing activities. As we look at these principles, we must keep God's truth in perspective. Jack Sparks, retired Chairman of the Board of Whirlpool Corporation, gave the precaution in opening his acceptance speech of the W. Arthur Cullman Executive Award: "Today we look at all sides and all directions for ethics in the Eighties. We see plusses and minuses, pros and cons, goodness and badness, positives and negatives . . . sometimes to the degree that the Ten Commandments begin to look like Ten Suggestions."[9] As we continue in this chapter, we need to view God's Word as truth, not "suggestions."

SELECTED RELEVANT BIBLICAL PRINCIPLES

As stated at the outset, this chapter relies on the truths of 2 Timothy 3:16-17, which says that all Scripture is inspired by God and given to help us in all aspects of our lives. Many special principles, however, can be identified that have special bearing on the manner in which businesspeople should behave and marketing activities should be undertaken. In this section some of those principles will be briefly presented along with appropriate implications for marketers.

A Pharisee lawyer once asked Jesus, "Which is the great commandment in the Law?" Jesus, quoting from Deuteronomy 6:5, responded, "You shall love the Lord your God with all your heart, and with all your soul, and with all your mind" (Matt. 22:37). His response is, of course, consistent with the first of the Ten Commandments (Exod. 20:3) and many passages throughout the Old and New Testaments (Deut. 11:13, 22; 19:9; 30:6, 16, 20; Ps. 31:23; Jude 21). This truth is expanded in Deuteronomy 11:1: "You shall therefore love the LORD your God, and always keep His charge, His statutes, His ordinances, and His commandments." Each of us is also called to remember that "whatever you do, do your work heartily, as for the Lord rather than for men; knowing that from the Lord you will receive the reward of the inheritance. It is the Lord Christ whom you serve" (Col. 3:23-24).

The key principle from which all the others flow, therefore, is *loving God and serving Him*. In all that we do as marketers we should ask ourselves, "Are we really loving the Lord, are we really serving Him, and are we doing all for His glory?" Only from such a focus on our relationship with God and our desire to serve Him (the necessary vertical relationship) can we truly work with and serve others properly (our horizontal relationships).

Numerous scriptures comment on the ways we are to respond to the laws of the land and to those people and organizations having authority over us. "Let every person be in subjection to the governing authorities" and "Render to all what is due them" (Rom. 13:1-7); "Be subject to rulers . . . to authorities, be obedient" (Titus 3:1-2); "Slaves, in all things obey those who are your masters on earth" (Col. 3:22); and "Render to Caesar the things that are Caesar's" (Matt. 22:21)—all relate to this general topic. In fact, Jesus in the Sermon on the Mount taught that His followers should go that extra mile to be an example to those in authority (Matt. 5:41). These scriptures imply two basic principles to guide marketers: *obeying the law* and *being loyal to our employers and professions*. Of course, if an employer or a profession behaves contrary to the law or if God's law is threatened, "we must obey God rather than men" (Acts 5:29). The discussion here ties in with the points made in the section, "An Ethical Framework."

Christ's answer to the Pharisee lawyer's question about the greatest commandment contained another part: "The second is like it, 'You shall love your neighbor as yourself'" (Matt. 22:39). This quote from Leviticus 19:18 brought loving God and loving others together with the truth that "on these two commandments depend the whole Law and the Prophets" (Matt. 22:40). Loving others, even your enemies, is a common theme throughout the Bible (see Matt. 5:44; Luke 6:27; 1 Cor. 14:1; Gal. 5:13; Eph. 5:2; James 2:8; 1 John 4:7).

The love mentioned in these passages refers to a kind of love that only God can give us to pass on to others. It is the kind of love described in John 15:13: "Greater love has no one than this, that one lay down his life for his friends." This, of course, refers to the love that God has for us, "in that while we were yet sinners, Christ died for us" (Rom. 5:8) and the good news passage of John 3:16. In fact, 1 John 4:19 asserts, "We love, because He first loved us."

The resulting principle quite simply is *loving others*. A detailed explanation of this type of love appears in 1 Corinthians 13. From a marketing perspective, then, this principle tells us to really care about the needs of others. It ties in directly with the explanation of marketing given earlier in this chapter.

Other scriptures provide additional insights into ways we can objectively put this love principle into marketing practice. The next six principles relate to or support the so-called Golden Rule, namely, "Therefore, however you want people to treat you, so treat them" (Matt. 7:12) and "Just as you want men to treat you, treat them in the same way" (Luke 6:31).

Two such principles are *not stealing* and *being honest*, which are included in the Ten Commandments: "You shall not steal" and "You shall not bear false witness against your neighbor" (Exod. 20:15-16). These principles also appear in other scriptures, such as "You shall not bear a false report" (Exod. 23:1), "You shall not steal, nor deal falsely, nor lie to one another" (Lev. 19:11), "You shall not have . . . differing weights" (Deut. 25:13-16), "Do not lie to one another" (Col. 3:9), and Matthew 19:18-19 where the Exodus passages are quoted by Jesus. A number of Proverbs reinforce these two principles (see Prov. 6:12-13, 16-19; 11:1; 12:22; 14:25; 19:9; 20:17; 26:18-19; 28:6; 29:4; 29:24; and others). The applications for marketers are clear: Be honest and truthful in all of your activities, and do not take advantage of anyone.

This latter point leads to another biblical principle for marketers, *not showing partiality*. We are told that God does not show partiality (see Matt. 22:16; Acts 10:34; Rom. 2:11) and that He "desires all men to be saved and come to the knowledge of the truth" (1 Tim. 2:4). Likewise, we are reminded, "To show partiality is not good" (Prov. 28:21); and we are urged to do nothing "in a spirit of partiality" (1 Tim. 5:21) and to "honor all men" (1 Pet. 2:17). In our marketing activities we should show equal concern for all customers and not give preferential treatment to some without making it available to all.

Another appropriate biblical principle for marketers is *being at peace with others*. Mark uses this very phrase, "be at peace with one another" (Mark 9:50). Other scriptures affirm that "God has called us to peace" (1 Cor. 7:15); that we are to "live in peace with one another" (1 Thess. 5:13); and that we should "pursue peace with all men" (Heb. 12:14). The implication for marketers is that we should do all that we can to resolve any dissatisfactions or disagreements between us and our customers and suppliers.

Paul declares that we are to "be imitators of God" (Eph. 5:1). Perhaps, in a very limited way, we can see ourselves as marketers imitating the principle of *filling needs* by examining the ways that God promises to fill our needs. Joseph told his brothers that God would surely take care of them (see Gen. 50:24). Can we not expect the same promise, especially in light of "the LORD is my shepherd, I shall not want" (Ps. 23:1)? From the New Testament, we learn that our "Father knows what [we] need, before [we] ask Him" (Matt. 6:8) and our "God shall supply all [our] needs according to His riches in glory in Christ Jesus" (Phil. 4:19). The writer of Hebrews reassures us that "He who promised is faithful" (10:23). Jesus announced, "I am the good shepherd; the good shepherd lays down His life for the sheep" (John 10:11); "I came that they might have life, and might have it abundantly" (John 10:10); and "I go to prepare a place for you" (John 14:2). God has truly taken care of all of our needs for our salvation, for our abundant life here on earth, and for our eternal existence with Him. As marketers, we cannot begin to take care of all of our customers' needs, but taking care of some of them is the role we should play within the business arena.

We can also be partial imitators of Christ by following the principle of *being compassionate*. Psalm 111:4 teaches that "the LORD is gracious and compassionate." It is wise to cast "all your anxiety upon Him, because He cares for you" (1 Pet. 5:7) and because "the Lord is full of compassion and is merciful" (James 5:11). Colossians 3:12 brings this principle to us personally by reminding us to "put on a heart of compassion, kindness, humility, gentleness and patience." Other scriptures call for us to comfort one another, take care of one another, be devoted to one another, and be kind (see Rom. 12:10; Eph. 4:32; 1 Thess. 4:18; 2 Thess. 2:17; 2 Tim. 2:24). We can do a much better job of serving our customers and working with our suppliers if we can see them from this perspective rather than view them as existing to satisfy our needs.

Planning for the future seems to be another appropriate biblical principle for marketers. A study of the Bible from the beginning of Genesis to the end of Revelation makes it clear that God had and still has a plan. We should make plans but count on God to direct us (see Prov. 16:9). This dependence on the Lord is reinforced in Psalm 127:1 and 1 Corinthians 3:10-11. Jesus reminds us to "calculate the cost" before undertaking something, especially spiritual service in context (see Luke 14:28). Proverbs 19:21 and 20:5, 18 also mention plans and planning. The Bible does not speak against planning; in fact, it seems to support the idea, with the obvious importance of depending on the Lord in the design and execution of such plans.

A recurring scriptural principle is *not loving the world*. The point is made quite plainly: "Do not love the world, nor the things in the world. If anyone loves the world, the love of the Father is not in him" (1 John 2:15); "For what will a man be profited, if he gains the whole world, and forfeits his soul?" (Matt. 16:26); "And the worries of the world, and the deceitfulness of riches, and the desires for other things enter in and choke the word, and it becomes unfruitful" (Mark 4:19); and "Do not lay up for yourselves treasures upon earth. . . . But lay up for yourselves treasures in heaven . . . for where your treasure is, there will your heart be also" (Matt. 6:19-21). Marketers need to think through the role that they might be playing in leading people into a love affair with the world and its many things. Perhaps through product offerings and communications strategies, we may influence customers to strive for "the things of this world" rather than the more enduring "treasures in heaven." More will be discussed in a later section on this principle and the marketing issues involved.

Having a ministry is a principle that can be applied to everyone. The Great Commission, "Go therefore and make disciples of all the nations, baptizing them in the name of the Father and the Son and the Holy Spirit, teaching them to observe all that I commanded you; and lo, I am with you always, even to the end of the age" (Matt. 28:19-20), does not end with the clause, "except those of you who are involved in the profession of marketing." The book of Acts talks about "the ministry of the word" (6:4); Paul said to Archippus, "Take heed to the ministry which you have received in the Lord, that you may fulfill it" (Col. 4:17); and he encouraged Timothy to "be sober in all things, endure hardship, do the work of an evangelist, fulfill your ministry" (2 Tim. 4:5). Jesus, just before He ascended to Heaven, told His disciples that the Holy Spirit would come upon them and give them the power to become His witnesses throughout the world (see Acts 1:8). That same Holy Spirit is in Christians today, providing us with the power to be Christ's personal ambassadors in the world, including the marketplaces in which we work.

Throughout the Bible are examples of the need for wisdom, requests for wisdom, and God's giving His people wisdom (see Exod. 31:3-5; 36:1-2; 1 Kings 4:29; 2 Chron. 1:10; Ps. 111:10; Prov. 2:6; 3:13; 4:5; Acts 6:3; 1 Cor. 1:24; Col. 1:9). *Asking for wisdom* is a key principle for marketers since we face many situations where the Bible is not explicit about what we should do. Jesus promised that He would give "utterance and wisdom" to His disciples (see Luke 21:15). When we are not sure about something, we can ask God, and He will give us the necessary wisdom. That promise is stated, "But if any of you lacks wisdom, let him ask of God, who gives to all men generously and without reproach, and it will be given to him" (James 1:5). The next verse of James, however, warns that the person must ask in faith without any doubting—in other words, with the right heart attitude.

Having the right heart attitude is an appropriate principle with which to conclude this section. All of the other principles discussed here make sense only if the marketer has the right heart attitude. As Dennis McCallum remarks, "Any system which ostensibly follows the letter of the law in the Old *or* New Testaments, while making it possible to hide one's true feelings behind a mask of perfunctory nomism is decidedly sub-biblical in tone."[10] We can go through the right motions, hear and say the right things, even achieve some successes, but if the heart is focused on "self" or the "world" rather than on God and our "neighbors," our labors will be in vain.

The world may call this wrong attitude looking out for number one, but God's Word refers to it as "self-willed" and has some harsh things to say about such people who are "lovers of self," and "double-minded" (see 2 Pet. 2:10;

2 Tim. 3:2; James 1:8). The Bible encourages us to prove ourselves "doers of the word, and not merely hearers who delude" ourselves (James 1:22). We are reminded that God knows the "motives of men's hearts" (1 Cor. 4:5), that the "word of God . . . [judges] the thoughts and intentions of the heart" (Heb. 4:12), and that we are to do things with "sincerity of heart," pleasing Christ not men (Eph. 6:5-7; Col. 3:22-23).

The psalmist asks, "Create in me a clean heart, O God, and renew a steadfast spirit within me" (Ps. 51:10). May our prayer be the same as we strive to have the right heart attitude and apply the rest of these principles to our marketing activities.

TWO COMPOSITE PRINCIPLES

In this section two composite principles will be examined. The first involves dealing with others, and the second focuses on dealing with the world. Both build on the principles and scriptures presented in the previous section.

Dealing with others—Man is special. God said, "Let Us make man in Our image, according to Our likeness" (Gen. 1:26). From the beginning God has been concerned about each of us; even the very hairs of our heads are numbered (see Matt. 10:30). God loves us so much that He sent His Son to die for our sins in order to give us eternal life (see John 3:16; 1 Cor. 15:3), and He wants all to be saved and come to a knowledge of truth (see 1 Tim. 2:4).

The Scriptures also teach us that we are to love one another as Christ loved us (see John 15:12). In fact, Paul wrote that the whole law is fulfilled in the statement, "You shall love your neighbor as yourself" (Gal. 5:14).

In the previous section we discussed the significance of loving others as it relates to marketing. The principles of being honest, not stealing, not showing partiality, being at peace with others, filling needs, and being compassionate and understanding are all ways we can put into practice, from a marketing perspective, the idea of really caring about our customers and suppliers. We can be imitators of Christ by showing love and concern for others in the ways He teaches us through His Word.

Tied in with this specifically is the Golden Rule of treating others in the ways we would like to be treated. Just as we would like others to take care of our needs, we should focus on satisfying the needs of our customers. As stated earlier, this is what marketing is really all about.

The Bible also gives us additional insights into ways we can deal with others in our roles as marketers. We are called to "avoid worldly and empty chatter" (2 Tim. 2:16) and to not deceive with "empty words" (Eph. 5:6). We are to be honest and forthright in our communication with customers and suppliers. Likewise, we are to provide our customers with value for their money. Jesus taught, "Give, and it will be given to you; good measure, pressed down, shaken together, running over, they will pour into your lap. For by your standard of measure it will be measured to you in return" (Luke 6:38).

Jesus also advised, "Beware, and be on your guard against every form of greed; for not even when one has abundance does his life consist of his possessions" (Luke 12:15). We should not take advantage of our customers or suppliers to enhance our position unfairly; instead we should "pursue righteousness, faith, love and peace" (2 Tim. 2:22) in working with others.

As marketers with a desire to operate from a scriptural basis, it is not enough just to know and even understand these biblical principles. Our faith in Christ and knowing what He wants us to do is dead if we do not follow through with the proper "works" (see James 2:17, 20, 26). Indeed, in dealing with others we are called to "not love with word or with tongue, but in deed and truth" (1 John 3:18).

Dealing with the world—Now let us look at principles for dealing with the world and the things of the world. We are warned not to love the world (see 1 John 2:15). In fact, the end of 1 John says to "guard yourselves from idols," or as Kenneth Taylor puts it, "Keep away from anything that might take God's place in your hearts" (TLB). Such an explanation really brings into focus what might be considered an "idol." We are also warned about idols in Acts 15:20 and 1 Corinthians 10:19.

The Bible declares that "the earth is the Lord's, and all it contains" (Ps. 24:1; 50:12; 1 Cor. 10:26), but we are also told that "the whole world lies in the power of the evil one" (1 John 5:19). The world and everything in it belong to God, but at the present time He has allowed Satan to establish and control a world system, which Satan challenges us with as an alternative to serving God. This world system is a counterfeit of God's Kingdom. We are to avoid getting caught up with and pursuing this system.

The message comes to us in several ways. In one of the Ten Commandments, we are told not to covet (see Exod. 20:17), and the New Testament reminds us that the love of money is the root of all evil (see 1 Tim. 6:10). In very harsh terms, we are asked, "You adulteresses, do you not know that friendship with the world is hostility toward God? Therefore whoever wishes to be a friend of the world makes himself an enemy of God" (James 4:4). In a parallel passage to Matthew 16:26, we are warned again: "For what is a man profited if he gains the whole world, and loses or forfeits himself?" (Luke 9:25). Jesus was firm in His statement that "no one can serve two masters; for either he will hate the one and love the other, or he will hold to one and despise the other. You cannot serve God and mammon" (Matt. 6:24).

As marketers, we have to be "in the world." We interact with other businesspeople to buy and sell the things of the world. But we must keep the right heart attitude about why we are in the world. We are not there to get rich and lay up treasures on earth. We are there to earn a living through meeting the needs of our customers so that we can have the necessary resources to take care of our families and ourselves, and at the same time we are to serve the Lord. When we lose sight of this perspective, it is easy to fall in love with the world and turn our backs on or give only the leftovers to God.

We also need to be careful that through our marketing activities, we do not cause our customers to fall in love with the world. Through our product offerings and communication strategies, we may create inappropriate wants for things that lead our customers away from God and into a relationship with the world system. They may spend most or all of their time, energies, and resources on striving for and accumulating things of temporal importance rather than the more important spiritual things with eternal significance. Marketers who encourage materialism as a way of life are running counter to the truths of the Scriptures. We must not motivate our customers to pursue products or lifestyles that might separate them from God's love.

ADOPTING A BIBLICAL PERSPECTIVE

The composite principles just discussed and the principles reviewed earlier provide guidelines and directions for marketing decision making. There are few absolutes. Many decisions require careful consideration to ensure they are consistent with God's will. Toward this end, spiritual marketers need to adopt a biblical approach toward decision making, which involves prayer, the Word, and fellowship with others who are knowledgeable about marketing and share the desire to seek God's will in all aspects of life.

Prayer—Prayer can be the first line of defense in making proper marketing decisions. Paul encourages us to devote ourselves "to prayer, keeping alert in it with an attitude of thanksgiving" (Col. 4:2). James teaches that "the effective prayer of a righteous man can accomplish much" (5:16). And the Lord Jesus asserts "Ask, and it shall be given to you; seek, and you shall find; knock, and it shall be opened to you" (Matt. 7:7). Does this mean that we will automatically receive anything that we ask for in prayer? No. The idea is that if we ask according to God's will (see John 15:7, 16), He will respond by doing what is best. For example, as discussed earlier, if in faith we ask for wisdom, God will give it to us (see James 1:5). In some cases God will provide us with direction from the Word or through counsel from other Christians.

The Word—We need to be students of God's Bible so that we can make correct marketing decisions by "handling accurately the word of truth" (2 Tim. 2:15). People in the early Church "received the word with great eagerness, examining the Scriptures daily" (Acts 17:11). It is appropriate that we do the same. Jesus taught, "If you abide in My word, then you are truly disciples of Mine; and you shall know the truth, and the truth shall make you free" (John 8:31-32). It is of value to repeat again, as stated at the beginning of this chapter, "All Scripture is inspired by God and profitable for teaching, for reproof, for correction, for training in righteousness; that the man of God may be adequate, equipped for every good work" (2 Tim. 3:16-17).

Fellowship—God can also speak to us through other Christians and use us to assist others in their decision making. The Old Testament offers this advice: "Listen to counsel and accept discipline, that you may be wise the rest of your days" (Prov. 19:20). We are also warned, however, to "test the spirits to see whether they are from God" (1 John 4:1). We can best accomplish this by knowing the Word of God and ascertaining that the specific counsel we receive is consistent with biblical teachings. Other scriptures advocate sharing and fellowship with other believers (see Gal. 6:2; James 5:16; 1 John 1:7). The writer of Hebrews specifically encourages us to "consider how to stimulate one another to love and good deeds" (10:24).

Adopting a biblical perspective and seeking God's principles to guide us as we carry out our marketing activities can be summed up by Paul's words: "Finally, brethren, whatever is true, whatever is honorable, whatever is right, whatever is pure, whatever is lovely, whatever is of good repute, if there is any excellence and if anything worthy of praise, let your mind dwell on these things" (Phil. 4:8). Through the power of the Father, the Son, and the Holy Spirit, in our willing hearts, may this and the other words of God be the ways we conduct our careers in marketing and all other aspects of our lives.

Members of the American Marketing Association (AMA) are committed to ethical professional conduct. They have joined together in subscribing to this Code of Ethics embracing the following topics:

Responsibilities of the Marketer
Marketers must accept responsibility for the consequence of their activities and make every effort to ensure that their

It is understood that the above would include, *but is not limited to,* the following responsibilities of the marketer:
In the area of product development and management.
- Disclosure of all substantial risks associated with product or service usage.
- Identification of any product component substitution that might materially

decisions, recommendations and actions function to identify, serve, and satisfy all relevant publics: customers, organizations and society.

Marketers' professional conduct must be guided by:

1. The basic rule of professional ethics; not knowingly to do harm.
2. The adherence to all applicable laws and regulations.
3. The accurate representation of their education, training and experience; and
4. The active support, practice and promotion of this Code of Ethics.

Honesty and Fairness
Marketers shall uphold and advance the integrity, honor, and dignity of the marketing profession by:

1. Being honest in serving consumers, clients, employees, suppliers, distributors and the public.
2. Not knowingly participating in conflict of interest without prior notice to all parties involved, and
3. Establishing equitable fee schedules including the payment or receipt of usual, customary and or legal compensation for marketing exchanges.

Rights and Duties of Parties in the Marketing Exchange Process
Participants in the marketing exchange process should be able to expect that:

1. Products and services offered are safe and fit for their intended uses.
2. Communications about offered products and services are not deceptive.
3. All parties intend to discharge their obligations, financial and otherwise, in good faith, and
4. Appropriate internal methods exist for equitable adjustment and of redress of grievances concerning purchases.

Any AMA members found to be in violation of any provisions of this Code of Ethics may have his or her Association membership suspended or revoked.

change the product or impact on the buyer's purchase decision.
- Identification of extra-cost added features.

In the area of promotions.
- Avoidance of false and misleading advertising.
- Rejection of high pressure manipulation, or misleading sales tactics.
- Avoidance of sales promotions that use deception or manipulation.

In the area of distribution.
- Not manipulating the availability of a product for purpose of exploitation.
- Not using coercion in the marketing channel.
- Not exerting undue influence over the reseller's choice to handle a product.

In the area of pricing.
- Not engaging in price fixing.
- Not practicing predatory pricing.
- Disclosing the full price associated with any purchase.

In the area of marketing research.
- Prohibiting selling or fund raising under the guise of conducting research.
- Maintaining research integrity by avoiding misrepresentation and omission of pertinent research data.
- Treating outside clients and suppliers fairly.

Organizational Relationships
Marketers should be aware of how their behavior may influence or impact on the behavior of others in organizational relationships. They should not demand, encourage or apply coercion to obtain unethical behavior in their relationships with others, such as employees, suppliers or customers.

1. Apply confidentiality and anonymity in professional relationships with regard to privileged information.
2. Meet their obligations and responsibilities in contracts and mutual agreements in a timely manner.
3. Avoid taking the work of others, in whole, or in part, and represent this work as their own or directly benefit from it without compensation or consent of the originator or owner.
4. Avoid manipulation to take advantage of situations to maximize personal welfare in a way that unfairly deprives or damages the organization or others.

Figure 4.3
CODE OF ETHICS OF THE AMERICAN MARKETING ASSOCIATION

EDITOR'S PERSPECTIVE

Is it possible to read Wayne Talarzyk's chapter and come away without a renewed appreciation for what it means to have God develop a biblical world and life view in us that includes the integration of Scripture with our calling? I believe not. The very beauty of his chapter, however, only intensifies my anguish over the spiritual malnutrition condoned and fostered in Christian circles today by the continuous serving of an imbalanced spiritual diet that falls short of helping people understand God's will for their vocational callings.

When an angel of the Lord came and released some of the apostles from the public jail, he instructed them, "Go your way, stand and speak to the people in the temple *the whole message of this Life*" (Acts 5:17-20, emphasis added). The Apostle Paul told the elders of Ephesus, "I did not shrink from declaring to you *anything that was profitable*. . . [or] shrink from declaring to you *the whole purpose of God*" (Acts 20:20, 27, emphasis added). Peter declared, "Gird your minds for action . . . do not be conformed to the former lusts which were yours . . . but like the Holy One who called you, be holy yourselves also *in all your behavior*; because it is written, 'You shall be holy, for I am holy'" (1 Pet. 1:13-16, emphasis added). And finally, Christ said, "Man shall not live on bread alone, but *on every word* that proceeds out of the mouth of God" (Matt. 4:4, emphasis added). These four statements point to our need for the whole message, the whole purpose, every word from God so it can be incorporated into every facet of our lives.

The whole counsel of God is frequently missed, however, because of emphasis on particular aspects of God's Word. Let me illustrate. Some churches attach such importance to evangelism that one is made to feel guilty for expressing an interest in other aspects of the Great Commission where "making disciples" and "teaching them to observe all that I commanded you" are *equally* significant. In this environment, even the saved who gather regularly are so committed to rehearing the salvation message again and again in the hope that the "outsider" visiting the "family" may be saved that they do not even seem to be aware of the rest of God's concerns. "Family" members are served a biblical milk diet, which leaves them babes. They are saved, but undernourished and ill-prepared to function as light, salt, and leaven in the marketplace. There may be much discussion of Christ as Savior, but there is generally little reference to Him as Lord of every area of life.

In the "personal holiness" churches a person's lifestyle frequently becomes the standard of measurement by which he or she is perceived to be holy. Church and program attendance become marks of people's piety. Their personal habits with regard to tobacco, alcohol, literature, movies, dance, card games, profanity, sex, music, and other recognized worldly dangers determine their sense of personal holiness, not how they do justice and love kindness in the marketplace.

Orthodoxy—the accurate propounding of the historic doctrines of Scripture—is also "the" mark for a number of churches. Their focus is generally on strong doctrinal teaching that provides members with an accurate intellectual knowledge of biblical truths as they pertain to the nature of God, His acts of salvation, the nature of man, and other theological information that is worked out in (1) the observance of worship carefully regulated by Scripture, (2) discipline of the members when there is known sin, and (3) the careful and proper administration of the sacraments. The maintenance of sound theological teaching that works its way out in these three ways, as important as they are, does not mean the diet of teaching is balanced (food for worship, family, and work) or only being heard and intellectually acknowledged without being applied.

Bodies with a "personal experience" orientation should not be forgotten, either. Here one's conversion experience, baptism experience, mystical experience, or special gifts experience (miracles, healing, tongues, etc.) promises assurance of one's membership in the Kingdom of God. Their times together are spent in giving testimonies, stimulating one another to new experiences, and seeking to get the "inexperienced" into the fellowship through opportunities for them to have a valid religious experience.

It is not the editor's intention to speak against any of the four fellowships outlined above, or any of another four or five types that could easily be illustrated, but three vital characteristics seem to be missing from the outline. Pointing these out does not in any way imply that the characteristics already listed are somehow unimportant, less important, or perhaps in some circumstances even more important. They are being pointed out in the spirit of calling for the teaching of the *whole message*, the *whole purpose*, and *every word* from

God. And they remind us of what Dr. Packer and Dr. Talarzyk have already called us to remember and practice. Dr. Packer concluded his chapter by stating that three things were necessary for relational holiness in the marketplace: prayer; honest fellowship with other Christians in accountability relationships; and constant reflection before God on what is *best*, according to the Bible's instruction regarding righteousness, love, and wisdom. Dr. Talarzyk has just concluded his chapter with the section "Adopting a Biblical Perspective" in which he says that if we are to know God's will, we must be in *prayer*, abide in Christ's *Word*, and *fellowship* with other Christians so we may encourage and "stimulate one another to love and good deeds" (Heb. 10:24).

Therefore, my questions are these: Where are the churches in which prayer is a distinguishing characteristic of their ministry? Or putting it another way, what churches are known as praying churches? I contend that the hardest work to engage Christians in is the labor of prayer because no work so acknowledges our utter dependence on God, indicates our trust and hope in His sovereign rule, and helps us focus on the Alpha and the Omega, the beginning and the end of the purpose for everything. We exist for God. He has created us so that we might truly know Him, love Him, obey Him, and enjoy all of the blessings derived from His purposes.

Where are the churches known for their accountability relationships that offer much encouragement and strength for doing battle in the world? What church invites people serving in the trenches of the marketplace to bring their particular struggles to the group in order to receive counsel, be affirmed, and be infused with a renewed hope that Christ is indeed present with them as they pursue His objectives in His prescribed manner? If that does not exist, are we who spend the vast majority of our time engaged in God's dominion enterprises going forth to labor without being helped where the acid test of life is encountered? Surely we do not come to church to be entertained, seek an existential experience, or accumulate religious credits. We come to worship, fellowship, and be built up in Christ so we can be effective servants and stewards.

Finally, where are the churches with specific ministries targeted at helping businesspeople flesh out the Word of God so that they know what it means to do justice to their employees, employers, competition, customers, suppliers, and larger community? Who is helping these people face the challenges of their profession and learn how to effectively cope with the many temptations they encounter?

I am sometimes afraid that we have been trained too well by the clergy to focus on Paul, Peter, John, David, Moses, Isaiah, Samuel, Abraham, Jacob, and yes, even Christ as if they are great works of art in a museum. We need to hear the Word in obedience and identify with the tax gatherers, slaves, soldiers, shop owners, farmers, laborers, traders, fishermen, fathers, mothers, children, law-yers, teachers, tent makers, yarn merchants, and the others to whom the biblical messages are directed. In my case, I am to apply God's Word where I teach, write, travel and give lectures, sit on the executive committee of a board, hire a man to care for my property, deal with an automobile dealer or mechanic, respond to my boss's requests, meet with my colleagues, and engage in hundreds of other daily relationships while doing many tasks. God's Word is intended for the marketplace as well as for the family and church environments. Wayne Talarzyk's chapter is surely a breath of fresh air to those who love Christ and work in marketing.

PART V

ADVERTISING: INFORMATION, STIMULATION, AND MORE

Advertising in many ways is a public display, in bite-sized chunks, of one's values and as such is subject to everybody's moral review. But advertising is universal and unavoidable. Personal advertising (clothes, makeup, hairstyle, body language, mannerisms, etc.) and commercial advertising have much in common. They both find us trying to put our best foot forward in public. Intentional deceit is never defensible, on either the private or the public plane of life, but neither should we always expect people in private or public to expose all their shortcomings. It is picking the place to stop on the slippery slope that runs from absolute disclosure to full disclosure to appropriate disclosure to appropriate nondisclosure to material nondisclosure to intended deceit that makes agreement on what is good and bad advertising so difficult to come by.

This chapter, authored by Thomas Dunkerton, is one of the two in this book reflecting a profound personal faith that has been fired and tested in the marketplace. You may not agree with some of Tom's observations about where Christians can stand on "the slippery slope of advertising." The other scholars did not always agree with him or with one another. His position reflects a heart filled with Christian liberty, not an insensitive or a market-oriented one.

The reader needs to approach the chapter knowing that the writer expresses where he believes our Lord allows His children to stand when they are devoid of impure intentions and motives. For example, Tom is not going to deny his brother or sister the privilege of working out, before God, the question of whether or not it is right to be involved in advertising tobacco products. There are places our author would let others stand, without judgment, that he would not stand in personally. Tom Dunkerton worked for years on Madison Avenue in New York with the following scripture as his daily guide:

Trust in the LORD with all your heart,
And do not lean on your own understanding.
In all your ways acknowledge Him,
And He will make your paths straight. (Prov. 3:5-6)

He went to work every day assuming that he might return home in the evening
without his job. He went to work with God's standards in his heart, as he
understood them, and he went to work with the commitment to uphold them
with the full awareness that many around him did not subscribe to his beliefs. He
can tell many "war stories" of times when he was asked to become the account
executive for products he could not endorse or to use publications that violated
his standards or to handle advertising copy that "missed the mark." He told us
that he would say, "Lord, You have led me into this situation, and I now look to
You to either get me out of it or be pleased to work Your will in my life as my job
comes down around my head." Proverbs 3:5-6 was ever before him. The Lord
sustained him in a long and successful career in what is now the world's largest
advertising agency, but not without testing him by fire.

CHAPTER 5

BIBLICAL PRINCIPLES APPLIED TO ADVERTISING

Thomas H. Dunkerton

Thomas Dunkerton was a Senior Vice President and member of the Board of Directors at Saatchi & Saatchi Compton, Inc. He joined Saatchi & Saatchi Compton in 1950, left in 1955 to join Vick Chemical Company as Market Research Manager, and returned to Saatchi & Saatchi Compton in 1961 where he worked until his retirement in 1986. Prior to 1950 he worked with the National Biscuit Company and A. S. Bennett and Associates in the field of market research.

Over the years Tom Dunkerton has been very active at the national level in the advertising industry. He was a member of the Research Committee of the American Association of Advertising Agencies (AAAA) and of the subcommittee of the AAAA and the Association of National Advertisers (ANA) that planned the Federal Trade Commission hearings in Washington, D.C., in 1971. In addition to being on numerous committees of the Advertising Research Foundation, he was a member of their Board of Directors from 1970 to 1979. He is also a member of the American Marketing Association, Alpha Delta Sigma, Copy Research Council, Market Research Council, and the Advertising Research Committee. He served on the Market Research Committee of the Proprietary Association, which he chaired from 1977 to 1981.

Dunkerton has worked with the Gideons International, having held many offices in the Westchester County Chapter in New York. He is a past director of Rockmont College in Denver, Colorado, and was involved in starting the Community Bible Church in Northern Westchester. He sits on the Board of Directors of InterVarsity Christian Fellowship, Chapel of the Air, Neighborhood Bible Studies, the Greater New York Fund, and the United Way of New York State, and he is a trustee of David C. Cook Foundation.

Mr. Dunkerton attended Wheaton College in Illinois, graduated with a B.S. in marketing from N.Y.U. School of Commerce in 1948, and did graduate work at N.Y.U. Graduate School of Business in marketing and statistics.

A dvertising is a business. It is engaged in many normal business functions, such as accounting, office services, personnel, and management, and must contend with all the details these functions entail. Three specialized functions set advertising apart from the other more normal business functions, though, and these are creative, media, and specialized marketing functions. Not all advertising agencies have marketing departments, but most have creative and media departments. This chapter will deal with issues faced in the latter two.

Honesty in advertising—The most serious questions raised in the industry revolve around issues of *honesty*. Are you truthful in your advertising? Are you telling the whole truth or bending it a little to make the sale? The issue of honesty has been debated by the industry, by government officials, and by many self-appointed experts from various backgrounds.

Advertising has a poor reputation in the minds of many people, and terms such as *huckster* and *charlatan* have frequently been used to describe its practitioners. Advertising, however, is a very broad field, and it has many practitioners. You, the reader, have probably been an advertiser. Did you ever sell a car or a house and place an ad regarding it? If so, you were practicing advertising. Maybe you were responsible for an advertising campaign at your church when it had a two-week series of evangelistic meetings, and you prepared the publicity for it. If you did, you were practicing advertising—but the fact that you were, probably never crossed your mind.

My point is simply this: With such a wide variety of practitioners it is difficult (impossible) to control everyone who advertises or to get all to agree on a statement of standards regarding the practice of advertising.

Advertising also includes the ads of local retailers, auto dealers (new and used), food retailers, discount stores, and fast food franchises. These are just a tiny sample of the many who use advertising. Some of their material is professionally produced, but much is not.

Politicians are also big users of advertising. Their election campaigns depend heavily on it, and the industry has suffered some of its worst moments because of their unconstrained practices.

Honesty is generally the first biblical principle that comes to mind when advertising is considered. The Bible clearly teaches that we are to be honest in all our dealings. We are to be truthful in all that we say or imply (see Exod. 20:16; Prov. 12:17).

Is our advertising truthful, or does it stretch the truth and prevaricate? We have all seen false or misleading advertising, and that has caused many people to condemn all advertising. But wait, we should not judge all by the behavior of a few. Remember, too, that with real estate ads and used car ads (placed by the general public and by many practitioners at the local retail level), we have lots of opportunity for shady/shoddy advertising to appear in the public arena. This advertising, however, does not represent the work of advertising professionals.

I helped arrange a two-week educational program in advertising for the Federal Trade Commission (FTC) in 1970. It was an industry-wide effort to inform and educate the commission about the advertising business. As a result of that experience, the FTC decided to monitor national advertising more closely and to allow advertisers to name competitors in their ads. Today, the FTC gets an advance copy of all advertising that is going to appear in the national media. In addition, the industry set up the National Advertising Review Board and the National Ad Division to police and monitor advertising. This self-regulatory effort has been most successful, and because of it, practically all national advertising is honestly presented today.

Disclosure or deceit—Another problem for the industry is that of *full disclosure*. Most advertising, particularly broadcast advertising, tells very little about the product or service being sold. How much should one be required to say in an ad? How much can one say and not bore people to death? What are the most important points to put across if one is to make a sale? Again, people in and out of the industry have debated—and still debate—this subject at great length.

A word to the skeptics. You have to realize that billboards cannot effectively communicate more than eight or ten words (that is about all you can read at fifty miles per hour). Radio and television commercials are shrinking in length—fifteen-second commercials are popular today, and one cannot say much in fifteen seconds. In fact, not much more can be said in thirty or sixty seconds. Studies have shown that in broadcast advertising all one can hope to communicate well is *one* idea.

If I am trying to sell you a Jeep, there is not much I can say about the vehicle in thirty seconds. It has four-wheel drive, a new six-cylinder engine, and starts at twelve thousand dollars. To purchase a Jeep intelligently, you are going to have to visit the dealer, read the brochures, compare it with other and similar vehicles, and talk with owners of the vehicles. Then you are ready to make a purchase that could be called an intelligent one. There is no way that advertising could provide in an interesting way all you need to know to make an informed decision.

The same is true for a cough syrup. I will tell you it could stop a cough and it tastes good so the kids will not fight it. But to make an intelligent buying decision, you need to get advice from your doctor or pharmacist, read the label and material packed in the box, and possibly talk with users of the product. Advertising simply cannot provide all you need to know.

Has advertising therefore been wrong or misleading if it has not told you everything? I do not believe it has been. In the time or space allowed, advertising can communicate one idea and certainly no more than two ideas about a product or service.

Let me illustrate in another way the advertiser's problem. You have sat through countless sermons in your lifetime, and they have each consumed twenty to forty minutes. How many of these can you recall in detail today? Remember, we are now talking about thirty minutes versus the thirty seconds an advertiser has. People have short attention spans, and we are dealing with a brain that cannot absorb and recall everything that has been put before it. Studies show that after twenty-four hours the average person cannot recall eighty-five percent of the previous day's information.

If people can routinely recall only fifteen percent of yesterday's information, the job of the effective communicator is to try to increase that percentage to twenty or twenty-five percent. One can do that only by having a narrowly focused, simple, and interesting message. It is better to communicate one point well than to tell people everything and end up registering nothing.

Challenging the status quo—Basically, advertising (for most products or services) *promotes dissatisfaction with the status quo* in an endeavor to get you to purchase a particular product. Is stimulating discontent with the status quo an ethical way to sell? Is that compatible with biblical principles? Are we not supposed to be content with what we have (see Phil. 4:11; Heb. 13:5)? Do we really need the latest model car, can opener, refrigerator, or microwave oven to find contentment and satisfaction? I believe that making one dissatisfied with the status quo is an important way to sell. But is the approach biblical?

It would be very difficult to sell you a new car if we did not make you dissatisfied with your current model. The latest style, antilock braking systems, a more powerful engine, smoother ride, and an air bag system are all improvements that just might make a new car purchase worthwhile. For most people, a new car every year would be a waste of money, but it could be a viable purchase every three to five years.

The United States economy thrives on change and new products. A deodorant that worked for up to seventy-two hours would be better than some current brands. Getting people to switch products because of some dissatisfaction with their old one is a legitimate function of advertising. When such changes enhance people's well-being, I believe it is appropriate to promote dissatisfaction with the status quo, and I can see nothing wrong with this from a biblical perspective.

Product restrictions—A battle is raging in the industry today over the advertising of certain products. For example, should we allow cigarettes to be advertised? Should we allow alcoholic beverages to be advertised? The stated position of the industry is that if it is legal to sell the product, it should be legal to advertise it. Is that biblical? How does one reconcile the fact that we can sell alcoholic beverages and advertise them in the print media but cannot advertise them in the broadcast media? Why can one advertise beer on television, but not liquor? Factors of both governmental policy and societal mores affect a fair discussion of this matter. The Bible does not condemn drinking, but it certainly does not encourage it, either. It is very specific, however, about condemning drunkenness (see Prov. 20:1; Isa. 5:22).

Most people have little objection, if any, to the advertising of most products or services. When products can be deleterious to one's health, though, many people feel they should not be promoted in any way at all. In the United States today, by common consent, cigarettes and liquor ads are excluded from the broadcast media, although they can appear in print, in outdoor media, and at promotional events such as auto racing and tennis matches. Currently some people are agitating to remove beer advertising from all sporting events because of the many impressionable young people who watch these events. A few people in government would further restrict these products and would not allow them to be advertised at all. But why should one be allowed to advertise in one media and not another?

Regulation—Another lively issue concerns regulation of advertising. Much local and regional advertising is not regulated—yellow pages, classified ads, local retail advertising. National advertising, on the other hand, is regulated to some extent by the media, the Federal Trade Commission, and a relatively new self-regulatory body set up by the industry—the National Advertising Review Board. From a biblical perspective, one has to consider whether advertising should be regulated at all. If so, who should do the regulating? Who will be the arbiter?

Whenever an individual is appointed to be an arbiter, one has to wonder what values that person will bring to the decision-making process. The arbiter, in effect, becomes a "god" and has the final say on what one can or cannot do. Can fallen people regulate themselves? Is it really a government function? In Europe today there is considerable fear on the part of many in government over the ability of the local residents to pick up television broadcasts from other countries via satellite. European governments control their television broad-casts, and a program or commercial coming in from the United States, Luxembourg, or wherever undermines their control and makes them nervous.

Conflicting interests—From the client (advertiser) side of the fence also comes the question of client conflict. Can an agency handle advertising for two competing motor car companies or two competing detergents? If your client makes a cake mix, but your ad agency does not handle it, can you handle a competitor's cake mix? There are many such conflicts. Does the Bible have anything to say about such matters? Our inability to serve two masters at one time (see Matt. 6:24) might apply, but that really refers to serving God and things of the world, not two different manufacturers. Yet, is it really different?

The point made by the Bible that one cannot serve two masters is probably loved by all clients and hated by all ad agencies. It is well established in the industry, though, that if you handle Tide detergent, for example, you cannot handle a competing detergent, even from the same manufacturer. But why not?

It gets even murkier as we go behind the scenes. If you advertise Colgate toothpaste, does that mean you cannot handle any products from Lever Brothers—products like margarine, shampoos, or deodorizers? The agency that handled the ads for Northwest Airlines when it made all its domestic flights nonsmoking also handled Planters Peanuts and other products for the tobacco giant, RJR. The agency was summarily dismissed by RJR when the Northwest Airlines' ads appeared. Was that ethical?

As clients get more acquisition minded and get bigger and bigger, the whole question of conflicting interests will get larger as well.

Pursuit of excellence—Much has been said in this country about the pursuit of excellence. We all give lip service to it, but who determines what that is in advertising? By what standards is it to be determined? How do you make intelligent judgments about what is excellent in advertising? Does the Bible address this topic? It is obvious that we need God's standards so that we may approve what is excellent (see Phil. 1:10), but much of that judgment is left up to us to make. What may be an excellent ad for a local retailer would probably not do for a large packaged goods manufacturer whose very existence depends on excellent advertising. Excellence in the field of advertising has many differing standards.

Child-oriented advertising—Many people question whether advertisers should advertise products and services directly to children. There has been some self-regulation here, and some at the government level, but the question persists.

Should one advertise directly to children? Does the Bible give us any help here? It tells us to train up our children in the way they should go (see Deut. 6:6-7; Prov. 22:6; Eph. 6:4), and it instructs parents to make sure their children are instructed in biblical matters (see Prov. 6:20; 13:1; 15:5). The onus in this case is on the parents, not on those who advertise or those who govern.

Advertising and programing—Also, in the minds of many people, advertising and broadcast programing are inseparable. They feel that television advertising and programing have an undue influence on our society and that both should be highly regulated. But who is to do the regulating? Whose standards are to apply? Whose world and life view will be presented? Can Scripture help us with this? The industry has an obligation to influence society for good, not bad, but whose definition of good or bad are we to use? As long as we live in a pluralistic society, such questions will not be answered easily.

Television, in particular, has changed this country in ways we have yet to begin to fathom. I personally believe that one of the driving forces in our race relations problems of the sixties was the fact that the Black community had observed on television for some years how the other eighty percent lived, and they wanted a share of the good life. Their desire was not inherently bad.

As television has matured, it has taken more and more excitement to catch and retain the viewers' interest. It takes more stimulus to get people to listen. Because of this reality, television programing has too often focused on the base, sensuous, and violent aspects of life, which in turn affect our social values. It is one thing to see a movie once a week or once a month, but to see one or more a day, day after day, is incredibly influential. That does things to people. Because of this more base diet and the amount of television we watch, we have become more prone to violence and a lot more accepting of perverse conduct than we used to be.

Selections of media vehicles—Advertisers buy space and time in the media. They are looking for efficient ways to reach their target audiences. Then what obligations do the advertisers and ad agencies have to place their advertising in wholesome media vehicles? What can Scripture do to help us sort this out? Certainly, we are to promote wholesome living, and we are not to encourage licentiousness. Scripture is filled with admonitions of this type.

But let us not overlook the fact that major advertisers are also interested in protecting their good name. They understand the prudence of Proverbs 22:1: "A good name is more desirable than great riches." For them, however, the good name is a means to the end of riches.

Skin books like *Playboy* and others have great demographics for male-oriented products. They effectively deliver large numbers of upscale young males to the advertisers. If numbers are all you use as your measure of acceptability, you will advertise in those magazines. Most advertisers do not use them, and many that once did have gotten out of them because of the pressure generated by the Reverend Mr. Donald Wildmon, Executive Director of the American Family Association, and others. We need advertisers who will promote wholesome advertising vehicles and will stand up against the crowd when that is appropriate.

Current or long-run objectives—Most American advertisers take a very short-run view of things—make the sales quota this year and worry about next year at another time. Because of people's job mobility today, many decision makers know they will be somewhere else next year, and because they are primarily judged on this year's results, they do not worry about next year. But is it biblically correct to ignore the long term in your decision making for the short haul? What obligation do I have to think about what the next branch manager will inherit from my decisions? Scripture calls us to have a strong interest in the long haul.

Religious and public service advertising—What obligation do advertisers have to promote and support good causes with advertising? Should they support religious broadcasting and other religious media vehicles? Which ones should they support, and which ones should they not support? Should they support public broadcasting and cable television? Should advertisers be concerned about public service advertising and programing? If so, how should that concern be manifested?

The sponsorship of religious programing and print vehicles has given advertisers more gray hairs than they would want to publicly admit. If you sponsor one religious group, how do you screen out the others without making the public mad at you? It is such a "can of worms" that most advertisers simply will not support any religious vehicle of any sort. "Better to be neutral than offend many" seems to be the reasoning.

Most advertisers and media support public service advertising, however. It is in many respects some of the finest advertising done in the United States today. Generally, the media run it at no charge, and the ad agencies produce it for their out-of-pocket expenses. The American Red Cross, United Way, and Smokey the Bear are a few that have done a lot of good, at little or no cost to the sponsoring agency. Freely giving of oneself, I believe, is a sound biblical ideal that can be applied correctly in religious or nonreligious areas of advertising.

What can we conclude? For years, the advertising industry has taken the position that advertising does not establish standards of conduct; rather, it mirrors what is currently going on in the public. Television programing and movies, however, do influence behavior—and in increasingly ungodly ways. Advertisers do not produce media vehicles; they purchase ad space and time in the vehicles they believe will aid their sales efforts. Advertisers and agencies have an obligation, though, to see that their ads appear in a wholesome viewing environment. They do not have to advertise in degrading programs or magazines. Most advertisers and agencies can and do avoid these vehicles. Unfortunately, other advertisers pick up this "distress merchandise," and the seedy and shoddy stuff continues to grow as the culture decays.

What does the Bible have to say about advertising? In specific terms, not a great deal; in terms of principles, a great deal. Advertising is a business, subject to all the forces that influence businesses in general. Advertising that is honest serves the good of the general public. To the extent that it is dishonest, it helps to sow the seeds of destruction for our society. The solution to the general problem of cultural decay must be found outside the business community, though. Only the power of the gospel can change the hearts of those who advertise and those who create and place the ads.

Tom Dunkerton has called it as he sees it. He does not apologize for the advertising profession and its work at the national level. While acknowledging that much could be improved, especially in local advertising, and while admitting that a wide range of preferences, tastes, nuances, implications, and intentions might be read into any ad, he basically believes that reading negative implications into most of our national advertising probably reveals more about the interpreters of the material than it does its creators: "To the pure, all things are pure; but to those who are defiled . . . nothing is pure" (Titus 1:15).

We should not expect the same standards of sensitivity, however, from those who work in the industry and do not love and obey Christ as we would from those who do. Advertising is in need of the salt, light, and leaven that sensitive but prudent Christians can bring to the profession. In fact, I would encourage creative and talented Christians who have aptitudes and opportunities to work in advertising to seek employment in the field.

Recently, a young man came to me in a state of depression because his Christian friends, upon learning that he had accepted employment with an ad agency, questioned the compatibility between his profession of faith in Christ and his choice of employment. I was—and am—grieved by the cultural world view that generates this kind of conclusion. That is like saying Christians should not own and operate secondhand car businesses because they have a stereotyped image distasteful to some. This kind of thinking should have no place in the Christian's life. There is nothing inherently wrong with either selling secondhand cars or advertising. Godly attitudes and conduct are needed in both, and in every other profession.

God gave the Church a number of genuine blessings during the Reformation, and one of those was the reaffirmation of the biblical truth that all honest employment is godly employment, glorifying and pleasing to God. This wonderful truth is operationally slipping through our fingers once again, though. Oh, lip service is still paid to it, like an historic relic, but there is little genuine support for it from our pulpits or in the seminaries. It is fast becoming an historic footnote, which is tragic because it fosters a resurgence of the false dichotomy between the sacred and the secular where the world is perceived to be bad. Christians must not retreat from the world.

Christians have a special contribution to make to the profession of advertising. Christians are *not*, as a group, likely to be more creative or capable of handling basic media decisions than nonChristians, but God provides His children with moral criteria to shape their skills of discernment that can be extremely helpful in elevating the standards of the advertising profession. Let me explain.

The world's ideas about morality are pretty much restricted to the overt activities of people. That is why if you try to tell people whose behavior is morally sound that they are sinners, they will be offended and think you are a self-righteous fanatic or a religious freak. People who are behaviorally moral but unregenerate seldom pay any attention to their attitudes, intentions, motives, and thoughts, which are critically important to God, for these really determine the character of all conduct (see 1 Cor. 4:5; 2 Cor. 5:12; 10:18). Christians have the advantage, because of their new nature, of understanding the relationship between the appetites of a fallen and base nature and those stimuli motivating people to try to satisfy their perverted drives in an inappropriate way. For example, there are false forms of security, false concepts of success, and false ways to seek self-esteem, and Christians in advertising have the opportunity to shape and direct creative advertising so it appeals to the best aspects of our nature, not to its worst qualities.

On the other hand, those who create advertisements are not responsible, per se, for the perceptions of those who hear or see them. The advertisers can work very hard to present a wholesome ad, and someone who sees it can still be perversely stimulated. This point is embodied in Titus 1:15, quoted a moment ago: "To those who are defiled . . . nothing is pure."

One last area of concern that troubles sensitive people—Christians and nonChristians alike—should be discussed. It is the issue raised by John Kenneth Galbraith, David Braybrooke, and others who have argued for years that advertising eventually will destroy the free market system. These people argue that advertising is so effective that it is *creating wants* and thus destroying consumer sovereignty. Classical economic theory holds that corporations are accountable to the marketplace where the consumers are deemed to be sovereign. The consumers vote by buying products of their choice, and in doing so, they reward the good companies and penalize the inefficient ones. The question being raised is a serious one, for corporations claim they are accountable to the marketplace and the legitimacy of this rests on the assumption that consumers are sovereign.

Tom Dunkerton addressed this matter, too, although from the opposite perspective, when he described advertising in the following way:

> Basically, advertising (for most products or services) *promotes dissatisfaction with the status quo* in an endeavor to get you to purchase a particular product. Is stimulating discontent with the status quo an ethical way to sell? . . . I believe that making one dissatisfied with the status quo is an important way to sell.

He did not glorify dissatisfaction but rejected the assumptions that the status quo in the marketplace is an acceptable modus operandi.

At the heart of the Galbraithian concern—the creating of wants through business advertising—is the assumption that mankind is somehow a deterministic being whose ability to be manipulated and controlled by the stimulus of others is a serious possibility. Tom Dunkerton, on the other hand, rejects this view of man. He sees the outcome of advertising as very beneficial instead—stimulating a dynamic economic system that generates a higher standard of living for everyone.

The introduction to Part IV of this book noted that God had created us with a seemingly inexhaustible capacity for desires, the capacity for creativity, the curiosity to forever seek to unlock the mysteries bound up in God's created order, and the motivation to strive to have dominion and rule over the universe. While it was acknowledged that the Fall opened the door to practical idolatry—materialism, hedonism, and even outright idol worship—it was still argued that mankind's unquenchable desires were the very avenue by which God would be glorified as His image bearers continued to discover the God-created potential locked up in the universe. I, therefore, also reject the Galbraithian argument against advertising.

The status quo should be an unacceptable state in the marketplace; Christians should always seek to create those things that will truly benefit their fellows. Certainly, some people express perverted values as the process is being carried out, but the waste and perversions of some should not become the grounds for limiting the efforts of the many who have proven over the centuries that there seems to be no limit to God's created opportunities for discovery.

PART VI

A THEOLOGICAL PERSPECTIVE ON ACCOUNTING

As this chapter was being created, and as we approach it now, I cannot help wondering how many of those who read it will have ever thought that biblical principles could be applied to accounting. Well, a lot of Scripture addresses the thorniest issues faced by those in the accounting profession, and Dr. Walter Harrison, Jr., identifies these issues and brings Scripture to bear on them. One need not have any interest whatsoever in the discipline of accounting to find this chapter both fascinating and enlightening.

Dr. Harrison demonstrates that accounting is, in truth, more of a social science, governed by behavioral factors, than it is a discipline governed by mathematical principles. It is a business function that rests almost exclusively atop moral judgments. While it is true that it is related to the natural law because its presentation is done through the language of mathematics, it is not otherwise truly governed by natural law principles.

The chapter also shows how God's revealed moral principles are so encompassing as to include something that seems, on the surface at least, to be so removed from theology. Walter Harrison indicates that accounting is close to the heart of theology.

The reader should emerge from Dr. Harrison's chapter with a deeper appreciation for the integrity required by any public accountant if he or she is to fairly present financial information that takes into account the legitimate needs of both those presenting the information (directors and managers in particular) and those needing to use that information for purposes related to their special interest (bankers, investors, suppliers). Accounting information is the bridge between the two sides, but when managers have personal reasons for wanting to look their best through their financial reports, the accountants can be faced with some real tests for their integrity. Not only dishonest people like to appear favorably to others. We all rationalize and justify our actions and seek to put the best light on them. This is natural, a reflection of our fallen nature, but persons in accounting are charged with the responsibility of maintaining the integrity of the reports and with not allowing the darker side of our nature to deceive us or others.

The chapter is fun to read because we get a glimpse into the inner workings of the accounting profession. And we learn of the realities of "creative account-ing," "cooking the books," "shopping for opinions," and other similar practices that have very legitimate places in accounting, but also open the doors wide to the abuses and deceits that can and do occur in the accounting profession, as in all others.

Dr. Packer, the only theologically trained scholar attending the Collo-quium where these chapters were presented, exclaimed, "Oh, that is what my accountant has been trying to explain to me all these years," when Dr. Harrison was describing "cooking the books." We all laughed with Dr. Packer at his sudden realization that there are "different accounting strokes for different folks." The tax agent, for example, does not necessarily get the same informa-tion, in the same form, as the banker—and for justifiable reasons.

The reader should enjoy this chapter on the integration of biblical princi-ples with accounting where debits, credits, trial balances, income statements, balance sheets, and other accounting jargon never appear. It is truly a journey into the *heart* of accounting.

CHAPTER 6

BIBLICAL PRINCIPLES APPLIED TO ACCOUNTING

Walter T. Harrison, Jr.

Walter T. Harrison, Jr., Ph.D., CPA, is Professor of Accounting and holder of the KPMG Peat Marwick-Thomas L. Holton Chair in Accounting at Baylor University. A graduate of Baylor, Oklahoma State University, and Michigan State University, he has also taught at the University of Texas and at Stanford University. His research has been published in Journal of Accounting Research, Journal of Accounting, Journal of Accounting and Public Policy, *and* Economic Consequences of Financial Accounting Standards. *He has coauthored* Intermediate Accounting, *fifth and sixth editions, published by Richard D. Irwin, and* [Principles of] Accounting, *published in 1989 by Prentice Hall.*

Dr. Harrison is married with two children. He has been a Christian since 1953.

A ccounting is a system for gathering, classifying, and communicating financial information for use in decision making. The main types of decisions based on accounting data are investments—at all levels. Corporate managers select among alternative plant facilities based on the cash flows and net income amounts they can expect from the respective investments. Bank loan officers make loans whose terms depend on customers' financial statements. Personal investors choose stocks based on the companies' prospects for profitability and dividends.

This chapter works with two of the five functional areas of accounting—financial accounting and auditing. *Financial accounting* deals with reporting an entity's activities, in financial terms, to persons outside the organization, primarily to its present and potential stockholders and creditors. *Auditing* involves examining accounting records for the purpose of expressing an independent, objective opinion on the fairness of the related financial statements. These two branches of accounting are linked by the requirement for reporting to outside parties. The tension of players with competing motives—managers on the one hand and stockholders and creditors on the other—spawns the need for a standard of conduct to regulate the information with which companies represent themselves to the public. In this chapter we blur the distinction between managers and accountants because top managers bear final responsibility for the information that companies disclose publicly, and the chief financial officer, often an accountant, is a member of top management.

An example will illustrate the need for an ethical standard for the provision of accounting information. Managers have incentives to convert business assets to their personal use. In corporations this conversion process is relatively easy because the stockholders have only a distant voice in management. Where manager bonuses are tied to reported income, accounting manipulations can bolster income and thus the bonuses. One way to control such excesses is a monitoring system, often involving a committee of the board of directors. In this setting, the directors are actually incurring costs to control the entity's most trusted employees, top management! The need for a standard of behavior and thus the application of biblical principles is clear-cut here.

A third branch, *tax accounting*, takes a subsidiary role in this chapter. Tax accounting is the system for planning the entity's affairs to minimize taxes and for complying with the law. This branch is also accountable to an outside party (the government), but decisions based on tax information differ substantially from the investment and credit decisions of financial accounting and auditing.

Managerial accounting is the system for providing managers with information for their use in directing the entity's operations. This topic is not treated in this chapter because its nature is akin to management, which is the subject of chapter 3. We defer *accounting information systems*, a fifth branch of accounting, to the broader subject of information systems in chapter 9.

THE ACCOUNTING SETTING

Accounting is a financial model of an organization. Like any model, it is not a full description but instead obscures much detail. Inevitably, some aspects of the entity and its setting are overlooked in the modeling process. For example, businesses have investments in their work forces that do not appear on the balance sheet because accountants record employee compensation as it is earned, and not before. Some pension and lease liabilities likewise are omitted from the balance sheet. How many of these facts can be lost before the model's acceptability is affected?

The principal users of accounting information are investors and creditors. These parties want accurate, truthful information about the entity's success. The fundamental issue addressed in this chapter is, What is truth in accounting? Answering this question is complex because of these reasons:

1. Accounting, a subset of economics, is a social science governed more by behavioral factors than by mathematical principles. Therefore, the link between accounting and natural laws is not obvious.
2. Accounting practice is developed from logical principles (rationalizations) that, because of the social nature of the discipline, are often internally inconsistent.
3. Accounting is largely an estimation process because the cost of providing precise data would be prohibitive.
4. Professional standards, called generally accepted accounting principles, allow wide diversity to accommodate the different views on how to account for most phenomena.
5. The judgment of an accountant is present in virtually all accounting information.

Success in business is measured primarily by net income, the excess of revenues over expenses from the business's operations. Investors and creditors cannot be certain of the ultimate success of an entity until it liquidates. However, their decisions cannot await liquidation, so accountants slice time into periods such as years and quarters for reporting on the activities of the business. Transactions are accounted for on the accrual basis. Revenue is recorded in the period earned, regardless of when cash is received, and expenses are recorded in the period incurred, regardless of when cash is paid. The accrual process introduces the potential for managers to manipulate the period when revenues and expenses, and thus net income, are recorded.

The estimation processes inherent in accrual accounting provide most of the opportunity for abuses that beg for standards of ethical conduct. For example, a bank can overstate reported income by underestimating the expense associated with bad debt losses. Another potential for "creative accounting" arises from the difficulty of pinpointing the timing of revenue earned prior to the collection of cash. For example, a manufacturer can bolster, or depress, current-year revenue by shipping, or failing to ship, goods to customers immediately prior to year end. Circumvention of forthright accounting can also result from changing accounting techniques. Suppose a company is having a bad year, and net income is lagging behind analysts' expectations. The company can change from one accounting method to another in order to increase its reported income.

This blatant activity is regulated, however, inasmuch as companies are required to report their accounting changes and disclose their effects on net income.

This third situation illustrates our legalistic way of curbing abuses in business—by a growing set of specific rules to cover all possible occurrences. This plan is flawed because it is impossible to foresee all types of unethical behavior, and an effective monitoring system imposes costs that society is unwilling to bear. Another possibility is an ethical system that changes from situation to situation. The prevailing social mood identifies acceptable accounting behavior. One difficulty with situational ethics arises during transitions. Behavior undertaken under one regime is pronounced unacceptable by the next regime, and confusion reigns.

In my opinion, the setting governing the provision of accounting information in the United States reflects a combination of legalism and situational ethics, and that, coupled with the fallen nature of man, explains most accounting failures. I am not arguing that accounting needs an overhaul, but that the accounting setting is imperfect. Interestingly, the conservative nature of most accountants suggests that many in the profession adhere to some notion of truth in accounting. This is probably a holdover from the anchoring of earlier generations in biblical principles.

I believe biblical principles provide the ideal basis for identifying fairness in accounting. Outlined in sufficient detail to give workable guidelines and effected by the Holy Spirit, the principles provide insights into the very mind of the infinite personal God. With a God-centered world view, God's Word can be applied to all accounting determinations. This chapter builds the case for its application.

In the preceding paragraphs, I have discussed the design of information for decision making in business—the paramount use of accounting information. A corollary objective is to report information that owners of the business can use in assessing how well the managers have discharged their *stewardship* responsibilities—a familiar theme in the Bible. Reporting on stewardship and providing predictive data for decisions come together in that most predictions are based on historical data designed to report on stewardship.

The remainder of this chapter discusses the application of biblical principles to the following topics: accountability, stewardship, sin, deceit/honesty, disclosure, and monitoring/auditing.

ACCOUNTABILITY

The Bible has a lot to say about accountability, so this topic introduces the application of biblical principles to accounting. In God's economy every person is accountable. Children are accountable to parents, friends, and school authorities. Adults are accountable to spouses, the Church, friends, employers, customers, banks, governments, and so on. Organizations are accountable to other organizations. To receive money from United Way, for example, welfare agencies must give an accounting of their use of the funds. Ultimately, all persons and all organizations are accountable to God because He owns all things (see Gen. 1:1; John 1:1-3). The principle of accountability runs throughout Scripture (see Ezek. 18:20; Matt. 12:36; 25:14-30; Luke 16:2; 19:12-27; Rom. 3:19; 14:12; 1 Cor. 4:5; Heb. 4:13; 1 Pet. 4:5).

Accountability pervades all aspects of life and is related to the social nature of God (see Gen. 1:26; 3:22) *and of man* (see Gen. 2:18). Let us consider what an accountability-free environment would be like. It seems that this environment could exist only where there is no Creator and there are no other people. The existence of a Creator poses at least the possibility of personal accountability: One is accountable to his owner. Couple this possibility with a personal God who has made man in His own image (see Gen. 1:27; Col. 1:15), has clearly demonstrated His presence and activity in the affairs of men (see Exod. 14:21-22; Josh. 6:20; John 11:38-43; Acts 28:1-6; 1 Cor. 15:6), and demands man's allegiance (see Exod. 20:3, 5; Acts 16:31), and the implication is clear: Man is accountable to the Creator.

Because of man's social nature, we must be accountable to other people in order to interact with them. People need other people for personal fulfillment because without others, life is not interesting for very long. We learn from others and take pleasure in contributing to their well-being. But we are also selfish, and this tendency causes us to exploit other people. One way society maintains a balance among persons is through rules of mutual accountability. This is the basis for contracting.

People need other people in business affairs. For example, Sears could not continue in business without customers to buy its products. Organizations raise capital from people and employ it for the common good. The high standard of living available to most persons in developed countries derives from cooperative efforts that can accomplish more than by individuals working alone. Consider the corporate form of business, which combines the capital of investors, the loaned funds of creditors, the talents of managers and employees, and the preferences of customers. A small business would find it very difficult to move fresh bananas economically from the rain forests of Central America to breakfast tables in the United States and Canada. Business operations require complex social interactions among people with diverse personal goals.

These achievements exact a cost on the participants in terms of their need for accountability to others. To raise the capital necessary to finance such endeavors, businesses must make promises, and managers must keep the promises. Borrowed funds require the payment of debt and interest. Owners' equity requires the earning of profit sufficient to attract investors' money and the payment of dividends. How do businesses convince investors and creditors that they will keep these promises? A key ingredient is establishing a track record of accountability—evidenced by earnings trends and dividends, debt payments and credit ratings. Investors make a continuous set of predictions about whether the entity will continue its record in the future. Accounting provides a large part of the information for these predictions.

Accountability is related to God's system of order and authority. God sits at the apex of the authority chain and grants authority to governments for the maintenance of an orderly society (see Dan. 4:17; Rom. 13:1-6). He is the Architect of the authority that employers hold over employees (see Mal. 1:6; 1 Cor. 4:2; Eph. 6:5; Col. 3:22; 1 Pet. 2:13, 18) and the authority of overseers in the church (see Acts 20:28; Heb. 13:17; 1 Pet. 5:2). God's system of order and authority is a clear indication of His common sense. Organizations simply run more smoothly when someone in charge is held accountable for results. Though marred by human imperfection, human entities benefit from God's organizational largesse. Consider the alternative—a world with all authority derived solely from men. The result would be survival of the fittest with a despotic trampling of human rights, paralysis due to the player's inability to follow a common leader, or pursuit of unworthy goals. Fortunately, in God's authority structure, submitting to leaders fosters the restraint of natural passions and lends stability to social relationships. Since all authority is God-given, submission to authority frees managers from wasting undue energy policing errant employee behavior. It enables those in authority to concentrate on projects for the common good. In His wisdom, God mandates that we are to obey all authorities (see 1 Pet. 2:13-15).

In democratic social structures, accountability runs both ways. Leaders are accountable to the people whose conduct is then measured against laws set by the leaders. In business, employees (including managers) are accountable to owners for giving a day's work for a day's pay. The owners must pay fair wages to keep employees on the job. The wage rate is judged ultimately by whether the business can pay the wages and also earn sufficient profit to attract the capital necessary for survival. This returns us to the familiar investment decisions based on accounting information. Without accountability evidenced by truthful information, people find it difficult to make the predictions that underlie their commitments of resources to ventures with uncertain outcomes.

STEWARDSHIP

Stewardship is closely related to accountability. Stewardship is the discharging of agency duties on behalf of a principal—an operating activity—whereas accountability deals with reporting the results to the principal—an accounting activity. In one sense, then, stewardship is more management than accounting. For fear of repeating the management material of chapter 3, I will abbreviate this discussion and focus on stewardship's interaction with accountability.

God is the principal, and people are His agents (see Eph. 6:6-7; Col. 3:22-23). Teaching on the stewardship of possessions is found in the parables of the talents (see Matt. 25:14-30; Luke 19:12-27) and of the unjust steward (see Luke 16:1-2). This indicates that an employee is supposed to carry out the work intended by the employer. This sets the stage for the link to accountability.

After performing the work, the agent must choose how to report the results to the principal. He can give an honest accounting, or he can lie. In the parable of the talents, the stewards reported truthfully. But Saul lied about his disposition of the enemy's possessions (see 1 Sam. 15:1-23), and Ananias and Sapphira lied to God about the proportion of funds they were contributing to His work (see Acts 5:1-10). In each instance, God dealt severely with the one who gave a dishonest accounting.

Reporting on management stewardship to a corporation's stockholders can be likened to the servants' reporting of investment results in the parable of the talents. In each instance, the employer entrusted goods to the employee with an understanding of the desired result. In my opinion, the main complicating factor in contemporary accounting for large organizations—vis-á-vis the master-servant relationship in the parable—is the distance between the owners and the employees. Typically, the stockholders of a corporation want and hire managers to produce profits. In turn, managers hire employees to carry out the work. As the incentive structure passes from stockholder to manager to employee, bit by bit the owners' wishes can be diluted among those of the managers and employees. Managers control the business on a daily basis and can convert enterprise wealth to their personal wealth under the guise of working for the firm. Examples include company hunting lodges, beach resorts, travel abroad, and the like. Costs of such management perquisites are immaterial in a large corporation and can be buried in accounts such as Promotional Expense or Management Development Expense. The owners never examine the accounts, preferring instead to view the business through its financial statements that report only summarized data.

In some organizations, employees feel estranged from the employer and give less than a full effort on the job. Managers pressured to report a certain level of profits can force accountants to explore alternative ways of bolstering profits. After "cooking the books," managers often seek other employment. It is common for the incoming management team to "take a bath"—report low profits—during the first year because of the need to clean up the accounts left by the old management.

What is the solution to these apparent breakdowns in stewardship? Colossians 3:23 gives the answer: "Whatever you do, work at it with all your heart, as working for the Lord, not for men." This admonition was directed at slaves who had little or no control over their work environments. In democratic countries, we have it much easier. We are free to pursue employment with an entity whose goals are consistent with ours. For many, it is relatively easy to find a work setting in which we can give a day's work for receipt of a day's pay. God's Word directs employees to be diligent even when the employer is absent (see Col. 3:23), ready for the employer to return (see Luke 12:35-48), faithful (see 1 Cor. 4:1-2), and blameless and not working to pursue dishonest gain (see Titus 1:7). When this occurs, employees have nothing to hide. They give a full effort and can report the results of operations with no fear of punishment for dishonesty. Christians in less desirable jobs are also directed by God to give a full effort, "since you know that you will receive an inheritance from the Lord as a reward. It is the Lord Christ you are serving" (Col. 3:24).

Let us now consider corporate accountants who report the entity's financial results to the stockholders and creditors that finance the business. What is the biblical standard for the financial statement information? The concept of sin is relevant to this question.

SIN

The Financial Accounting Standards Board (FASB), the body that sets accounting standards in the United States, identifies *relevance* and *reliability* as holding primary importance for making accounting information useful. The FASB further states that reliability is a function of *representational faithfulness*, which I shall call honesty. How is honesty in accounting determined? (This section uses the term *honesty* in applying the concept of sin to accounting. The next section discusses honesty as contrasted with deceit in accounting.)

Another way to pose this question is, What is the standard for determining honesty in accounting? *FASB Concepts Statement No. 2, Qualitative Characteristics of Accounting Information*, defines *representational faithfulness* as "agreement between a measure or description and the phenomenon that it purports to represent." Most persons—Christian and nonChristian—would agree that this means accounting information should be honest, should tell the truth. Why is this desirable? From a purely amoral, economic efficiency stand-point, people acting on the basis of honest information have a higher probability of allocating their resources to worthy users of those resources than if they act on dishonest information. There is less "noise" in an honest information system than in a dishonest system. Why is this true, and where does the relationship between honesty and efficiency arise?

I believe the basis for the efficiency of an honest information system lies in the character of God. He loves truth because He is truth (see Deut. 32:4; Ps. 119:160; John 14:6). Because God is whole, His truth produces reasonable results. Though His ways are inscrutable (see Ps. 145:3; Rom. 11:33; Eph. 3:8), His outcomes are efficient (see Exod. 14:13-25; Josh. 6:20; 1 Sam. 17:48-49; 1 Kings 18:25-38; Neh. 6:15; Matt. 14:15-21; Mark 5:22-42; John 5:1-9; 20:1-31; Acts 2:1-41; 10:1-48).

A corollary to God's truth is that He hates dishonesty. Dishonesty is a form of sin, which in the Bible means a missing of the mark. The reference is to an archer shooting an arrow and missing the bull's-eye. In Christian thought, humans miss God's target of perfect conduct. How, then, can accountants provide thoroughly honest information?

As mentioned previously, accountants must use *estimates* because account-ing requires the forecast of the future effects of current transactions. However, future outcomes are uncertain, and accountants' foreknowledge is imperfect. No one can predict accurately the useful life of a building or which customers will fail to pay their credit accounts or which warranted products will prove defective and need repair or replacement. Nevertheless, under the accrual basis of accounting, these events cause expenses that are estimated and subtracted from revenues to measure the net income or net loss of the period.

In many situations, the cost of a precise accounting would be prohibitively expensive. Consider all the wastebaskets, pencil sharpeners, and staplers that Goodyear uses in its corporate offices and retail stores. Setting up depreciation schedules and recording depreciation for these insignificant assets would proba-bly cost as much over their ten-year lives as the items cost new. In recognition of this apparent waste of resources, accountants expense low-cost assets at acquisi-tion. Admittedly, this method is less than perfect accounting. Is it wrong? Does it miss God's mark of excellence? How does God's notion of sin—missing the mark—map into the contemporary setting of accounting?

For the purpose of this discussion, let us assume God approves of account-ing shortcuts of this nature. Where, then, does He draw the line of unacceptable accounting? By shading an estimate a bit, the accountant can change a net loss into net income. In a later period when doubt is cast on the earlier estimate, the accountant can simply admit misestimating the amount. Changed estimates are common in accounting. Where does good accounting end and bad accounting begin? Where does truth end and sin begin?

Another issue arises in the application of the biblical concept of sin to accounting because accounting standards are specifically designated as "generally accepted accounting principles." Their authoritative support comes from a political process in which interested parties lobby the FASB in support of their views on acceptable and unacceptable accounting methods. This looks like a situational ethic in that accounting standards can—and do—change with the latest mood. How does a Bible-believing Christian who knows a God of absolute truth function in this environment?

I believe answers to these questions are the province of the Holy Spirit. In John 16:7-12, Jesus describes the Spirit's three-fold work of showing us sin (wrong), righteousness (truth), and judgment (final outcomes), and promises to guide Christians into all truth. In Philippians 2:12-13, we are encouraged to "work out [the implications of our] salvation with fear and trembling, for it is God who works in [us] to will and to act according to his good purpose." And James 1:5 states, "If any of you lacks wisdom, he should ask God, who gives generously to all without finding fault, and it will be given to him." In combination, these verses say that God recognizes that our experiences will span a wide variety of circumstances requiring value judgments. The Holy Spirit residing within Christians (see Jer. 31:31-34; John 14:17; Rom. 8:9-11; 1 Cor. 6:19) will help us distinguish truth from falsehood. When a Christian accountant faces a vexing question, all he or she must do to obtain the benefit of God's infinite wisdom is to ask Him for it, expecting to receive it in full (see James 1:6-8).

DECEIT/HONESTY

Deceit poses a particular challenge to the Christian businessperson and has direct application to accounting. This topic is a special case of the broader concept of sin. As such, God hates deception (see Ps. 5:6) and cheating (see Deut. 25:13-16; Prov. 20:10). Deception is part of man's natural state (see Jer. 17:9; Mark 7:20-23), so accountants, like everyone else, must deal with it.

Enough diversity exists in accounting for managers and accountants to "cook the books." Elaborate disclosure rules are intended to render such antics a waste of time. In fact, most large companies (IBM, Eastman Kodak, Coca-Cola, among many others) appear to have reasoned that deceptive accounting practices are dysfunctional, and leading companies are known for impeccably high standards of financial information. At the other end of the spectrum, other companies are known for using every opportunity to present the best possible face to the public—without breaking an accounting rule. During the 1970s, a column in *Barron's* regularly castigated companies, by name, for what the author, Professor Abraham Briloff, considered bad accounting. Subsequent empirical research published in the top accounting journal showed that companies' stock prices suffered immediately after a Briloff article.

Other research indicates that the stock market is not fooled by accounting manipulations—if enough information is available for the public to evaluate the message conveyed by the information. For example, the stock prices of companies that change accounting methods in an effort to increase net income usually decrease in value. The market appears to see through the attempt to create income in the boardroom rather than in the factory. Moreover, companies that use methods known to bolster reported income are not priced higher by the stock market than companies that use more conservative methods, even though the former group reports higher income. It is difficult for unscrupulous managers and accountants to fool the market with public information. The stock market is said to be *efficient* in that prices fully reflect all publicly available information. However, managers can deceive investors and creditors by withholding, or biasing, information that would be detrimental to the company.

How should a Christian accountant behave in this setting? By doing his or her job in keeping with this advice: "Blessed [happy] is the man . . . in whose spirit is no deceit" (Ps. 32:2; see Zeph. 3:13). The opposite of deceit is honesty, and God requires honest information. A key area involving deceit/honesty is the demand for honest weights and measures. Apparently, this problem was not unusual in Bible times as merchants would try to cheat customers by using dishonest weights—perhaps selling three-fourths weight of a commodity while charging, for example, the price of seven-eighths (see Lev. 19:35-36; Prov. 11:1; Ezek. 45:10; Amos 8:5). God recognizes that the seller normally provides the scales and thus has the opportunity to cheat for personal gain. In the same way, managers and accountants have inside information about their companies. Literature on principal-agent relationships explores the implications of manager incentives to provide honest or deceitful information. Without safeguards, managers could cheat on the information the company provides. Four safeguards are the prohibition of misleading information, laws prohibiting trading securities based on inside information, and the requirements for fair disclosures and for an independent audit of the financial statements.

DISCLOSURE

A key biblical basis for truthful accounting disclosures—in addition to God's demand for honesty and hatred for deceit—is that no secrets are hidden from God (see Ps. 44:21; Eccles. 12:14; Jer. 17:10; Rom. 2:16; 1 Cor. 14:25;

Heb. 4:12-13). All deceptive disclosures, which must be known by a few insiders, are known by God and will haunt the deceivers someday. The financial press publishes stories about persons who tried to deceive others in business for personal gain. Two examples illustrate the need for full and fair disclosure in accounting. The first situation yields a clear result; the second is less clear.

Suppose a mining company makes a valuable mineral strike. Its top managers, who own some of the company stock, have competing incentives about when and how to disclose this information to the public. They could quietly purchase more of the stock immediately before disclosing the mineral strike, hoping to benefit from the inside information. This act would violate insider trading laws. In the press release, they could overstate the significance of the strike in the hope that the price of their personal holdings of company stock would skyrocket. Of course, this, too, is illegal. The deceivers would be criticized in the financial press, and their careers might be ruined.

Suppose a company is named as defendant in a lawsuit, and in the best judgment of attorneys, the outcome, with a fifty-five percent probability, will go against the company in a significant way. How should the company disclose this event in its financial statements? If managers disclose these facts as related here, disclosure could become a self-fulfilling prophecy, serving as tacit admission of guilt. On the other hand, a slightly less forthcoming disclosure may convey the seriousness of the litigation without biasing the outcome. How should managers, accountable to their stockholders, report this event?

Perhaps the most obvious setting for deceit in accounting is the attempt to make a company's financial statements present a picture that differs from the company's true condition, as in the disclosure of the pending litigation. This matter is so serious that the Securities Acts of 1933 and 1934 impose stringent standards on the information that companies disclose to the public. The legal standard is simply that the information must not be misleading. One who can show a financial loss as a result of reliance on misleading information has a case against the entity that presented the information. To date, American society has evidenced a strong commitment to truthful information in the securities markets, which probably explains why our markets are the envy of the world and contribute to our high standard of living.

How does the legal standard compare to God's standard? It appears that they are similar. Both standards—God's and man's—are concise and sweeping. The legal standard that the information not be misleading looks much like God's standard for an honest report (see Exod. 20:16; Prov. 12:17). The correspondence of man's standard with God's is the business community's recognition of the importance of truth in financial disclosures. It is man's admission that God's Word is true.

MONITORING/AUDITING

Accountants make honest mistakes that affect the company's financial statements. And managers cannot always be relied upon to present unbiased information. Even a person with the purest motives is subject to sin (see Ps. 51:5; Isa. 53:6; Rom. 3:23; Gal. 3:22) and under certain circumstances may bias the data in the company's financial statements. These reasons explain why public corporations are required to have their accounting systems and financial statements audited by independent accountants. The auditors are part of an elaborate monitoring system, including laws discussed previously, designed to ensure the validity of the reported information.

Monitoring/auditing can be related to the biblical role of a witness in developing objective evidence about a transaction or an event. Why is objective evidence needed? An individual, left to his own devices, will rationalize the facts to fit his perspective and be more likely to hold an erroneous view than if held accountable to the consensus view of a group. Each member of the corroborating group also needs this monitoring mechanism. With outside evidence, established facts of a matter are less disputable and more likely to result in common agreement. This social structure recognizes that man is fallible and prone to err.

As recorded in Genesis 23:10-18; Ruth 4:1-9; and Jeremiah 32:10, land was purchased in the presence of witnesses. John 8:17 reiterates the Old Testament law that the testimony of two men is needed to prove the validity (truth) of a proposition. Jesus spoke this in response to the Pharisees' challenge that His messiahship was invalid because it was not confirmed by an external witness. (The witness was God the Father.)

A new challenge has entered the auditing environment. Some companies, unsatisfied with their auditor's stance on an accounting matter, shop around for an auditor who agrees with the company position. In the interest of free trade, this situation is allowed by government regulatory bodies. However, the practice makes many professional accountants uncomfortable. They wonder if it is unethical for companies (clients) to seek an independent auditor with a stipulated view of acceptable accounting. Recently, clients have been more open than in the past about discussing areas of potential disagreement with auditors. Is this setting of openness desirable, or is it evidence of a decay in moral conduct—companies, like people, wanting their own way (see Deut. 12:8; Judg. 17:6; Prov. 18:1) and going to great lengths to buy a particular audit opinion?

There is intense price competition for audits. Auditors are pressured to keep audit fees low, which suggests that auditors decrease the amount of work performed to arrive at their opinions. Auditors may be reluctant to take an engagement with a company known to prefer accounting alternatives that lead to an overly favorable view of the client, for fear the client will expect an audit of unacceptable quality. An inadequate audit may fail to uncover something damning to the client and may subject the auditor to legal exposure.

Discomfort with "opinion shopping," as the practice is called, may be rooted in the belief that an absolute truth exists in each audit situation. Traditionally, the auditor has examined sufficient evidence to form a professional opinion of the client's accounting system and financial statements. Essentially, this is what the Securities Acts require. An alternative view of opinion shopping is that some clients pose greater risks than others and that auditors should be free to work for a risky client. Because expected returns (income) move in direct proportion to the risk taken, the auditor of a risky client should expect higher income than the auditor who works only for safe clients. Fully aware of the situation, the accountant can assess the risks involved in auditing the client and decide whether to accept or reject the engagement. How does God view opinion shopping?

The biblical application to monitoring/auditing is rooted in man's propensity to sin, outsiders' desire for honest information about matters of social importance, and the reasonableness of having external observers validate the facts of an occurrence.

SUMMARY AND CONCLUSIONS

This chapter has focused primarily on the application of biblical principles to financial reporting, by which companies represent themselves to the public. The central theme has been the biblical requirement for truth. By that standard, accounting information should be true and should be presented in sufficient completeness not to be deceptive. The many estimates inherent in the accrual basis make it difficult at times to distinguish true information from untrue information. The estimation process offers the potential for abuse resulting in deceptive accounting disclosures. The Bible speaks to this issue.

Accounting's bible is the body of generally accepted accounting principles (GAAP), which identify acceptable practices. In some ways, these principles are like biblical principles in that they set forth general guidelines, with supporting detail where needed. Like the Bible, GAAP are not comprehensive rules, so their application requires judgment. This chapter argues that biblical principles should mold the accountant's judgment and that the Holy Spirit can enable him or her to make professional decisions consistent with God's will.

EDITOR'S PERSPECTIVE

Accounting and accountability are obviously twins, but not identical ones for there are differences in their content and broader purposes. Clearly, though, the central purpose of accounting (especially public accounting) is to provide information on the operations of a business that allows an entrepreneur, a corporate manager, or an outsider to assess the financial quality of the operating results for a period of time. Dr. Harrison rightly uses the subject of accountability as the governing framer for his chapter. He identifies numerous scriptures revealing the importance of accountability as a biblical principle that should play a role in our lives. He even demonstrates that accountability "is related to the social nature of God (see Gen. 1:26; 3:22) and of man (see Gen. 2:18)," as well as "to God's system of order and authority." The other five topics he covers—stewardship, sin, deceit/honesty, disclosure, and monitoring/auditing—could almost be interpreted as subsets of accountability because of its subsuming character.

The concept of accountability is so packed with vital "ends" affecting every area of our lives that I want to unpack it a bit more for the purpose of stimulating further thought about it. To do this, I want to briefly examine accountability as (1) a functioning part of biblical love; (2) a stimulus for self-control; (3) an integral part of sanctification; (4) a provider of freedom; and (5) a guardian of positive fear.

Accountability as an aspect of biblical love—Accountability needs to be discussed in the context of biblical love if it is to be correctly understood and embraced (even sought for one's own good). Because the world has a perverted concept of love and hates accountability, it seems bent on pursuing and glorify-

121

ing some form of "autonomy" that generally leads to an unbiblical notion of self-rule and independence distancing people psychologically from the wholesome, God-intended aspects of accountability. The concept of the "autonomous will," long debated by philosophers and theologians, has been captured by secular thinkers; it has become more than a subtle force in the minds of most intellectuals where autonomy, not accountability, is held up as a "good." In God's economy, accountability is an aspect of love, autonomy a sign of pride.

Love, a commitment to seek what is truly best for the upbuilding of another person, is never naive. Love acknowledges the reality of our fallen nature. Love accepts us where it finds us; love will not, however, leave us where it finds us. Love will correct and discipline us for our own good; love will hold us accountable every step of the way so that we can be built up in Christlikeness. Love is in touch with the fact that we are self-deceived, temptable creatures, prone to self-justifying rationalizations. Love recognizes that we have a nature incapable of being just, righteous, and holy apart from God's special help and the help of others who are appointed by God to hold us accountable for our conduct. If we love certain persons, we will want them to be accountable to other people and to God. If we are mature, we will want to see to it that we are accountable to a body of responsible people, also.

Accountability as a stimulus for self-control—Self-control, one characteristic of the fruit of the Spirit (see Gal. 5:23), is the only effective means of control available to us in this universe. All other so-called controls, even a system of accountability, are but stimuli reminding us to exercise self-control. God alone has the authority (actual power) to redirect the hearts of men and women according to His good purposes and pleasure (see Prov. 21:1). Only God can constrain and release the minds and hearts of people, but even God normally allows His image bearers to exercise their will according to their predispositions and frames of mind. God's hand is not always pressing down on us, even though He is the Potter and we are the clay (see Isa. 45:9; Jer. 18:5-12). He calls us to righteous behavior; He does not force us to be righteous.

We mortals, thank God, have no such power over others. We can change no one. We can do no more than stimulate people, and they, in turn, must decide if they will or will not respond to the stimulus (speed limits, corporate policies, etc.) and obey the expressed will of those in authority over them. This reality reflects one of the most fundamental and basic truths about our nature—we are moral beings responsible for our own choices and actions; we are not free to shift the responsibility for our actions to another person (see Deut. 24:16; Jer. 32:29-30; Ezek. 18:4, 20).

Accountability as an ingredient of sanctification—Growth in godliness does not occur apart from much discipline. Hebrews 12:5-11 makes this very plain:

> "My son, do not regard lightly the discipline of the Lord,
> Nor faint when you are reproved by Him;
> For those whom the Lord loves He disciplines,
> And He scourges every son whom He receives."
> It is for discipline that you endure; God deals with you as with sons; for
> what son is there whom his father does not discipline? . . . But [God]
> disciplines us for our good, that we may share His holiness. All
> discipline for the moment seems not to be joyful, but sorrowful; yet
> to those who have been trained by it, afterwards it yields the peaceful
> fruit of righteousness.

The most basic objectives of accountability are to afford intermediate points in an process where evaluations can be made and either affirmations offered or corrections (discipline) made. But godly corrections should always be administered in the context of love—being truly concerned for what is in the best interest of the person being instructed or disciplined. We should not concentrate solely on the improvement of a person's job performance, as important as that may be. If people are to grow professionally as well as spiritually, they need to be in a system where accountability is required and is lovingly practiced. For accountability to be practiced in love, the expectations and attitudes by which others are to be evaluated have to be clearly communicated and understood and fairly administered.

Accountability as a provider of freedom—There is no greater myth than the belief that somehow, somewhere, there is a quantity of absolute freedom available to those who can find it. Absolute freedom does not exist. Even God is not absolutely free. He is free only to be God. He is not free to violate His nature or defile His character. For example, He is not free to entertain evil. We, too, only to a much greater degree, are constrained by who we are.

All freedom, true freedom as defined by God, is bounded or limited. Freedom that exceeds the God-ordained limits can only be rightly described as license—the excessive, undisciplined abuse of freedom. For example, a person has one set of freedoms in God's mind before he or she is married and another set after marriage, and God has revealed these freedoms. If someone acts as a single person in the context of marriage or as a married person while single, he or she violates God's established bounds of freedom. A man, for example, has no "headship" authority over his fiancée; a woman has no right to expect her fiancé to provide for her materially prior to their marriage.

Fallen people too often confuse their ability to do something with the notion that they are, therefore, free to do it. Our ability does not give us permission. True freedom is discovered and enjoyed inside those limits that are legitimately defined for us. A sound system of accountability helps us define true freedom and encourages us to live within its bounds.

Accountability as the guardian of positive fear—Unconditional love is the greatest motivator in the universe. Positive rewards are the next best motivators, and the fear of negative consequences is the poorest motivator of all in the repertoire of motivators. But positive fear (not negative fear) is nevertheless an indispensable motivator, especially in a fallen world where our tendencies to self-justify and rationalize our thoughts and behavior are so strong.

It is good for all of us to know that we must account to others for how we have borne our responsibilities and used the authority entrusted to us. The knowledge of accountability quickly causes us to place the governing expectations (standards) of those evaluating us before us as we plan and work. This typically motivates us to seek the positive rewards associated with good performance. But love is absent from an evaluative system unless the person being evaluated is certain that there will be negative consequences meted out for any inappropriate conduct. Love and justice are absolutely compatible concepts biblically, and both require the presence of negative consequences. There is little growth without discipline, and discipline is incomplete without the possibility of constructive correction.

Positive fear is the kind of fear that prudent persons possess. It resides in the background of their minds. It comes to the front only when they are tempted to procrastinate, slack off in their efforts, take a shortcut, disregard a known policy, or take a selfish action that could embarrass the organization. Positive fear provides an internal brake on the old nature. In this sense, positive fear is internally activated in the face of a known consequence. People possess this kind of fear when those in authority are willing to love them and do whatever is necessary to enhance their well-being, even to the extent of disciplining them. In God's economy is a constructive form of fear—it is positive and godly fear.

PART VII

ORGANIZATIONS AND THEIR PATTERNS OF BEHAVIOR

Fashion trends are phenomena we associate with the garment industry, and style trends are noted in the automobile industry. Trends are also found in sports—formations used in football, for example. Even breeds of dogs become popular for a while and then fade into relative obscurity. Organizational behavior is no different. It, too, is subject to fashions and fads as those who lead business organizations look for ways to gain an edge on their competitors or those who follow fall into line lest they miss out on the opportunity to be more successful.

As we examine the subject of organizational behavior, several things should be kept in mind. First, an organization is different from the individuals who manage it and work there, yet it is a complex, dynamic composite of the historic and contemporary thoughts and behavior of the individuals who have made up and do make up its employment. An organization is people and a "thing" simultaneously. People work for the organization as well as for people. Organizational behavior takes on a character of its own as people assume distinctive roles, share in the unintentional creation of a group psychology, and participate in a collective endeavor that results in a synergistic outcome transcending what the individual participants could accomplish individually. An organization obviously has no soul or personal life, but it does have a community or collective life that is very real and alive.

Next, we need to be aware that when an organization gets well enough established to generate and communicate a collective ethos, the organization has suddenly taken on a life of its own that will mirror its peculiar culture, personality, set of values, and political processes. This, in turn, opens a subtle door in the minds of many people. This "living" organization suddenly affords them the opportunity to serve the organization—a "thing" at one level and a

125

collective group of people at another level. This understanding can be psychologically dangerous in the sense that the organization can be perceived as the satisfier of their personal identity needs, which allows them to ascribe great worth (worship?) to the organization—a not too subtle form of idolatry (see Rom. 1:25). (See the "Editor's Perspective" following chapter 3 for a brief discussion on our inherent identity needs and how God intends them to be satisfied.)

Finally, the behavior of business organizations, especially the larger ones, reflects an internal community ethos *and* the broader society's "social contract." The social contract is not written down anywhere, but it is as real as any identifiable force in the marketplace.

Our society accepts a particular economic structure (basically a free market system) and certain types of business organizations—entrepreneurships, partnerships, corporations—because there is broad consensus that these institutional structures serve us better than others could. But these institutions are "kept in line" through the maintenance of an elaborate and complex social contract determined by (1) society's generally accepted presuppositions about economic and distributive justice; (2) a body of common law brought to this country by our forefathers and other nationally established common law; (3) local, state, and federal legislation and regulations; and (4) an historic body of judicial decisions set forth at the various court levels. The content of and interaction between these four repositories of our national economic ethos create a powerful social contract that guides and manifests itself in the behavior of our business entities. For example, the social contract has made most businesses conscious and responsive to many environmental issues in the past quarter century.

Dr. John Haggai's chapter provides a sketch of the historic trends in the changing dynamics of organizational behavior and puts the motives behind organizational behavior in clear focus. Businesses are established for economic purposes, not beneficent ones; businesses change their behavior for the "ends" of efficiency, productivity, and profits, not goodness and kindness. He goes on, however, to show how biblical principles have a lot to say to Christians confronted by the many issues associated with organizational behavior. In addition, he raises some critical questions, reminding us that every area of economics must at all times be ready to be subjected to the searching light of Scripture.

CHAPTER 7

BIBLICAL PRINCIPLES APPLIED TO ORGANIZATIONAL BEHAVIOR

John Haggai

John Haggai, born in Louisville, Kentucky, now lives with his wife, Christine, in Atlanta, Georgia.

Dr. Haggai is a prolific writer. His best-selling first book, How to Win Over Worry, *has surpassed the two million mark and has been translated into nineteen languages.*

His most recent book, The Leading Edge, *tells of his founding Haggai Institute for Advanced Leadership Training in 1969. Haggai Institute conducts seminars for Christian leaders from Asia, Africa, and Latin America. Nearly seven thousand graduates work in 120 countries.*

John Haggai's international influence touches millions of people. He has completed his sixty-fifth journey around the world—and his ninth visit to China.

Jethro's advice to Moses provides the first instance in biblical history of a change in management structure:

> So Moses gave heed to the voice of his father-in-law and did all that he had said. Moses chose able men out of all Israel, and made them heads over the people, rulers of thousands, of hundreds, of fifties, and of tens. And they judged the people at all times; hard cases they brought to Moses, but any small matter they decided themselves. (Exod. 18:24-26)

It also helps us to define terms. Management and organizational behavior are, after all, intimately connected. Any study of organizational behavior must cover the behavior of managers, and any study of management must reflect a manager's interest in the behavior of his organization. Yet the two remain separate, as the passage from Exodus shows.

The delegation of Moses' responsibility to a system of judges does not change the art of management—in that the "able men" presumably employ the same skills as their leader. But the structure has changed. In other words, the total required work input, previously handled by one man, is now covered by several. That Moses implemented Jethro's idea so rapidly is proof of his astuteness as a manager, but the idea itself goes beyond management, drawing on a discipline whose subject is the relation of workers to their work and of organizational structures to organizational goals.

Our primary purpose in this chapter might be called "business as a social entity." The skills and responsibilities of management per se, dealt with elsewhere in the book, will be treated tangentially here. But even granted this high degree of specialization, we must be realistic. How far organizational behavior can be criticized from a biblical perspective and improved by the application of biblical principles is a complex issue, deserving more detailed consideration than we can afford in the pages ahead. For that reason, the bulk of the chapter will be devoted to exploring organizational behavior as a field of study and to examining some of the ideas that underpin it.

ISSUES ARISING FROM ORGANIZATIONAL BEHAVIOR

At the most general level, it is impossible to study organizational behavior without making some reference to its economic foundations. Here we depart from the Exodus model. Although Israel possessed a form of economy, the nation did not exist to create wealth, and Moses' position was not analogous to that of a managing director. Furthermore, Jethro (who today, no doubt, would be lecturing on effective management technique) offered his advice out of consideration for Moses' health: "What you are doing is not good. You and the people with you will wear yourselves out, for the thing is too heavy for you: you are not able to perform it alone" (Exod. 18:17-18).

Fundamentally, a business is a unit of wealth creation. That is the reason for its existence. To remain viable, it must sell its products or services, survive competition, and keep its income higher than its costs. That is not to deny the part played by the business community in public welfare projects and the endowment of education and the arts. However, these contributions are not the criterion by which business success is measured. In that, the dollars count.

This fact immediately suggests two lines of inquiry. The first, which does not primarily concern us here, relates to the ethics of the whole financial system. It could be asked, for instance, whether our present economic structure is the best means of generating and distributing the world's wealth. The point at issue is simply that in the application of biblical principles to the world of business nothing should be taken for granted. Every concept goes back on the negotiating table.

More immediately relevant to the topic of this chapter is that wealth creation (as an organizational goal) inevitably affects organizational behavior. The significance of this fact is seen in the horizontal division of most business enterprise into management and work force. Historically, considerations of strategy—and, by extension, of the desirability of widening profit margins—belong to management. The worker is there only to "do the job"—to pick the tea, service the loom, operate the word processor. From one point of view, of course, this is a demarcation of roles. But from another, it is tantamount to a loading of the financial dice. Looked at in terms of its economic objectives, business is concerned about the worker only insofar as he or she provides a labor input. In the last analysis, what benefits the balance sheet maximizes the worker's productivity and keeps down his wage.

If this seems crude, reflect for a moment on the ease with which the powerful often mistake profit for something like a moral absolute. We could wax lyrical about the slave trade (as hard a drive for low-wage labor as you are likely to find); about the British factory owners of the eighteenth and nineteenth centuries who cheerfully subjected their employees to subsistence pay and twelve-hour working days; about the millions of underpaid migrant workers; and about the connivance of some multinational corporations at corrupt employment practices in the Third World. There is, it seems, some form of complicity between wealth creation (in itself morally neutral) and selfishness (which derives from the Fall). The result is a rule of thumb that management will tend to abuse a work force, either through direct exploitation or neglect, rather as a tree will bend with the prevailing wind. The more absolute the managerial force—the stronger the wind—the greater the danger of abuse. In the West, where extreme exploitation is proscribed by statute, the influence of economics is more subtle.

The founding father of organizational behavior as a discipline is Frederick Taylor. A shop floor-worker turned senior executive, Taylor noticed that working practices in the industry of his day were passed on haphazardly from one generation to the next, with the supervisors doing little or nothing to streamline production. In the 1880s, committed to eliminate the wastage resulting from inefficiency, Taylor developed his concept of Scientific Management—a system that formalized the now familiar roles of workers and managers and reserved to the latter sole responsibility for deciding how work should be organized.

That Taylor implicitly, at least, regarded the work force simply as labor is clear from the principles he laid down for deploying it. Managers were to use "work studies" to break down each job into its elemental activities. Each activity was to be systematically analyzed, and more efficient working methods, abetted by bonus schemes, developed to effect the maximum increase in productivity. Each revised activity was to be timed at a standard rate of work to help managers fix manning levels and set output targets.

The popularity of Taylor's idea, which could be summarized as trimming the worker to fit the job, is evidenced by the number of efficiency-gaining techniques it has begotten—for instance, O and M (Organization and Methods). From the worker's point of view, however, Scientific Management can be less than satisfactory. For example, a work process like issuing company receipts, previously performed in parallel by three individuals, will (to achieve economies of scale) generally be divided into three separate activities, each performed by one individual. The resulting loss of variety makes the already unfulfilling work numbingly repetitive and dull. Fatigued, allowed no sense of achievement, and assumed to have no interest in his job except as a source of income, the worker will quickly identify the manager only as a figure of authority. In ethical terms the system is questionable; in practice—despite enormous gains in structural efficiency—it is often counterproductive, fostering alienation and breeding disputes over pay and conditions.

What constitutes fair treatment in terms of wages, hours, shifts, and job environment is a vital issue under any kind of management. It has numerous other aspects, too: color and sex discrimination, age, qualifications, sick pay and maternity leave, recruitment policy, training, pensions, and compensation for job loss. Ironically, though, experience has shown that satisfactory pay and conditions—even in businesses that do not use Scientific Management—have a minimal impact on worker *motivation*. This problem was first addressed in 1924 by the General Electric Company of Chicago. They engaged the services of the professor of industrial research at the Harvard Graduate School of Business, Elton Mayo. Mayo's five-year research program revealed what was then a startling piece of information. Workers, it turned out, were motivated by material factors, such as bonus schemes and job security, and by factors relating to the social and psychological environment.

Mayo's lead was followed up—and his results clarified—by other researchers, notably Abraham Maslow and Frederick Herzberg. Maslow's Hierarchy of Needs Theory is well known. He suggests that a worker will not be fully motivated unless his work enables him to satisfy five categories of need. These progress from low-level material needs (food and shelter, safety and security) through social needs (belonging and affection) to the higher ego and self-actualization needs (esteem and self-respect, self-fulfillment and release of potential). Individual workers, Maslow concedes, may be motivated more by one need than another; for instance, one man may feel an overwhelming need for job security or status. Nonetheless, in general, a worker will have to be offered satisfaction in every category to be fully productive.

The problem with Maslow's theory is its rigidity. All these needs exist, but satisfaction of one—say, of adequate food and housing—does not always lead, as Maslow claimed it would, to desire for the next. A man with enough money to rent an apartment may be more concerned about buying a house than with the threat of being laid off, and so fail to rise from one category of need into the next. A more useful model, therefore, is the one developed by Herzberg in the 1950s. Herzberg accepts the role of need in worker productivity, but distinguishes between what he calls "hygiene factors" (necessary to avoid dissatisfaction) and "motivation factors" (necessary to incite extra effort). Paradoxically, according to Herzberg, while a worker deprived of adequate pay and conditions will perform poorly, the same worker supplied with these material needs will not be motivated to perform well. For that he will have to be offered prospects beyond the merely adequate: status, higher income, and a job structure that allows him to fulfill his potential.

In the praxis of organizational behavior, techniques based on Herzberg's and Maslow's work (now known as the Human Relations Approach) are gaining ground on Taylor's Scientific Management. In keeping with the terminology of Douglas MacGregor (*The Human Side of Enterprise*, 1960), Theory Y management is starting to replace Theory X. In other words, managers are now less likely to view their subordinates as constitutionally lazy and amenable only to the motivation of carrot and stick, and more likely to value them as creative individuals, capable of handling responsibility and solving managerial problems.

Consequently, significant innovations are appearing in modern business. Under Scientific Management, personnel were deployed in such a way as to achieve maximum efficiency in the production process; under the Human Relations Approach, the production process is adjusted so as to achieve maximum efficiency in the personnel. Herzberg calls the strategy "job enrichment." The extreme fragmentation engendered under Taylor's system is reversed by reassigning work in whole tasks, with discernible end products. Furthermore, responsibilities that Taylor had placed firmly in the hands of the management are returned to the work force, encouraging consultation, initiative, and social contact between sections. Some companies (for instance, Ford and ITT) have gone as far as adopting the Japanese concept of "quality circles"—voluntary groups of about ten workers who meet regularly to discuss and find solutions to technical or organizational problems affecting their work area—in the hope of matching Japan's outstanding record in the field of work-force motivation.

Given this trend, it might be assumed that, in the West at least, management and work force are soon to attain a threshold of mutual respect and humanitarian concern that will transform forever the spirit of business enterprise. But this is not the case. In fact, all we are seeing is a shift in organizational behavior on a par with Jethro's advice to Moses. The goal of business is still purely economic. And if greater attention is now being paid to the human welfare of the work force, it is hardly cynical to suggest that this tactic has something to do with higher productivity of a satisfied and motivated work force. The point is this: We must never make the mistake of thinking that humanitarian treatment of employees in business is self-sustaining, or that progress in technology, wealth, and education is matched automatically by progress in ethics and behavior.

You do not have to look far for evidence of the worker's critical dependence on the forces of economics. For many industries in the West (and countless industries in the Third World), a Human Relations Approach to work-force motivation is more or less impossible to apply. A struggling company that uses assembly-line production, for example, may be forced to maintain a system of Theory X worker control based on Scientific Management, even though the workers would respond well to Theory Y. If the company is of the labor-intensive type common in developing countries, low wages and the neglect of potentially costly improvements in the work environment probably keep its prices competitive on the world market.

Even in the Third World these problems may eventually be solved by the most recent and pervasive influence on organizational behavior—the microelectronics revolution. The chief advantage of the new technology is that routine tasks can be automated, giving some manual and clerical workers a widened area of responsibility and therefore a higher quality of working life. For others, of course, automation means a layoff. It is debated whether the financial benefits of automation outweigh the social costs. So far in the United States, employment levels do not seem to have been reduced significantly by the arrival of the silicon chip, and indications are that job losses at the lower end of the scale are almost matched by job gains at the higher end. This pattern may or may not be duplicated in other countries. Either way, the microelectronics revolution furnishes yet another example of the way in which changes in the organizational behavior are, ultimately, to be traced back to the dictates of economics.

How much freedom is given to economic considerations in business must be a major area of concern for anyone examining organizational behavior from the Christian perspective. Other issues are numerous, but for the most part these can be summarized by addressing three questions. First—and for the purposes of this chapter indirectly—is it possible to affirm from a biblical standpoint the economic context within which business operates? Second, what models of interpersonal cooperation within a business are accordant with biblical principles? And third, can a firm ethical basis be found—and implemented—to decide appropriate pay and conditions for employed personnel?

BIBLICAL PRINCIPLES FOR ORGANIZATIONAL BEHAVIOR

Biblical teaching that casts light on the issues of organizational behavior is found in five main areas of doctrine: man, justice, work, love, and vision.

Every individual is of value to God—The Creation story presents man as the crowning glory of God's creation: "Then God said, 'Let us make man in our image, after our likeness. . . .' So God created man in his own image, in the image of God he created him; male and female he created them. And God blessed them" (Gen. 1:26-28).

The "image" conferred on man seems, in essence, to be a gift of responsibility to the Creator. Man is set aside not so much by his intellectual capability (a God-given attribute) as by the relationship God established with him in Eden. That relationship was not entirely broken by man's disobedience, for God still addressed him with the personal pronoun "thou" (Gen. 3:9, KJV). From this point, to the end of time, God is pictured as reaching out to redeem the human race. That redemption is fulfilled in a renewal of man's responsibility, a completion of the image. So John recalls, "I heard a loud voice from the throne saying, 'Behold, the dwelling of God is with men. He will dwell with them, and they shall be his people, and God himself will be with them'" (Rev. 21:3).

What provides fallen man with the means of responding to God's love is the event that is also His love's highest expression—the incarnation of Christ. And here we find positive affirmation of the value God places on man both individually (see, for instance, Matt. 18:12) and corporately (see Matt. 9:36). The scene of the returning prodigal perhaps helps us to grasp something of the meaning of this value: "But while he was yet at a distance, his father saw him and had compassion and ran and embraced him and kissed him" (Luke 15:20).

As might be expected, there runs alongside this teaching about the value of man another teaching demanding that the value be recognized. It finds its clearest expression in the Old Testament Law ("You shall love your neighbor as yourself" [Lev. 19:18]). Consequently, when Paul tells the Romans, "Owe no one anything, except to love one another" (Rom. 13:8), he is not so much advocating gratuitous acts of piety as reminding his readers to respect one another's rights.

Justice must be done—Justice in the Old Testament is more than a legal concept. Justice as a rule to guide judges (Hebrew *mispat*) is closely connected with justice as righteousness (Hebrew *sedeq* or *sedeqa*). Both are rooted in the ultimate justice of God. To quote Zephaniah, "The LORD within her is righteous, he does no wrong; every morning he shows forth his justice, each dawn he does not fail" (3:5).

Acting with justice is equivalent, in the general sense, to upholding the moral standard set in the Law. So God says of Abraham, "I have chosen him, that he may . . . keep the way of the LORD by doing righteousness and justice" (Gen. 18:19). Contained within this, however, and reiterated in the New Testament, is a more specific Old Testament call:

> Cease to do evil,
>   learn to do good;
> seek justice, correct oppression;
>   defend the fatherless,
> plead for the widow. (Isa. 1:16-17)

The abuse of power is a recurring theme in the Prophets. Malachi sums up the position of the Law that justice is not to be talked about but actively performed in the honoring of contracts and the discharging of social responsibilities: "I will be a swift witness against . . . those who swear falsely, against those who oppress the hireling in his wages, the widow and the orphan, against those who thrust aside the sojourner, and do not fear me, says the LORD of hosts" (Mal. 3:5).

Work is to be kept within limits—The Bible does not assume that work is enjoyable. "In the sweat of your face you shall eat bread," says God to the fallen Adam (Gen. 3:19). On the other hand, there is no shortage of reproof for those who make work unnecessarily burdensome—who, as it were, demand bricks yet withhold straw (see Exod. 5:6-7). Overall, the pattern recommended by the Old Testament is one of regular labor balanced by regular rest, allowing the land and its occupants a long-term and productive coexistence.

Behind this lies an important implication. Nowhere in the Bible, in either Testament, does work appear as an end in itself. It is viewed as necessary for material sustenance, even as a moral duty (see Paul's teaching in 2 Thess. 3:10), but always secondary to the principal aim of worshiping God. Amos offers the following corrective to an obsession with making money:

> Hear this, you who trample upon the needy,
>   and bring the poor of the land to an end,

saying, "When will the new moon be over,
    that we may sell grain?
And the sabbath,
    that we may offer wheat for sale,
that we may make the ephah small and the shekel great,
    and deal deceitfully with false balances?" (8:4-5)

Once again, the Bible requires justice, but not only justice. In common with the concept of Jubilee as taught to the Israelites, this passage sets bounds to the whole process of wealth creation. Hard work and productivity are encouraged up to but not beyond the point where (under the Jubilee regulations) they result in permanent distortions in the pattern of ownership and (under the Sabbath law) they interfere with the society's religious life. Work is to be kept in its place.

Man's first duty to his neighbor is one of love—The so-called double commandment of love, coined by Jesus as a summary of the Old Testament Law, is so familiar as to be almost platitudinous: We are to love God, and our neighbor as ourselves. For that reason, it is worth remembering two points. First, this love is affirmed throughout the Bible as being characteristic of the ideal human relationship. In other words, we can do nothing better, and nothing more important, for our fellowman than to love him. It may be that love proves to be a facilitator and that loving another person results in the greater cooperation or productivity we might otherwise seek to attain by another means. But even if this is not so, the commandment stands. Our first duty is one of love.

The second point is complementary: Love is a matter not of emotions but of the will. Therefore, we have no excuse for neglecting it. Love is the outgoing of the totality of one's being to another in beneficence and help, and it takes its cue from the love God Himself expressed through the redemption of the Cross. Whether we feel love or not—and with our natural enemies we are unlikely to feel it—we are obliged under the Spirit to act toward others as God has acted toward us.

Successful enterprise demands a shared vision—Another frequently quoted verse is this one from Proverbs: "Without a vision, the people cast off restraint" (29:18). The more literal translation is better than that of the King James Version ("Where there is no vision, the people perish") because it pinpoints the role of discipline. A lack of common vision—a lack of shared goals—results in confusion, disorder, and uncontrolled license. Vision binds together, unites behind a common purpose.

Ample proof of this truth can be gleaned from the pages of secular history.

But it is demonstrated, too, in the Bible. The early Church, the campaigns of David, even Babel—all these illustrate the necessity of shared objectives if an enterprise is to be successful. It is not sufficient for the leader alone to possess the vision, though vision is a key component of effective leadership. Thus, we witness a crucial refusal in the Israelites' progress to the Promised Land:

> Joshua the son of Nun and Caleb the son of Jephunneh . . . said to all the congregation of the people of Israel, " . . . do not fear the people of the land, for they are bread for us; their protection is removed from them, and the LORD is with us; do not fear them." But all the congregation said to stone them with stones. (Num. 14:6, 9-10)

The entire history of Israel in the Old Testament is, from one perspective, an object lesson in the failure to achieve a common vision. And the principle contained in that story is as valid for a partnership of two people as it is for an entire nation.

BIBLICAL PRINCIPLES APPLIED

The issues relating to organizational behavior are interconnected. On the face of it, the two most pressing needs are for an ethically satisfactory model of personnel structure and a firm foundation for deciding what constitutes fairness in pay and conditions. In practice, however, these questions cannot be isolated, either from each other or from the more general tension between the economic aims of business and the social and moral responsibility of those who run it.

On models of personnel structure, it is not hard to find fault with Taylor's concept of Scientific Management. So far as raising operational efficiency is concerned, the technique is certainly effective and in many instances saves unnecessary wastage of labor and time. But this benefit has its price. A deliberate move toward fragmentation and repetitiveness in work is difficult to square either with respect for the worker's humanity (because it tends to treat him as a machine) or with the biblical principles of love and justice (because life for the worker becomes considerably less fulfilling). In most cases, also, Scientific Management is destructive of the shared vision that inspires productivity.

By contrast, the Human Relations Approach is far more sympathetic. Positive emphasis is placed on meeting the individual worker's needs; efforts are made to stimulate his interest in the job and to foster a sense of responsibility to company and colleagues so that the result is a happier employee. This point in itself, however, does not place the Human Relations Approach above scrutiny. As noted earlier, it shares with Scientific Management an ultimate preoccupation with profit, which might merit careful examination in the light of the biblical teaching on work as sketched above. But even if we take the pragmatic view that profit is an acceptable governing principle in business life, we may find the Human Relations Approach being applied in contexts that raise questions of their own. A relevant example is the paternalistic attitude to workers adopted by some of the larger Japanese industries. From the standpoints of fairness and common vision, a company that provides everything from housing to holiday resorts is to be commended. But at the same time, such a powerful motivational structure need not be set up on, or deployed under, the biblical principle of love. In theory, it could be just the opposite.

At a more specific level a number of broad statements can be made from the biblical standpoint on the subject of fairness in pay and conditions. The problem here, though, is that they are very broad. Any analysis of the biblical notion of justice, for instance, must conclude that exploitation of the work force is wrong. That is a judgment with which almost any thinking person would concur. Difficulties arise only when you attempt to work out what, in fact, constitutes exploitation. In the face of widely differing rates of development, for instance, you will be hard-pressed to find a definition of *minimum wage* that holds for all nations and cultures. Establishing universal standards for work conditions is even worse. First, a poor worker in, say, India may declare himself satisfied with a situation that would be outrageous judged by the standards of the United States; second, even if you could get everyone to agree on a set of minimum requirements, these would, in practice, be well beyond the financial reach of businesses in most of the Third World.

Answers in this area are probably to be found in two directions: (1) in world economic policy, which to a large extent influences the national and local economic conditions under which individual businesses operate; and (2) in a vigilant application of principles like love and justice within the framework of what is economically feasible. It could be objected that this approach betrays a certain apathy toward reforming the economic system. But that is not quite true. An economic system may need to reform; ultimately, with the return of Christ, the very concept of economics will be reformed. But until that time, and in order to see the will of God worked out in organizational behavior here and now, it will be necessary to devise temporary and provisional solutions. In the words of the writer of Hebrews, "Here we have no lasting city, but we seek the city which is to come" (13:14).

EDITOR'S PERSPECTIVE

Dr. John Haggai's observation that the contemporary Human Relations Approach to the management of organizations is more humanizing than the older Scientific Management approach is on target. His further observation that the newer approach is just as profit driven as the older one is just as true and is an important point for Christians to remember lest they overlook God's deep concern for motives and attitudes (see 1 Cor. 4:5; 2 Cor. 5:12). To put it bluntly, love is not the motivating force behind the modern changes in organizational behavior. This truth is readily apparent as one scans the business literature pouring forth from both the academic community and the hands of business practitioners.

A great deal of interest is currently being paid, for example, to the following subjects: (1) conflict management and negotiations, (2) transformational leadership theory, (3) influence tactics and power, (4) organizational change processes, (5) organizational cultures, and (6) career development. The focus is on efficiency, productivity, and profits—good goals, but not sufficient ones—and God's love is rarely a primary concern. It would be hard to find a richer array of topics, though, to which biblical principles could be applied, for God's Word is full of commands and wisdom that bear on conflict management, leadership, politics in business (influence and power), a personal calling (career development), and so forth. We will take a brief excursion into the world of biblical politics, the godly management of anger (conflict management), and the true nature of leadership to stimulate still further biblical exploration and thinking about these and other matters pertaining to organizational behavior.

Some people would prefer that I not use the term *biblical politics*, for few areas of life are held in such low esteem today as the everyday notion of

138

politics—and for good reasons. Our contemporary view of the subject is so negative that it creates an immediate aversion to the idea that the Bible should somehow be related positively to the political process. It should be positively related, however; from a biblical perspective, the ability to be political means one has practical wisdom and the ability to diplomatically employ it in a prudent, sound, discreet, circumspect, and informed manner. Politics need not, therefore, become synonymous with behavior that is duplicitous, hypocritical, and self-serving. While acknowledging that the political process—whether in business, the Church, or government—has come to be characterized as a subprofessional aspect of life in the public arenas, we must nevertheless remind ourselves that the political process is not inherently evil. We should, in fact, want to learn how to be political.

The Apostle Paul, for example, was acting prudently (politically) when he went to Jerusalem to discuss the Judaizers' efforts to have the gentile Christians circumcised and "submitted to [the church council] the gospel which I present among the Gentiles, but *I did so in private to those who were of reputation,* for fear that I might be running, or had run, in vain" (Gal. 2:2, emphasis added). Paul took a tough question to the church leadership in a private setting rather than first putting it before them in a public forum. His approach was a political one that allowed "those who were of reputation" to raise discreet questions in private, and have them answered, without having the added pressure of taking preliminary positions in public. Major differences can be discussed and resolved more easily in a more intimate setting, as a general rule. This is prudent—sound politics.

The book of Proverbs is full of "political advice." For example, if you have been snared by the words of your own mouth—promised to do something you now believe you cannot do—"Do this then, my son . . . go, humble yourself, and importune your neighbor. . . . Deliver yourself like a gazelle from the hunter's hand" (Prov. 6:2-5). And we are told, "A gentle answer turns away wrath" (15:1); "The tongue of the wise makes knowledge acceptable" (15:2); "The heart of the wise teaches his mouth, and adds persuasiveness to his lips" (16:23); "He who restrains his words has knowledge" (17:27); and "Keeping away from strife is an honor for a man, but any fool will quarrel" (20:3). These prudent insights are full of political implications, as is all the wisdom literature. Being political (prudent), in the biblical sense, is never to be equated with being deceitful. It has nothing to do with buttering up someone. It is acting in accordance with God's wisdom, that puts another's interests in the forefront, without forgetting that there is a godly form of self-interest. True self-interest is prudent, not selfish. It is courteous, polite, discreet, circumspect, diplomatic, and practical.

The second excursion will be in the area of conflict management and negotiations. Generally, conflicts arise when people perceive that others do not care about them or things that affect their sense of self-worth. When this occurs, anger and distrust easily develop, communications become strained, and our imaginations (regarding others' motives and behavior) turn negative and dominate our perceptive patterns.

Concealed and suppressed anger can do no one any good in the marketplace—or anywhere else for that matter. That is why God has *commanded*, "Be angry, and yet do not sin; do not let the sun go down on your anger, and do not give the devil an opportunity" (Eph. 4:26-27). Most of us have been poorly trained in our families and elsewhere to properly obey this relatively simple, four-part command.

Being angry does not necessitate or imply the need for any violence, loudness, intemperate language, or discourteous conduct. We can be very angry and at the same time be very calm, very polite, and very concerned for the well-being of the person with whom we are angry. Anger (not God's righteous anger but our normal variety), however, is almost always rooted in our having been *hurt*. When we are hurt, we can do one of two things: (1) we can expose the fact that we have been hurt, when the hurt occurred, and why it hurt; or (2) we can verbally pour out our anger on someone with the almost certain result of making him or her extremely defensive. The first approach helps us guard the integrity of the command: "Be angry, and yet do not sin." The first approach lets us talk about our hurts and encourages the other person to reflect on the conduct that may have hurt us. Most people do not like to willfully hurt other people. The first approach opens many doors for reconciliation. The second approach makes reconciliation more difficult.

The second part of the command ("Do not let the sun go down on your anger, and do not give the devil an opportunity") calls for our dealing with our hurts as quickly as possible—at the moment they occur or, minimally, in the day they occur. By doing that, we keep our imagination in check, prevent the emotional infection from spreading to innocent third parties, and speed the chances for healing. These positive factors help shut the Devil out of any further meddling.

The key, of course, to conflict management is the assumption that all parties really want to be reconciled, live in harmony, and have respect for one another. Reconciliation is impossible when pride and hate are dominant attitudes. And occasionally we encounter people who enjoy being angry, and they bring additional baggage to the situation.

Finally, a few comments will be made about leadership. Leadership is an ability that embodies both subjective and objective elements, such as the ability to elicit the trust and confidence of others so that they will voluntarily choose to follow a particular leader—leadership is given, not taken. Leadership brings forth in the followers the belief that their own best interests will be served by following the designated leader—leadership is strengthened by serving, diminished by taking. A leader projects a believable vision, the presence of knowledge, the skills necessary to fulfill the vision, and a level of unflagging confidence from which others can draw strength and hope.

Leadership, if it is to be designated as Christian, must also be characterized by the fruit of the Spirit, attitudes that reveal a godly character, and a pattern of righteous behavior. These qualities, and these alone, distinguish Christian leadership from worldly leadership. After all, the world has experienced many leaders with plenty of charisma, knowledge, and ability, but poor character or little interest in righteous behavior. Christian leadership should encompass the best the world has gleaned from God's common grace and the best of God's special gifts.

PART VIII

HUMAN RESOURCES: MEANS OR ENDS

John Haggai observed in the previous chapter that business managers alter their organizational behavior for the "ends" of efficiency, productivity, and profits, not out of the goodness and kindness of their hearts. An integral component of business that is entwined with its purposes, behavior, and accomplishments is its enlistment and employment of people. But people are employed in the market-place because of what they know and the tasks they can do, not for the purpose of developing personal relationships. Businesses are formed to perform specific tasks, not to nurture those employed (which is a primary function of the family and church).

This very truth—that businesses are formed to perform an economic function rather than pursue interpersonal ends—is all too frequently an Achilles heel for business. No country in the world has a better educational process preparing people for business careers than the United States, yet students are given the predominant impression that employees (laborers in particular) are just another factor of production along with capital, raw materials, and management. In this framework, employees represent only a cost factor to be factored into cost/benefit analysis, break-even point, input/output analysis, variable costs, or "means" analysis. Quite frankly, students are largely left with the impression that people are nothing but a means to a greater end—efficiency, productivity, and profits—because in the final analysis, when the choice is between people and profit, profit usually wins.

The lone voice addressing the other side of this phenomenon is sometimes found in courses, seminars, and programs dealing with Human Resource Management. Here the language tends to be much more humanizing and sympathetic to matters addressing human values and dignity. But even this is justified in the marketplace by making reference to matters of productivity, long-term costs, and profits. For example, providing a positive work experience helps reduce personnel turnover, which in turn eliminates the cost of securing and training new people, which should result in both higher productivity and higher profits. Productivity and profit, not justice and righteousness, are appealed to. Indeed profit generally pushes aside declarations of concern for people when an economic showdown comes.

This propensity to seek profits through enlightened Human Resource Management is not bad in and of itself. Christians should be grateful that God's perfect creation reveals that the accurately understood natural laws and moral laws mirror each other in matters of conduct and relationships. Christians observing the development of the field of Human Resource Management have long recognized the growing compatibility between secular theory and principles found in Scripture.

The field of Human Resource Management is rife with opportunities to integrate biblical principles with the many concerns under the big umbrella of Personnel matters. Christians, however, should never be content with limiting their interest in employees to the functional practices they perform or to the "bottom line" of profits, as important as these are. Surely God sees people as "ends" as well as "means." For example, salvation and discipleship are the "ends" sought in presenting the gospel, while people presenting the gospel are the "means" by which the task is accomplished. Christians should have the same understanding about people in business—people are a means of production, and their personhood should be nurtured and cared for as a godly end of business.

Dr. David Hoover approaches this troublesome reality in four meaningful ways: (1) he presents an overview of the immense size of Human Resource Management; (2) he raises twelve sample questions that need to be addressed from a biblical perspective in the field; (3) he provides a sample of the biblical principles available for coping with the main issues in the field; and (4) he focuses on two of the more difficult questions he raised. He calls the Christian working in the marketplace to employ God's principles as a means of fostering renewal in both the lives of individuals and the affairs of institutions.

CHAPTER 8

BIBLICAL PRINCIPLES APPLIED TO HUMAN RESOURCES

David J. Hoover

David J. Hoover, Associate Professor at Covenant College, earned his Ph.D. in business at Virginia Polytechnic Institute and State University majoring in Human Resource Management with minors in Labor Relations and Industrial and Organizational Psychology. For three years, he was on the faculty of Miami University's School of Business Administration. He has also worked and consulted in the private, public, and not-for-profit sectors. In addition, he is an ordained pastor in the Presbyterian Church in America. He served in five pastorates over twelve years, having earned an M.Div. at Westminster Theological Seminary.

GeORGE and Sylvia Stratton along with their two children just moved to Atlanta, Georgia. Having accepted a position as a senior engineer with Signal Technology, Inc. (STI), George looks forward to settling down and advancing in his career. Like most people, though, George is only partially aware of all that has gone into obtaining this new job. If an organization is going to make good hiring decisions, a lot of skillful effort must be expended in the selection process. Yet, when George reports to work next Monday, that will be just the beginning of a complex relationship. Decisions and actions (or lack of them) by both George and STI will affect the quality and duration of their relationship.

Although George's job is important to him, giving meaning and status to his life as well as providing a living for him and his family, the viability of STI depends on his capabilities and productivity. Therefore, the company needs to be vitally concerned about the attraction, selection, maintenance, development, health and safety, and retention of competent, motivated workers. Employees' concerns about their jobs and organizational concerns about employees are of interest to Human Resource Management.

For some readers, the term *Personnel* might be more familiar. However, within the last decade the dominant term used in academic literature has been *Human Resource Management.* This new name was devised to reflect the elevated status of this area of management due to its recent inclusion in the strategic planning of sophisticated firms. Nevertheless, it would be a mistake to think that one particular department actually can manage an organization's human resources. No matter what size the organization, or whether it has a Personnel/Human Resources department, for an organization to be effective, all managers must be active in managing their human resources. Therefore, this chapter is intended for all businesspersons who have subordinates, not just managers whose primary responsibility lies in the area of Personnel or Human Resources.

To lay out the boundaries of Human Resource Management, we shall consider in our first section a description published by the Academy of Management. We shall also look at a model that appeared in a popular textbook on this subject, *Personnel/Human Resource Management.*[1]

Significant questions or topics that need to be explored from a biblical perspective are identified in the second section. In the third section, biblical principles that may apply to Human Resources are identified. Finally, two of the issues are examined in the light of biblical principles in the fourth section.

THE DOMAIN OF HUMAN RESOURCE MANAGEMENT

According to the Academy of Management's 1989 *Call for Papers* for its annual meeting, the domain of Human Resources is "content relating to administering the Personnel/Human Resources office, and to external influences upon the administration of work activity." Sixteen major topics fall within this domain. Although the Academy's list is not exhaustive, it should give the reader a good grasp of the broad range of organizational issues covered:

- recruitment;
- selection;
- testing and staffing;
- Human Resource planning and forecasting;
- employee relations and information systems;
- design of policies and procedures;
- health and safety programs;
- job analysis and pay determination;

● compensation procedures, including benefits and services;
● design of performance appraisal systems, forms, and procedures;
● methods by which Human Resource programs are developed, adopted, implemented, and evaluated;
● the role and experiences of Human Resource managers;
● the impact of the Human Resource office on such outcomes as performance, motivation, attendance, turnover, occupational health and safety;
● such external influences upon work activity as unionization, collective bargaining, industry councils, and other forms of formal employee participation;
● labor force participation rates and the supply of labor; and
● the impact of legislative, economic, and political developments relevant to administering Human Resource programs, including labor legislation, EEO/Affirmative Action, court rulings, and regulatory agency guidelines.

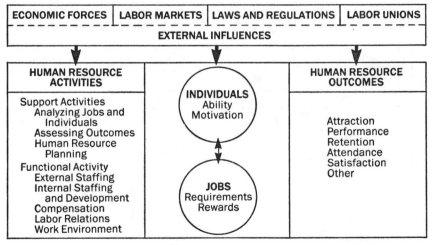

Figure 8.1
HUMAN RESOURCE MANAGEMENT MODEL
(Heneman, Schwab, Fossum, and Dyer)

Figure 8.1 is helpful for visualizing the relationship of the diverse Human Resource topics. The Heneman model indicates that the very heart of Human Resource Management is creating and maintaining a match between individuals and jobs. Three foundational or support activities undergird the five management functional activities, which facilitate the creation and maintenance of matched individuals and jobs. Effectiveness of those matches can be evaluated in terms of measurable outcomes like the five indicated. Yet, there is more to the model. Particularly since the 1960s, we have begun to realize how organizations are affected by events essentially beyond their control. External influences work on all aspects of management, including Human Resource Management. Therefore, four such influences are identified at the top of Heneman's model.

A Christian perspective makes a subtle yet substantive addition to the model (see figure 8.2). According to Scripture, God continues to be active in His creation (see Ps. 145:8-13). Therefore, God is a potentially important external influence on the functioning of an organization. How should we include Him in this model? Should God be placed to the left of "economic forces"? Would that be appropriate for the Sustainer of the universe, who lifts up and casts down entire nations and their economies (see Ps. 2)? No, He is above the external influences in the model. God affects the four external influences identified as well as individual businesses.

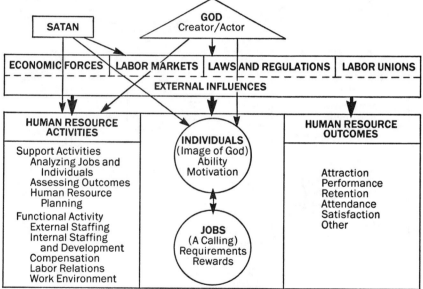

Figure 8.2
HUMAN RESOURCE MANAGEMENT
FROM A CHRISTIAN PERSPECTIVE

To have a proper perspective, it is necessary to begin with the distinction between God and His creation.[2] Here is a foundational biblical principle:

P1: God, who is above His creation, continues to be active in its history.

Thus, a new dimension must be added for a Christian model (see figure 8.2). What are the implications of adding the dimension of a God who is active in human history, a dimension noticeably absent from all major texts on this domain? God can and does intervene through His special grace, transforming individuals through salvation, and through His common grace, in restraining sin. The risen Christ who has all rule, authority, power, and dominion fosters hope (see Eph. 1:20-23).

Another related addition to a Christian model is Satan. He is the "ruler of the kingdom of the air" (Eph. 2:2), who is powerful and active in human affairs. Nevertheless, his power is limited. Christ, who dwells in the heart of Christians, is greater than Satan. As a matter of fact, through Christians in business, God is attacking Satan's domain. How exciting and challenging it is for Christian businesspersons to be a part of that extension of Christ's Kingdom! To be more effective in that pursuit, Christians need to approach their management of human resources in a biblical manner. In the second section, we shall identify Human Resource topics or problems that need to be explored from a biblical perspective.

SIGNIFICANT HUMAN RESOURCE QUESTIONS

Human Resource issues or questions that should be considered in light of God's special revelation are too numerous for a brief chapter. Consequently, our discussion is only representative of topics currently being addressed by researchers and practitioners. In keeping with our model, we shall list these topics by the categories of activities and then outcomes. First, we shall consider support activities.

Support activities—
Q1: *Is it possible to estimate individual motivation?* The significance of this question rests on the importance of individual and organizational effectiveness in an internationally competitive business environment. (Notice the external influence of economic forces that elevate the meaningfulness of this question.) What contributes to performance? Victor Vroom's view that performance is a function of ability times effort is generally accepted as accurate. Progress has been made in measuring individual abilities, but prediction of performance is not accurate. One reason is that very able people who are not motivated will put forth little effort, which lowers their performance. Other persons with

considerably less natural ability who are motivated can outperform their more able peers. Since individual motivation is an integral factor in performance, businesses would like to measure it in order to enhance predictions of who will have greater productivity. To this point, little progress has been made.

Q2: *Should employers be truthful in responding to inquiries by prospective employers about the performance of current or former employees?* If your answer is yes, you risk expensive lawsuits from those who fail to get a job due to your reference. If your answer is no, you potentially deny the prospective employer information vital to a good selection decision.

Q3: *To what extent should your organization become involved in and/or support affirmative action programs?* With recent changes in the composition of the United States Supreme Court, there may be new challenges to previous decisions. In Human Resource planning activities, do Christian businesspersons need to lead the way in providing employment opportunities for those who have historically been disadvantaged, or are such programs unfairly discriminatory against WASPs? (Note the impact of external legal influences on issues two and three.)

Functional activities—
Q4: *Should businesses require or be permitted to require drug tests in the final screening of job applicants?* Whereas businesses are required by law to provide a safe work environment and desire employees to have all their faculties when working, test results may be inaccurate. Furthermore, nonabusers are subjected to what many view as a major invasion of privacy. A related and more complex issue is whether current employees should be randomly tested for evidence of substance abuse. At their heart, these questions probe the right of employers to know versus the right of individuals to privacy.

Q5: *Should employers be permitted to consider the sexual orientation of applicants in staffing decisions?* While the law protects employees against gender discrimination (i.e., anything that would tend to place a male or a female at a disadvantage in the terms or conditions of employment due to gender), federal law does not prohibit discrimination against gays or lesbians. On the other hand, several cities and states have declared this latter type of discrimination unlawful. In these locales Christian businesspersons face an apparent dilemma. These laws are premised on the belief that homosexuality is an "alternate lifestyle"; that is, nothing is inherently wrong with homosexual relationships, and those who engage in them are perfectly normal. Yet Scripture clearly declares homosexuality to be a perversion (see Rom. 1:26ff). Therefore, Christians cannot condone such behavior. Recognizing that God has judged societies harshly for such practices (see Gen. 18:22-19:26), Christians are legitimately concerned for the welfare of the country as such laws are enacted across this nation. (See the final section for discussion of this issue.)

Q6: *Should a merit pay plan be imposed on teachers whose union is vehemently opposed to it?* Some critics fault the teachers for the dismal results of public school pupils on standardized tests. Merit pay allegedly would provide motivation for current teachers to improve their teaching plus attract more capable persons to the profession. Others say that it is virtually impossible to accurately capture all the dimensions of teaching performance. Such attempts could subvert the efforts of teachers by distracting them from educating to seeking to manipulate outcomes that are measurable. A related criticism is that merit pay systems become just another means of arbitrary subjective manipulation by administrators since many outcomes cannot be objectively measured.

Q7: *How should employers determine the pay scale for a job—by considering the labor market or by considering the value of the job to their organization?* That is the heart of the comparable worth controversy. Many females believe that the market is historically biased against jobs that have been held predominantly by females. Indeed, the wage gap—females on average earning roughly sixty percent of males on average—has been persistent. Furthermore, studies of jobs requiring equivalent skill, effort, and responsibility have found an unexplained gap between wages for male- and female-dominant jobs even after factors such as education, job experience, and tenure have been accounted for.

Based on such evidence, numerous legislative initiatives have required city and local governments to conduct comparable worth studies. Subsequently, taxpayer money is used to support above-market wages for female-dominant jobs such as nurse, librarian, secretary, and clerk. Is that just?

Q8: *How strongly should a business resist a union-organizing campaign?* Since penalties for violations of the National Labor Relations Act are light, should organizations do whatever it takes to win and then pay the delayed consequences? National Labor Relations Board appointees and federal judges under the Reagan administration have been generally sympathetic to business interests. Therefore, the interpretation of Labor Relations laws has loosened, and conviction and punishment of violators have been less aggressive. This trend may continue under the Bush administration. In the interest of greater autonomy, relaxed work rules, and the lure of greater productivity in a non-union environment, how should businesses respond to a union election?

Q9: *When hiring or transferring the spouse of a dual-career couple, what duty, if any, does a company have toward the other spouse?* With the significant increase in the number of females participating in the labor force, more and more couples can be classified as dual-career couples. This fact has served only to increase the visibility of this issue. A business's policy on this issue has considerable impact on family units. With a disgraceful national divorce rate, additional stress on society's basic unit, related to providing for that unit, may ultimately contribute to the demise of our nation.

Q10: *Should businesses provide daycare services for children of their employees?* With a tight labor market, many businesses have turned to providing day care as an effective means of attracting and retaining female workers. For the increasing number of single-parent families, this benefit is typically welcome. However, new studies indicate that such nonparental care during early child development generally has long-term negative effects on children.

Outcomes—

Q11: *How should businesses measure performance?* What should be the relationship between considerations of quantity and quality? Historically, our industrial society was preoccupied with assessment of quantity. Quality control was something placed at the end of our production process. The Japanese quality assurance, on the other hand, stresses quality throughout the entire process, resulting in superior products. As a consequence, even though many Japanese products are now significantly more expensive than American substitutes, there remains a strong consumer demand.

Q12: *How can companies reduce absenteeism, that is, improve attendance?* The cost to employers and our entire economy of employees not showing up when scheduled for work is in the hundreds of millions of dollars each year. After years of poor response to discipline, even of a progressive variety, by offenders, many employers are turning to new programs devised by behavioral scientists. Should we expect these programs to have a long-term benefit? Are they worth the cost? (See the final section for further discussion of this issue.)

The twelve questions listed above only scratch the surface of the ones businesses confront in the area of Human Resources. Without taking the space to indicate their significance, let us briefly suggest additional topics for which biblical principles could provide direction:

- To determine demand for labor, how should businesses forecast demand for their product or service?
- How much notification should be given to employees scheduled for layoff? How much when plants are scheduled to close?
- During periods of heavy customer demand, how should work be scheduled? How much overtime is reasonable? Should employees be expected to work seven days per week?
- With the cost of medical benefits soaring, should companies

implement wellness programs?
- What approach should an organization take toward the issue of sexual harassment?
- During a reduction in force, what is a company's obligation to released employees?
- How should a company establish cost/benefit standards for decisions involving employee risk of occupational accidents, illnesses, and/or death?
- How should jobs be designed? Should emphasis be placed on work simplification or job enrichment?
- Without regard to the economic forces of international competition, should management's relations with labor unions be adversarial or cooperative?
- Should attempts be made to control multinational corporations that use their ability to locate facilities in countries with lower labor costs in order to coerce concessions from their employees?
- To what extent should employers permit/tolerate religious witnessing or proselytizing by employees?

Our next section introduces several biblical principles broadly applicable to Human Resources.

BIBLICAL PRINCIPLES

The most obvious place to begin our discussion of biblical principles that apply to Human Resources is to investigate what the Bible says about man. There is, however, a more foundational principle. Earlier we noted this biblical principle:

P1: God, who is above His creation, continues to be active in its history.

Our second biblical principle pertains to one of God's creatures, the crown of creation:

P2: Man was created in the image of God.

As we shall see below, apart from God's continuing activity in history, we would be unable to grasp the true nature of man. A popular secular assumption about man is that he is an animal whose species evolved into its present form over millions of years. In stark contrast to that view, the book of Genesis reveals that man's creation was distinct from that of the animals (see 1:26-31; 2:22). Only of man is it said that he was created in the image or likeness of God. Moreover, man was to rule over the animals. (Note that there is now consensus among theologians that the terms *image* and *likeness* are synonyms.)

This second principle is clearly stated and repeated (see Gen. 5:1; 1 Cor. 11:7; 15:49; James 3:9), but its meaning is not so clear. None of the passages gives a systematic explanation of the concept. Consequently, in the history of Christian thought, much of the interpretation about man's being in the image of God has been speculative. For example, many theologians have believed that the Bible was referring to aspects of man that are distinct from animals, such as man's moral and intellectual abilities. However, the Scripture does not say that. Other theologians have sought to interpret this concept through more careful study of Scripture. John Calvin looked into the New Testament teaching on the restoration of the image of God. This method seems more appropriate than mere speculation. He identified three aspects of the renewed image: righteousness, holiness (see Eph. 4:24), and knowledge (see Col. 3:10).

Further insight has been gained through examining the original image in terms of Christ.[3] Christ is declared to be the image of God (see 2 Cor. 4:4; Col. 1:15). In Him, we can view the untarnished image. Thus, our understanding of man will derive from better understanding Christ, to whose image believers are being conformed (see Rom. 8:29).

This method of learning about the nature of man does not deprecate the physiological, biological, psychological, and sociological insights derived from scientific study of man. However, such studies are merely descriptive and, therefore, inadequate for determining the nature of man.

What do we learn from the New Testament about the image that relates to Human Resources? First,

P2a: Apart from renewal in Christ, man is distorted.

Or as Scripture puts it, apart from Christ, people are dead in sin. That is fundamental to understand when handling Human Resources. Secular approaches to Human Resource Management fail to consider man's sin nature. Scripture teaches that mankind has been radically affected by sin. Dealing with Human Resources, then, calls for realistic management actions that take into account this abnormal state of man.

Our second observation on what being created in the image of God means is that

P2b: The highest end of man is fellowship or communion with God.

Maslow's self-actualization, the epitome of his Hierarchy of Needs, is shown to be deficient. Man's ultimate fulfillment is found in relationship with God. A person's vocation cannot lead to such as achievement. Rather, only performing one's vocational calling to the glory of Christ, in fellowship with Him, realizes that basic need.

A third observation relates to the good news. All persons who trust in Christ are in the process of renewal. If any man is in Christ, he is a new creation. Old things have passed away, and new things have come (see 2 Cor. 5:17). A radically new lifestyle begins. There is the laying aside of the old self—corrupted in accordance with the lusts of deceit. The mind is renewed. The Christian puts on the new self in righteousness and true holiness (see Eph. 4:22-24). Look at some of the consequences in the following verses: telling the truth to one's neighbor (see v. 25); working instead of stealing (see v. 28); building up others rather than tearing them down with one's speech (see v. 29); drawing people together rather than isolating them (see vv. 31-32); and, finally, being able to imitate God (see Eph. 5:1-2). For God's beloved children, that means imitating Christ's love. In this age of the Spirit, there is an unveiling of the glory of God. When the image is renewed,

P2c: Christians actually image, reflect or mirror the glory of God and are being transformed into that same image (see 2 Cor. 3:18).

What a difference renewal makes in individuals in the workplace! How much profitability is lost due to strife among employees, lack of teamwork, feelings hurt by others' comments, employee theft, and reliance on false information? That principle leads us to our fourth principle:

P2d: In Christ there is corporate healing.

Man's creation in the image of God is presented in Scripture not primarily in terms of individuals but in terms of a community. Transformation of individuals brings about true community. Christ, our peace, has broken down partitions, making in Himself one new man (see Eph. 2:18-22). Ethnic barriers have been obliterated (see Col. 3:10-11). Gender no longer divides (see Gal. 3:28). The differences are not removed, but they no longer impede functioning as God originally intended. That is great news for managers and provides hope that the serious people problems plaguing businesses have solutions.

A final observation involves the tension in the biblical perspective. Although there is concrete renewal—believers actually reflecting God's glory, truly imitating Him—the full reality is yet to come. Now we know in part, but then we shall know fully (see 1 Cor. 13:12). It has not yet been revealed what we shall be (see 1 John 3:2). Consequently,

P2e: Neither individual Christians nor organizations composed of Christians will fully reflect the image of God.

P2f: Since individuals and communities are in the process of being conformed to the image of Christ, they are not yet perfect.

Until Christ returns, managers will be needed to plan, organize, lead, monitor, and take corrective action in light of man's fallen nature and in light of what renewal in Christ means. Many other biblical principles apply to Human Resources, but space constraints require that we briefly suggest just a few more.

With regard to one external influence, the Bible is very clear about laws and regulations (see Rom. 13; 1 Pet. 2:13).

P3: Officials and authorities must be obeyed.

There is one caveat (see Acts 5:29).

P3a: If there is a conflict between what God requires and what officials or laws require, obey God.

Ultimately,

P3b: Each individual is responsible to God (see Rom. 14:12; 1 Cor. 3:13-15; 1 Pet. 4:5).

In the area of compensation (see Deut. 25:4; Luke 10:7; 1 Tim. 5:18),

P4: Employees deserve fair pay.

P4a: They should make enough to be able to afford basic necessities.

P4b: We should not take advantage of the economically disadvantaged (see Prov. 14:21, 31; 22:16, 22; James 2:6).

On the other hand,

P4c: Employees should not be encouraged to love money.

It is not possible to serve God and riches. Furthermore, the love of money is the root of all types of evil (see Matt. 6:24; 1 Tim. 6:10). (Note the recent Wall Street scandals in this regard.) In the work environment, a guiding principle is the Golden Rule:

> **P5: Do to others what you would want them to do to you.**

This principle is also important for labor relations. Another principle relevant to that area and the area of assessing outcomes is this:

> **P6: Be truthful, which may include being angry** (see Eph. 4:21-29).

In the area of performance,

> **P7: God made work meaningful and gave it significance** (see Gen. 1:28; Gal. 6:5-6; Col. 3:22).

Confirmation of the positive nature of work is found in the next principle:

> **P8: We are not to subsidize persons who are unwilling to work** (see 2 Thess. 3:10).

God determines the work people should do.

> **P9: God gives people different abilities for accomplishing different tasks** (see Rom. 12:6; 1 Cor. 12).

Finally, in the area of health and safety, the Old Testament indicates that those who injure or kill persons unintentionally have certain responsibilities. Those who do so intentionally deserve more severe consequences (see Exod. 21; Num. 35; Deut. 4). At the risk of being controversial, I believe these points imply that

> **P10: No-fault workers' compensation insurance is an inadequate remedy for occupational illnesses and injuries.**

BIBLICAL PRINCIPLES APPLIED

In this final section, we will suggest responses to two Human Resource issues based on biblical principles, taking one question from the "Activities" section and one from the "Outcomes" section.

Q5: Should employers be permitted to consider the sexual orientation of applicants in staffing decisions? Three biblical principles are relevant to this question:

P3: Officials and authorities must be obeyed.

P3a: If there is a conflict between what God requires and what officials or laws require, obey God.

P3b: Each individual is responsible to God.

To determine if P3a applies, we must ask if these new laws conflict with God's law. If not, we must obey them until they are changed. Since homosexuality is such an emotionally charged issue, perhaps it would be helpful to look at how Christians have coped with other sexual sins in our pluralistic society.

How do Christian businesses treat adulterers and fornicators? While we probably discipline illicit behavior, we typically do not discipline on the basis of orientation. Should it be any different when a person's orientation is homosexual rather than heterosexual? Are not all sexual relations outside the bond of marriage wrong? Then it seems reasonable to treat all sinful behavior of a sexual nature in the same way.

As long as the laws protecting homosexuals against discrimination in the workplace are interpreted so that business can establish "reasonable work rules," which would include moral standards of conduct while on company time or property, such laws could not contradict God's law. Certainly God does not require businesses to impose His standards on persons dead in sin outside the workplace. If we look at the United States Supreme Court's landmark decision on sexual harassment (*Vinson v. Meritor Bank*), there is strong warrant for protecting employees from any sort of environmental harassment in the workplace.

Although state and city ordinances protecting homosexuals against employment discrimination do not appear to conflict directly with God's law, they reflect the distortion of sin in our society. Christians should confront that incorrect view of homosexuality lovingly but firmly. Legislators should know of our strong convictions in this area and should be held accountable on their voting record. Not only are they individually accountable to God, but they are accountable to their electorate.

The last question to which we shall apply biblical principles is this:

Q12: How can companies reduce absenteeism, that is, improve attendance? Studies of behavior modification conducted in business settings suggest that various techniques can be effective for specific behavior. Several successful organizations, such as UPS, have adopted certain practices based on that theory with a recent application to attendance.

The new techniques reward desired behavior. For example, all employees who report to work on time for an entire month would be eligible for a drawing for a color television. Such programs have sparked a lot of employee interest and resulted in significant improvement in attendance, at least for the short run. But there is some indication that as the newness fades, so do the excitement and the results. Perhaps identification of the root problems could suggest a more permanent solution. (If man were evolved from animals, modifying human behavior through positive and negative reinforcement techniques might be more appropriate.)

Companies that have designed jobs to be very simple and those where the jobs are dangerous seem to have the greatest attendance problems, which suggests that P2d concerning corporate healing is relevant. Employees need to have jobs designed to be significant, and they need to be treated individually as significant contributors to the organization. God gave meaningful work to man (P7). Simple, boring jobs provide no intrinsic motivation. Unsafe jobs motivate people to abstain.

Herzberg would classify safety as a dissatisfier and job design as a motivator. However, with man's sinful distortion, even correcting such deficiencies would not ensure good attendance. Nevertheless, such approaches should provide longer-term improvement. Ultimately, employees need to find their motivation in working for the Lord (P2b). In such circumstances, they could be motivated even as slaves to serve their masters. Furthermore, they would understand the importance of diligence, not just showing up for work (P7). Is that not more crucial? Look at what the Protestant work ethic has meant for Western civilization! While that work ethic was initially rooted in a relationship with God, we have had long-term benefits, even though its foundation has frequently been missing. The salt and light of Scripture have amazing power and benefit, even for nonbelievers.

Even where renewal in God's image is a reality, removal of progressive discipline is not recommended. Principle P2f suggests the necessity of controls since renewal is yet to be completely realized. As God graciously brings individual and corporate renewal to our country, and as businesses heed biblical principles, absenteeism should be less of a problem.

EDITOR'S PERSPECTIVE

David Hoover did not avoid the tough issues (sexual orientation of job applicants, the problem of absenteeism) when he selected those two Human Resource topics to examine in the light of Scripture. His analysis provides us with an excellent example of what is involved in seeking to understand and carry out God's will in the marketplace. Included are such essential topics as the biblical principles applicable to the specific issues; the identification of the deeper moral issues resting beneath specific concerns, for example, homosexuality is a subset of the broader issue of sexual immorality in its many forms (premarital fornication, postmarital adultery, etc.); and the simultaneous integration of the issues with public law and scholarly research theory.

Dr. Hoover also pointed out the advantages of identifying the root problems that give birth to particular Human Resource issues or circumstances. For example, better, long-lasting motivational results would be realized if workers were given meaningful tasks and treated as significant persons rather than merely rewarded for doing menial tasks. Without an understanding of the root causes, we will spend our lives working with surface issues rather than dealing with the deeper causes that give rise to them.

Until Christians discern practical ways to make application of basic biblical doctrines in their daily living, their Christian light will be dim and inadequate to lead the way to higher ground. The Apostle Paul was often led by the Holy Spirit to first set forth doctrine and then to illustrate what was to result if one truly believed the teachings. (Romans and Ephesians are examples of this doctrine/application format.) Dr. Hoover used this technique in the third section of his chapter. He began with a principle about God as Creator and His continuing activity in human history. Then he presented the doctrine of our being created in God's image, which was in turn followed by several biblical principles that relate to and should lead to particular behavioral consequences.

I want to briefly examine a foundational biblical doctrine and demonstrate its practical importance to the field of Human Resource Management as a means of encouraging all Christians to think deeply about the application of the great scriptural doctrines to life's daily affairs. I want to consider a few practical things, with business application, that fall out of an enlarged understanding of the doctrine of the Trinity. (For further discussion, refer to page 15 of *Biblical Principles and Business: The Foundations*, the first volume in the CHRISTIANS IN THE MARKETPLACE SERIES.)

It is my observation that few Christians have been exposed to much in-depth teaching on the relationship between the Persons of the Godhead, nor do they spend much time thinking about the practical things that can be gleaned from such an understanding. I was never taught to seek any particular applications that might be embodied in the doctrine of the Trinity. My exposure to the doctrine, besides my reading of Scripture and a handful of sermons that were doctrinally oriented (not application oriented), was limited to two sources. The first was the statement found in chapter 2, section 3, of *The Westminster Confession of Faith*:

> In the unity of the Godhead there be three persons of one substance, power, and eternity: God the Father, God the Son, and God the Holy Ghost (Matt. 28:19; II Cor. 13:14; Matt. 3:16, 17). The Father is of none, neither begotten nor proceeding; the Son is eternally begotten of the Father (John 1:14, 18; John 17:24); the Holy Ghost eternally proceeding from the Father and the Son (John 15:26; Gal. 4:6).

The second was a book by Edward Henry Bickersteth, *The Trinity*,[4] published in the 1800s to address the rising challenges of Unitarianism.

My personal spiritual pilgrimage aroused a deep internal interest in the attributes of God; Bickersteth's work stimulated me and laid an early foundation for my thinking about the equality of the three Persons of the Godhead. *The Trinity* cites numerous scriptures showing that every attribute of God ascribed to one Member of the Godhead is also ascribed to the other two Persons. Every Member of the Trinity is absolutely holy; every Person is all-knowing; and so forth.

Scripture also reveals definite diversity in the roles assumed by each Person of the Godhead. My growing awareness of this truth set me to thinking about its implications for human existence and relationships. I soon realized that Scripture, in speaking about humans and interpersonal relationships, was addressing matters perfectly modeled in the Godhead. I explored other ideas in Scripture as diverse as equality/inequality, authority/submission, rights/responsibilities, and being an individual while being in community.

Thus when I came across the third biblical principle Dr. Hoover identified for application in Human Resource Management ("officials and authorities must be obeyed"), I was reminded immediately that God has revealed a hierarchy within the Godhead. This does not do the slightest damage to the truth that each member of the Trinity is truly God and equally worthy to be honored and worshiped. Yet Christ came and took on flesh and completely submitted Himself to the will of the Father. So the taking on of authority does not make the person with authority inherently better than the person without it. Neither does the making of a volitional commitment to live or work in submission to someone in a position of authority demean or reduce the worth or dignity of the person assuming the subordinate role.

The attitudinal and behavioral implications of such truths are extremely important. How we treat people above us, beside us, and below us must reveal a deep respect and genuine concern for them, or we will exhibit an ungodly character and demeaning behavior. Those who appropriate the name of Christ in the marketplace ought to include in their search a sound understanding of the great doctrines of Scripture so that the broader implications are realized and applied in everyday decisions affecting behavior.

PART IX

HUMANS AMID BITS, BYTES, AND CHIPS

Does the Scripture, framed over two thousand years ago in an agrarian culture, address in a relevant way the issues faced by mankind in today's high-tech society? The chapter before us demonstrates precisely and unequivocally that God's Word speaks directly to the moral problems encountered in the most technically sophisticated realms of modern business: the information systems and operations research fields.

Many people are afraid to even attempt to think about the moral issues that might be lurking in the shadows of advanced technology because they misunderstand the technology involved. Dr. Joseph McRae Mellichamp, Director of the Artificial Intelligence Laboratory at the University of Alabama, and author of the upcoming chapter, has done a marvelous thing for the computer sophisticate and unsophisticate alike. He has opened before us the purposes, functions, and objectives of the information systems and operations research fields in language comprehensible even to those who have absolutely no training in mathematics, computers, or science. This ability to communicate is the hallmark of a master teacher. Of the fifty Chavanne Scholars who participated in creating the chapters for this series of books, Rae Mellichamp has the distinction of being the only scholar greeted by a round of spontaneous applause at the conclusion of his presentation to the others!

Dr. Mellichamp has also successfully delineated the distinction between the people who employ the technical "tools of the trade" and the sophisticated logical, mechanical, and technical contrivances they rule. He has stripped away any legitimate possibility that people might try to hide behind or blame the level of sophistication and complexity of the disciplines for inappropriate outcomes. The people who use the techniques and tools of the trade are morally responsible for their intentions, decisions, and actions. This is why Scripture has so much to say about the moral issues encountered there.

In bringing Scripture to bear on the broad moral issues encountered in these fields, Rae Mellichamp sets before us six biblical principles that can be applied to the fourteen moral issues he identifies—eight in information systems and six in operations research. I am aware of no other work that exposes the moral issues encountered in the information systems and operations research fields to the light of Scripture in such an understandable, useful way.

CHAPTER 9

APPLYING BIBLICAL PRINCIPLES IN INFORMATION SYSTEMS AND OPERATIONS RESEARCH

Joseph M. Mellichamp

Joseph M. Mellichamp is Professor of Management Science and Director of the Artificial Intelligence Laboratory at the University of Alabama. Dr. Mellichamp has published articles in numerous journals, including the Harvard Business Review, Management Science, Decision Sciences, Interfaces, Simulation, *and* AIIE Transactions. *His research interests are in the application of Artificial Intelligence techniques to problems in manufacturing, communications, and information systems. He has served as a consultant to a variety of organizations including General Motors, AT&T, NASA, and the United States Army (Strategic Defense Initiative). Dr. Mellichamp and his wife, Peggy, have served on associate staff with Campus Crusade for Christ since 1972.*

In this chapter, various issues in the fields of information systems and operations research will be examined from a biblical perspective. The objective is to determine what biblical principles are pertinent in the application of these two important areas of business administration. It should be helpful at this point to present operational definitions of information systems and operations research, since both areas are relatively recent additions to the functional areas of business. More details about the specific content of each area will be presented later in the discussion.

An *information system* is a system used to collect, store, process, and present information to support an organization's information needs.[1] The term *information systems* is generally construed to imply computer-based systems; hence such systems are the principal product of computer science and in an organization would include the personnel and computer hardware and software committed to the task of information support for decision making.

Operations research is a scientific approach to problem solving for executive management.[2] It involves the construction of mathematical and statistical models of decision problems and the use of such models to evaluate the relative merit of alternative courses of action. Operations research typically depends heavily on computer processing; thus, there is a logical connection between operations research and information systems, and it makes sense to examine the two areas together.

Upon initial consideration, one is inclined to wonder if there are moral and ethical questions associated with activities that appear to be concerned exclusively with the accumulation and assessment of numbers, data, and facts. To be sure, there are many complex and perplexing issues. Addressing the notion of problem solving, which is the objective of both information systems and operations research, Joseph Weizenbaum wrote,

> Real problems in the real world involve, among other things, conflicts of interest among real people. They cannot be understood, let alone solved, without first understanding what goes on in the hearts and minds of people.[3]

In the same connection, Ron Howard has written, "Since the formalism of decision analysis is amoral, like arithmetic, any moral considerations must come from the people involved in the application."[4] Human involvement in information systems and operations research has opened the door to an array of moral and ethical considerations.

We will examine these issues in the context of a hierarchy or classification. For this purpose we will need to consider information systems and operations research from the standpoint of ends, means, and methods. The first category of issues is concerned with the ends of these two areas of activity, that is, the intended and desired results of information systems and operations research. The second category relates to the means and methods of information systems and operations research—the actions (means) and strategies, tactics, and techniques (methods) used to achieve desired ends. The final category, related specifically to the human element, is designated the human factor.

Before we begin the examination of issues, we will present several key biblical principles relevant to the issues identified. The applicable principles for each issue discussed in subsequent sections of the chapter will be identified. The application of these biblical principles will also be discussed with specific emphasis on how that application might ameliorate tensions existing as a result of the issues.

BIBLICAL PRINCIPLES

Information systems and operations research are uniquely concerned with decision making. The major focus of both areas is

> . . . on individual decision-making because in a most important sense all decisions are individual decisions. Individuals making decisions as agents for others must conform to the agreement they have made in accepting the responsibility to act as an agent. This category includes all those who act on behalf of organizations. . . . Thus, whether as principal or agent, everyone is exercising individual decision-making.[5]

In attempting to apply biblical principles to these two areas, it will be necessary to present principles applicable to individuals and to businesses and governments.

Principles relating to individuals—We could develop scores of biblical principles relating specifically to individuals. But for purposes of applying biblical principles in the areas of information systems and operations research, four broad ones should be sufficient: the value principle, the integrity principle, the steward principle, and the others principle.

The *value principle* addresses the uniqueness of man vis-á-vis other elements of God's creation and the significant role man plays in the creation. Genesis 1:26-27 speaks of the uniqueness of man—man was created in the image of God. Other passages tell us that man was created with intellect, emotions, and will and that these attributes set him apart from other creatures in the creation. Every person is important to God as an individual (see Luke 12:7; 1 Tim. 2:4; 2 Pet. 3:9). Some passages suggest that meaning and purpose in life come from a proper relationship with God (see John 10:10; 1 John 1:3), and John 1:12 and 1 John 5:11-12 define the essence of this relationship.

The *integrity principle* defines the quality of character expected from the person in a right relationship with God. Individuals are to be holy as the Lord is holy (see Lev. 11:44; Matt. 5:45; 1 Pet. 1:16). Such persons are to be "blameless and innocent, children of God above reproach in the midst of a crooked and perverse generation, among whom you appear as lights in the world" (Phil. 2:15). Second Peter 1:5-10 encourages the pursuit of moral excellence.

The *steward principle* refers to the individual's responsibility before God. He intended for mankind to be stewards of the creation (see Gen. 1:28). The parable of the talents teaches that individuals are responsible for their actions (see Matt. 25:14-30). We are admonished to "do all to the glory of God"

(1 Cor. 10:31). Colossians 3:23-24 states, "Whatever you do, do your work heartily, as for the Lord rather than for men; knowing that from the Lord you will receive the reward of the inheritance. It is the Lord Christ whom you serve."

The *others principle* outlines how all individuals properly related to God should relate to others. In this regard, the Golden Rule is the underlying standard: "And just as you want men to treat you, treat them in the same way" (Luke 6:31). We are to love our neighbors as ourselves (see Matt. 22:39; Mark 12:31; Rom. 13:9) and to love one another (see John 13:34; 15:12). We ought to love our enemies (see Matt. 5:43-47) and think more highly of others than we do of ourselves (see Phil. 2:3).

Principles relating to businesses and governments—Books have been written detailing the scriptural patterns for businesses and governments. It is enough for our purposes to simply identify the major functions business and government are to play from a biblical perspective: the business principle and the government principle.

In regard to the *business principle*, scores of businesses and occupations are mentioned in Scripture. There are shepherds, farmers, doctors, lawyers, soldiers, sailors, merchants, jewelers, tax collectors, and on and on. From the sheer number of references, it may be concluded that the business enterprise is a normal and natural element in the human experience. Business activities should return a profit to owners (see Matt. 25:15-30; James 4:13-15). Laborers are entitled to receive wages for their labor (see Luke 10:7; 1 Cor. 9:1-18). And business practices must be fair and just (see Deut. 25:15; Prov. 11:1).

The concepts of profits and ethics in business are prominent in economics. Friedman wrote,

> [In] a free economy . . . there is one and only one social responsibility of business—to use its resources and engage in activities designed to increase its profits so long as it stays within the rules of the game, which is to say, engages in open and free competition, without deception or fraud.[6]

A strong case can be made from Scripture that the two fundamental responsibilities of government are to promote and maintain peace and order and to promote justice (the *government principle*). Governments are instituted so that citizens may lead a "tranquil and quiet life in all godliness and dignity" (1 Tim. 2:2). First Peter 2:13-17 suggests that the role of government is to punish evildoers and to praise those who do right.

Having presented these biblical principles, we are now ready to consider the various ethical issues in information systems and operations research and to show how the principles apply in each instance. We will consider information systems issues first, then issues in operations research.

INFORMATION SYSTEMS

In his best-selling book *Megatrends*, published in 1982, John Naisbitt pointed out the major transformation taking place in the United States, the "megashift" from an industrial to an information society.[7] All indications are that by the year 2000, information processing will be the largest sector in the United States economy. That this is true is intuitively apparent from the proliferation of computing equipment in our society. Naisbitt writes that "from the beginning of time through 1980 there were only one million computers." A casual look in practically any office complex today will reveal scores of computers—almost one computer for every desk, and many workers have more than one! Given the current importance of information processing, it is appropriate to consider the moral and ethical issues in the information systems arena.

Computer-based information systems are developed to support an organization's information needs. Decision makers require different types of information for different types of decisions. Strategic information is needed, usually at fairly high levels in an organization, to establish organizational goals and policies. Tactical information is needed to develop subordinate plans that can implement organizational strategy and control such implementations. Operational information is needed to measure performance against specific goals.

Information systems have historically been effective in providing information for highly structured operational decision making, for example, in accounting systems or inventory management/production scheduling systems. However, there has been a significant trend toward information systems that support more tactically and strategically oriented decisions, which are typically less well structured than operationally oriented decisions. Management Information Systems (MIS) were originally intended to support managers at all organizational levels for all types of decisions. Decision Support Systems (DSS) were conceived as very specialized systems to support a *single* decision of any type, usually in the low to semistructured category. A relatively recent phenomenon in the information systems arena is the emergence of Expert Systems (ES, a branch of Artificial Intelligence), which replicate the decision-making capabilities of genuine experts in very narrow decision domains.

Ends-related information systems issues—The preceding discussion makes it apparent that the ultimate objective or end of information systems is to support decision making in organizations. Regardless of the type of information system developed (MIS, DSS, ES, etc.), the type of hardware involved (mainframes, personal computers, workstations, etc.), and the specific implementation, the objective of such systems is to provide the information needed by decision makers to make effective decisions. Unfortunately, information systems methods are not always used to achieve this stated end.

Computer Crime. The proliferation of computers, especially microprocessors, and the simultaneous emergence of computer networks have created an environment in which a new type of criminal activity is flourishing. Rod Willis describes the situation:

> Along with giving managers instant access to information and making their jobs easier, it has made it relatively easy for a skilled bandit or dishonest employee with a personal computer and a modem to obtain confidential data—or millions of dollars—from unwitting companies, banks, and government agencies.[8]

Willis adds that the Department of Justice estimates annual losses to computer crime to exceed $100 million, excluding the costs of investigation and prosecution. Some experts believe that this is just the tip of an iceberg of enormous proportions.

What makes this type of crime attractive to individuals? For one thing, it is fast—it takes only a few microseconds to transfer millions of dollars from one account to another. It is also relatively safe—a good programer can make it extremely difficult to discover. Prosecuting a computer offense is time-consuming. And the victim is often a large, affluent, impersonal corporation or agency. Often, crimes are committed by employees to get even with the bureaucracy—an employee who has been passed over for a promotion or denied a pay raise.

What biblical principles apply to the phenomenon of computer crime? Certainly the integrity principle. Computer crime is frequently committed by a single individual acting out of frustration or for revenge; organized conspiracies involving groups of people are the exception. Employees who seek to please God by their actions are not likely to become involved in such activities. The steward principle also applies here. An employee performing his job to the glory of God is unlikely to become frustrated or motivated to seek revenge because of some circumstance at work.

Invasion of privacy—George Orwell's classic, *1984*, raises a specter that probably all of us have seriously contemplated in our imagination. I refer, of course, to the invasion of individual privacy by the government. In Orwell's portrayal, the government (Big Brother) had viewing and listening devices in every home. The devices fed computer data banks so that every move or word was recorded and available for use as evidence, if necessary, for "population control" purposes.[9]

When George Orwell wrote *1984* in 1949, such a situation was unthinkable not only from a technological perspective but also from a human rights viewpoint. But what about today; how far are we from events depicted in that novel? From a technological standpoint, awesome capability exists in both the public and the private sectors to accomplish the monitoring Orwell suggests. Some of the excesses of government agencies and private organizations with regard to monitoring the activities of individuals have come to light in recent years and have given cause for concern. The sheer volume of information routinely maintained on individuals by the Internal Revenue Service, by credit bureaus, by banks, and by corporations on employees provides opportunity for abuses.

However, if governments and businesses were to function strictly according to biblical principles as outlined in the preceding section, the opportunity for infringement on privacy would be significantly reduced. Oversight committees and commissions, federal and state government restrictions and regulations, and professional and business codes of ethics serve a good purpose; yet the only completely effective action against abuses in this regard would be for governments and businesses to limit their activities to those essential to fulfilling the role defined for them by Scripture.

Depersonalization—An unintended result of our computer-driven information society is the depersonalization of life. Much of our interaction with business organizations is computer driven. We get our utility bills and our department store bills from company-owned computers. We write checks and send them back to the computer. Our banking is computerized. We can make deposits, withdrawals, loans, and so on by interacting with a computerized teller. A computer diagnoses problems with our car; a computer tells us we have high cholesterol. And so it goes. We interact once a year with the federal government not as individuals but as SSN XXX-XX-XXXX. Anecdotes about exchanges between real people trying to straighten out an error in an account with the superintending computer abound, as does the frustration created by such encounters.

What does one do in the face of such impersonal encounters? What is the proper response to a society increasingly mechanized and computerized? The individual who understands Scripture understands that his or her individuality, uniqueness, and value come from a right and proper relationship with God. From this perspective, some of the encounters with computers may be annoyances; however, none are identity threatening.

Means- and methods-related information systems issues—We move now to issues related to the means and methods of information systems. They concern the potential complexity of such systems and the phenomena of espionage, piracy, and sabotage.

Complexity—In considering the whole area of information systems, one is immediately struck with the tremendous complexity of the systems currently being developed. Consider the magnitude of the system developed by the National Aeronautics and Space Administration for the space shuttle. The system consists of scores of computers networked together, tracking devices, weather and communications satellites, and literally hundreds of computer programs that accomplish the various tasks during launch, mission, and landing.[10] To place this in proper perspective, consider that the operating system alone on a current mainframe usually exceeds 100,000 lines of code. Thus, the entire space shuttle information system contains millions of instructions.

The magnitude of these systems means there is great opportunity for error. Often the development of information systems involves teams of programers working over months or even years. Some programs are so complex that it is virtually impossible to validate the various instructions contained in the code. Organizations and agencies in the information systems development mode must have workers dedicated to the success of the organization and to excellence in their work, and their integrity must carry over into their professional lives. Thus, the biblical principles of stewardship and integrity have application for the complexity issue.

Espionage, piracy, and sabotage—These are not new concepts; however, they have taken a new twist in the arena of information systems. Espionage is essentially an organizational perpetration while piracy and sabotage are usually accomplished by individuals.

A news item in *USA Today* described a judgment against a major Japanese computer manufacturer for unauthorized copying of IBM mainframe operating systems software.[11] The judgment required an initial payment of $237 million and "millions more in coming years." The item appeared as "a quick read on the top money news of the day." It was not a headline article; it was not even a major article in the money section because firms in the computer industry regularly market copies of the hardware and software products of technology leaders. Compaq, AST, and Amdahl have been quite successful at marketing IBM compatible hardware that, in some cases, outperforms the IBM original.

There is a very fine line between a compatible and a "knock off" or copy. Recognizing this and also the millions of dollars of profit to be made in the compatible market, we can expect that from time to time well-intentioned firms will get caught with their hands in the cookie jar. Even though the issues involved here are extremely complex, a biblical guideline has application in this area. The scriptural prerogatives for businesses allow businesses to pursue profits in "open and free competition," which, according to Friedman, means within the context of the "rules of society embodied in law and in ethical custom."[12] Thus, executives making product decisions in this area need to be acutely aware of the laws that apply and of the judgments of courts in applying the laws (which amount to ethical custom).

One of the most pervasive ethical issues in the information systems area is that of software piracy or "bootleg" software. It is practically impossible to measure the magnitude of the amount of unauthorized copying of software products. An appropriate descriptive adjective might be *colossal!* So many different software packages are available through such a variety of sources that it is extremely difficult to remain completely aboveboard. For example, I have repeatedly told my students that I do not want bootleg software in my laboratory, that I want to use only legally acquired packages for which developers have been appropriately compensated. Several weeks ago when I was overseeing the movement of an older personal computer from the lab to my office, I was appalled to learn that twenty percent of the packages of the system were bootleg copies!

Another disturbing ethical issue in information systems is computer sabotage. We have heard about individuals who, for one reason or another, have released destructive programs called viruses or worms, which spread from one computer to another with potentially disastrous results.[13] One such incident described in *TIME* reveals that a graduate student in computer science brought down the Department of Defense Advanced Projects Research Agency's entire network of sixty thousand computers with a virus, apparently for no other reason than to see if he could do it.[14] Such "experiments" pose an incredible threat not only to information systems used for defense and national security, but to *all* information systems—those used by private companies, universities, research agencies, medical centers, and so on. The obvious solution to the threat is to produce secure systems—an option that experts say will impose an overhead burden on systems of perhaps thirty percent of capacity, not to mention the millions of dollars required to develop such systems. A high price, indeed, to protect ourselves from a few misguided or malicious individuals.

The biblical principles that apply to piracy and sabotage are the others principle and the integrity principle. If we were serious about loving our neighbor (or enemy) as we love ourselves, we would not use his or her software without appropriate remuneration, and we would certainly not intentionally inflict damage to our neighbor's computer. The integrity principle applies in an obvious way.

Human factors issues in information systems—Perhaps the most significant ethical issue in the information systems area, if not in *all* of scientific inquiry, is currently being debated in the Artificial Intelligence (AI) community. The issue, in a nutshell, is whether there is any qualitative difference between the human brain and a complex computer. For at least twenty years, researchers in the AI community have been puzzling over the question: Can a machine think? Various arguments have been suggested and discussed at length.[15] With the recent advancements in the AI field, the controversy has assumed greater proportions.

An international, interdisciplinary symposium was held in March 1986 at Yale University to address the issue of Artificial Intelligence and the human mind. Some of the foremost members of the scientific community presented papers at the symposium—among the participants were four Nobel Laureates and two of the pioneers in early AI research. The debate, which was written up in *AI Magazine*, clearly impressed observers. Letovsky notes,

> I was struck by the historic proportions of the debate and the personalities involved. It reminded me of those debates which occurred in England after Darwin's theory first came out, when eminent scientists ridiculed the theory from the bedrock of common sense prejudices.[16]

The implications of this issue are indeed far reaching. An interesting parallel exists in the behavioral sciences; Kagan summarizes the issue:

> Do all facets of human nature lie on a continuum with animal nature, or are humans a qualitatively different creature because they possess a consciousness that evaluates the meaning of action, a conscience that characterizes people and their actions as good or bad, and a will that can control morally unacceptable behavior?[17]

According to Kagan, because of the impact of Darwin's theory and Freud's descriptions of the id, the ego, and the superego, the behavioral community has essentially decided that a continuum between man and animals is a more correct description. The unanticipated outcome of the wholesale acceptance of this notion is violence, manifested in incest, child molestation, child and spouse abuse, aggression, rape, and murder. Kagan concludes by saying,

> Some Americans have become too accepting of Darwin's view that "Man still bears in his bodily frame the indelible stamp of his lowly origin." I fear that an uncritical attitude toward that assumption could make it a self-fulfilling prophecy.[18]

Turning to the controversy in AI, what can we expect if our scientific community buys into the notion that the human mind is nothing more than a complex computer? One of the Yale symposium participants gives a partial scenario:

> Because the mind was now in software, you could back it up on disk. If you knew you were going on a dangerous mission, you could save a copy of yourself. If you get killed, your friends could resurrect the copy . . . with a short gap in memory corresponding in the time spent on disk . . . not too high a price: a small, finite interval of death in exchange for immortality.[19]

Some logical extensions of this mentality are euthanasia, unrestrained genetic engineering, and population control.

The controversy here is beyond simple answers. I participated in the Yale conference and presented a twenty-page paper detailing why I believe that there is a qualitative difference between human intelligence and machine intelligence.[20] The biblical answer is that man is unique because he is created in the image of God; he has intellect, emotions, and will; and he has meaning and purpose that can come only from a proper relationship with God.

OPERATIONS RESEARCH

Operations research (OR) is a scientific approach to management decision making that incorporates the following steps: problem definition, alternative generation, alternative evaluation, and alternative selection. The problem definition phase involves articulating or describing the exact nature of the problem (or decision) to be addressed. Relevant terms are defined, the scope of the problem is determined, and characteristics of an "efficient" and "effective" solution are stated. The alternative generation step is concerned with discovering feasible solutions to the problem without regard to efficiency or effectiveness. The emphasis is on the quantity of potential solutions uncovered, not on their quality.

The alternative evaluation phase of operations research seeks to assess each potential solution in the light of the characteristics of efficiency or effectiveness stated in the problem definition step. The outcome of this evaluation is a ranking of alternative solutions in terms of various measures of effectiveness important to the decision maker. The final step is alternative selection—the choice of one solution from among the potential solutions for implementation. In this phase of the process, the decision maker will consider various subjective factors not explicitly addressed in previous steps.

Operations research is differentiated from other approaches to decision making by several distinguishing characteristics. First, OR is fundamentally concerned with decision making. Second, OR usually incorporates an interdisciplinary perspective; an OR study may cut across a broad spectrum of organizational activity and involve individuals from diverse interests and viewpoints. Another characteristic, which has already been suggested, is that alternative evaluation is based on effectiveness criteria. One solution is chosen over another solution because the first "rates" better on the stated measures of effectiveness. Fourth, OR relies heavily on mathematical models. The fifth characteristic is a heavy dependence on computers. The OR study that does not incorporate some sort of mathematical model with computer-generated solutions is rare.

Ends-related operations research issues—What is important for our purpose is that the essential focus of operations research is decision making. Operations research studies are undertaken to enhance the quality of decision making in organizations, which is the intended objective or end of all OR activity. Unfortunately, OR studies have been conducted and most certainly will continue to be conducted that have altogether different objectives. We will examine three broad categories of such cases.

Rubber-stamping—One relatively common misuse of operations research is to validate or support the preconceived desires of a manager or managers rather than to gain a systematic, objective evaluation of the decision situation. In trying to assess the magnitude of this misapplication of OR, Ron Howard writes,

> I have recently been asking decision analysts how many of their studies were prompted by a belief in a systematic analysis per se rather than by a desire of some party to the decision to advance either his own proposals or to defend them against attacks. A very large proportion of the responses has been in favor of the self-interest hypothesis.[21]

Several years ago, a colleague and I were hired as consultants by a manufacturing concern to make recommendations regarding a proposed new computer installation. After studying the situation, we met with management to present our findings. Before we finished our presentation, the Vice President of Manufacturing produced typed, signed purchase orders for a system considerably smaller than the one we were recommending. He asked us to endorse the smaller (cheaper) system. We responded that we strongly believed they would be making a mistake by purchasing the small system since it simply could not support the requirements. The VP said he was sorry that we could not see the logic of their decision and then instructed the purchasing agent to acquire the system.

My associate and I later concluded that the managers really did not want our honest evaluation of their situation; they simply wanted an endorsement from two "external consultants" for a decision they had already reached. It was no great consolation to learn a few months later that the firm had scrapped the original system and was acquiring one similar to the one we had recommended.

Biased models —Another similar misuse of operations research occurs when the models used in a study are deliberately slanted to achieve a particular result. The so-called cost-benefit studies often used by government agencies to justify various government programs are especially vulnerable to the type of bias described here. It is often fairly easy to measure the costs associated with a given program; costs are usually tangible items, such as the cost of land, materials, salaries, and so on. On the other hand, benefits are often more difficult to quantify and measure. In such cases, it is not difficult to formulate a set of assumptions that will produce just the magnitude of benefits to yield the desired decision.

As a graduate student, I conducted a comprehensive study for a government agency to develop a methodology for measuring the benefits resulting from the projects the agency promoted. When my study was completed, it presented hard, objective data that the benefits used by the agency to justify projects had been grossly overstated. I was subjected to enormous pressures to change my findings. When I declined to do so, the study was relegated to a filing cabinet where it probably remains to this very day.

Whenever operations research studies are being used to promote inappropriate ends (e.g., rubber-stamping or the use of intentionally biased models), the applicable biblical principle is the integrity principle. It is never acceptable to participate in unethical activities; thus, the OR analyst confronted with such a situation has several possible recourses. He or she should probably seek other employment if there is no possibility of change or if the condition is pervasive in the organization. Another option is to refuse to participate, realizing that such refusal may very well result in losing the job or opportunity for advancement. One might blow the whistle as analysts do from time to time, most often with negative results for the analyst; on rare occasions, good results obtain from whistle blowing. Or as Nehemiah did, the analyst might offer a creative alternative: "We'll conduct the study and let the chips fall where they may. If the study supports the conclusions you want, fine. If it doesn't, you are free to go to Plan B however you define it" (see Neh. 5:1-13). Whatever response is elected, the guiding principle is that an OR analyst should not participate in studies with ethically unacceptable ends.

Destructive purposes—Another ends-related operations research issue is concerned with the purpose of the project or activity for which the OR study is to be conducted. Any number of potentially destructive programs might be cited here as candidates for concern: chemical and germ warfare, spy satellites, political assassinations, and so forth. An interesting example of what I am talking about here has occurred recently in the U.S. defense community with many prominent scientists refusing to participate in research related to the Strategic Defense Initiative. Some scientists have insisted that they refuse to be involved because the concept is infeasible; however, many have objected on ethical and moral grounds suggesting that the program is immoral or that it is an offensive weapons system, among other similar objections.

In such instances, the appropriate biblical principle to apply is the one that defines the proper role of government in God's order. If the activity passes the test of contributing to the government's ability to establish peace and justice, an OR analyst should feel no compunction toward participating in a study relating to the activity.

I have participated for over fifteen years as a consultant, contractor, and principal investigator on various defense-related projects and am currently involved in a research role with the Strategic Defense Initiative. I can remember early on in my involvement puzzling over the proper Christian response to defense-related projects. It is apparent to me that our country's history is characterized by nonaggression. We have been involved in numerous wars and conflicts, but our involvement has been either in our own defense or in the defense of our allies. With this record to go on, I am confident that when I participate in defense-related projects, the resulting products, systems, or weapons will be used for defensive purposes—for preserving or maintaining the peace.

Means- and methods-related operations research issues—Next we will consider issues related to the means and methods of OR. The OR approach is vitally concerned with "optimum" or efficient solutions to mathematical models of decision situations. Thus, the major issues we will examine are optimization and modeling.

Optimization—This is a hallmark of operations research. Many models employed in OR are optimization models, for example, linear programing, multiobjective programing, and nonlinear programing. Even when an optimization model is not used in an OR study as, for example, in simulation studies or waiting line analysis, the ultimate aim of most studies is to discover the best solution or solutions to the decision problem that is under investigation. This preoccupation with optimum solutions has led at least in part to two areas of criticism of the operations research approach.

The first is that OR studies tend to emphasize objective factors to the exclusion of subjective ones. In a sense, this criticism is valid. Objective factors are, by definition, more easily measurable and quantifiable; thus, it is natural that they would predominate in quantitative analysis. The OR analyst would agree, but would also argue that subjective factors not included in a particular OR model are considered by the decision maker in making the final choice of an alternative to be implemented. Although this argument may sound convincing, there are several reasons that it is often not true in practice.

For one thing, the very nature of subjective factors makes it extremely difficult to consider them even in an intuitive way apart from a quantitative model. How does one, for example, assess the impact to an organization's reputation from terminating thousands of employees as several major United States corporations have done in the last few years? The impact on costs of such a decision is quite easy to quantify. But what is the impact on customer attitudes and thus on revenues? What is the impact on shareholder impressions and thus on stock prices? It is one thing to say that these impacts will be considered apart from a model; it is quite another thing to undertake a rigorous, comprehensive assessment.

Another problem is that solutions from quantitative models have a subtle way of becoming more than just a possible solution. It is the "thus saith the model" syndrome—if the model says that such-and-such solution is the optimum solution, it must be the optimum solution. No matter that important subjective factors were omitted from the analysis because they could not be measured. No matter that the OR analyst expects management to give appropriate recognition to these factors in making a final choice between "the optimum" and some other "good" solution. In many cases the optimum solution will be selected because it is the optimum solution, and very little consideration will be given to what might be very, very important subjective factors.

A second area of criticism related to the optimum issue is that the OR approach tends to focus almost exclusively on organizational goals and objectives to the exclusion of other meaningful goals. Wagner writes,

> A second criticism is that formal model building is antagonistic to social values, morality, and recognition of the individual as a unique being. At best, say the critics, these considerations enter models as constraints and, therefore, are viewed as hindrances; at worse, they are simply ignored.[22]

My experience in the field of operations research confirms that OR analysts tend to concern themselves more with systems or organizational issues and leave the behavioral or human issues to the human relations or organizational behavior people.

Modeling—This is central to the OR approach. The OR analyst is interested in reducing a decision situation to a mathematical model that can be manipulated and massaged to generate desired solutions. That this is true is evident from a popular characterization of an OR analyst as "an analyst with a tool kit full of models in search of a problem to work on." This emphasis on modeling has generated controversy in at least two respects.

There is always a tension in model building over the complexity versus simplicity issue. Models are, by definition, abstractions of reality. A model including every detail of its actual counterpart would not be a model; it would be a duplicate system. Thus, every model will (and should) omit elements of the modeled entity. The key question in this regard is, How much of the real thing can be omitted? The appropriate OR answer is this: The model should include only those elements that are important with respect to the use to be made of the model. Thus, if a model is to be used to make decisions about various transportation options available to a firm, it is generally appropriate to omit detail that deals with procurement and, possibly, production activities of the firm.

Now, this distinction turns out to be arbitrary, and what might seem quite important to one analyst in a particular situation might seem quite unimportant to another analyst in the same situation. The obvious outcome of this tension between complexity and simplicity is described by Wagner: "Operations research models are, however, at best approximations to reality, and the concepts they embody are often fictions, figures of speech, and unreal entities."[23]

No significant problems would be posed if the users of OR model results recognized that this was the case and always tempered their decisions to compensate appropriately. Unfortunately, this is not always what happens. Again quoting Wagner, "It is virtually inevitable that a model that has been implemented should become a reality in itself and thereby compete with the real phenomenon it modeled."[24] Apparently, this concern with OR will persist; it is simply an inherent limitation of the OR approach.

Another concern raised by the OR emphasis on modeling relates to the reductionist approach implicit in OR methods, which is the notion that a decision problem can be decomposed into its components and then recomposed. It is certainly true that the OR methodology attempts to divide large problems into subproblems and then to concentrate on finding solutions to the subproblems. It is also true that most, if not all, OR analysts are keenly aware of the problems of suboptimization and the concomitant implications for partitioning oriented approaches. Still, it can be argued that this tension will exist on all but the most trivial OR applications and that by its existence, there is the possibility for misuse or misapplication of the methodology.

These key issues relate to the means and methods of operations research. They arise out of the OR interest in optimization and modeling. What biblical applications can be focused on these issues? I believe the relevant principle here is the steward principle. That is, OR analysts should strive for excellence in the development and use of OR models. Every reasonable effort should be made to include relevant factors in models—both organizational and behavioral/societal factors. Analysts should pay particular attention to the appropriate level of detail to be included in models and should be very careful to observe the interaction of problem components to avoid the pitfalls of suboptimization. Finally, much should be made of the assumptions, limitations, and concerns attending each model. If OR analysts are "up front" with these concerns, decision makers (users) might be more judicious in their use of model outputs.

Human factors issues in operations research—The final major concern to be raised in the implementation of operations research deals with the human element of OR, specifically the OR analyst. Howard has summarized this issue by writing,

> The quality of the analysis depends critically on the quality of the decision analyst. In perhaps no other form of analysis is it so easy for the analyst to produce any result he likes by taking advantage of his knowledge of biases and his modeling choices.[25]

In at least two respects the role of the OR analyst deserves serious attention. In the first place, the OR analyst is not likely to be an expert in the field of the particular decision problem of interest. Thus, his or her role should be that of an objective observer; the task is to understand the decision problem and, through that understanding, to develop an accurate representation of the decision problem. As Howard puts it,

> He is skilled in constructing the decision set using his imaginary and colorful friends, the clairvoyant (who knows all and who helps with defining variables and events unambiguously) and the wizard (who can do all and who helps with value assignment), but the information and preferences . . . must come from the decision maker and his delegates.[26]

In the second place, the OR analyst must be keenly aware of the distinction between analyst and advocate. Again, Howard underscores the issue:

To be an advocate while posing as an analyst is, of course, professionally unethical even if the position advocated is morally excellent to the individual. The problem is that one is using morally reprehensible means, fraud, to achieve an end.[27]

The temptation to slip over into the role of advocate will always exist, and in some cases the analyst will succumb without overtly realizing it.

The applicable biblical principle with respect to the role of the OR analyst is the integrity principle. The analyst who is acutely aware of the value God places on personal integrity is likely to be aware of the analyst-expert-advocate conflict and will be careful to make a clear distinction to keep the various roles in perspective.

CONCLUSIONS

We have discussed several ethical issues in information systems and operations research, and we have demonstrated various biblical principles that apply to each issue. Wagner makes an interesting point about the relationship between ethics and operations research:

Undeniably, an easy case can be made that as of today operations research lines up with the technocratic forces in our society. But I find it hard to believe that the ultimate success or failure of operations research will significantly alter our social ethics or undermine reverence for human values.[28]

The more fundamental issue involves the effect(s) of the ethical and value systems of our society on the practice of operations research and information systems. This chapter has shown that biblical principles can positively affect information systems and operations research at the points where tensions currently exist.

One final note for persons who might be skeptical about attempting to apply biblical remedies to problems in science:

It is not those of us who seek to understand the world from a number of different perspectives, including the scientific one, who prefer ignorance to knowledge. It is those who, blinded by their faith that science can yield "full" explanations, prefer to remain ignorant of whatever knowledge other ways of knowing the world have to offer.[29]

EDITOR'S PERSPECTIVE

Dr. Rae Mellichamp has laid before us the moral issues encountered in the information systems and operations research arenas. And he has simultaneously detechnicalized the subject matter and separated the human and moral elements from the technical elements that so mystify the uninitiated. His work makes it evident that God expressed, long ago, His concerns about human conduct in all fields, even the modern fields dominated by technology. I have nothing to add to the content of this incredibly cogent piece of work, but I want to point to it as an outstanding model of how Christians can bring God's Word to bear on areas of human endeavor that are both technical in nature and deeply immersed in relativistic, pragmatic, and utilitarian forms of reasoning. All too often, such efforts obscure the true moral issues lurking behind the technology that characterizes many sophisticated frontiers of knowledge.

I want to issue a call to those Christians who have been led by God's providence to work in other high-tech fields to seriously consider marshaling their efforts to address, in the light of Scripture, the major moral issues embedded in their disciplines. These are being swept aside or overlooked in the rising tide of practical atheism. Practical atheism—leaving God out of judgments that have moral implication—dominates a great deal of the thinking in our high-tech environments. The emergence of reasoning devoid of any thought or mention of God's concerns for what goes on in the high-tech fields has come about because of three dominant forces.

First, a new world view has emerged that isolates God from the mainstream of most people's thinking about common events like the weather, happenings in history, employment opportunities, and so forth. These things were routinely considered to be under God's sovereign control (see Ps. 16:5-6;

183

139:13-16). Farmers thought of God as the sender and withholder of rain. The word *providence* was sprinkled throughout the history books of the eighteenth and nineteenth centuries. God-fearing and not-so-pious people alike incorporated the idea of the divine into their thinking. Things are quite different now. God is not at the center of our explanations of earthly events as He once was. The "world according to God" has become the "world according to science."

Men like Francis Bacon insisted that reason and revelation were not compatible. Galileo stated that the universe could be better understood through the "book of nature" (written in the language of mathematics) than through theology. This type of thinking opened the doors to a new method of knowing dubbed the "scientific method." Mathematics, "natural law," experimentation, and the scientific method came to dominate our way of thinking. Moral issues, which do not yield their secrets to the scientific method, suddenly were perceived to be limited to the realms of feelings, intuition, personal opinions, personal experiences, and other nonverifiable dimensions of human analysis. This change in the method of knowing made theology, morals, and ethics less respected in intellectual circles.

The scientific method and its tools of experimentation are ideal to use when working on physical questions as we exercise dominion over God's created order. But this method of knowing can generate only agnostic conclusions when it becomes the basis of analysis in exploring metaphysical matters— questions about spirits, values, rights, duties, ethics, and other nonphysical realities. The analytical tools of the physical sciences simply do not fit such matters. Mathematics is a poor tool to employ when trying to comprehend love; the physical senses will not help when trying to understand God as a being of pure spirit. The physical and spiritual realms of reality simply do not yield their answers to the same methods of knowing.

One must use legal evidence and historic evidence, for example, to prove that General Sherman burned Atlanta during the Civil War—the particular event is not subject to replicable experimentation. The idea that *proofs* must be limited to what can be verified by the methods employed in the physical sciences is so pervasive in today's society that to be found even questioning its universal application subjects the questioner to charges of anti-intellectualism. But pointing this out does not change the fact that the scientific method has generally replaced historic and legal proofs as the fundamentally accepted way of knowing truth. This change in our approach to verifying reality has struck a crippling blow to the intellectual acceptability of the Scripture, which depends totally on historic/legal evidence for validation.

The second major contributor to the decline in God-centered reasoning in our culture has been the nature of the intellectual leadership of the organized

Church. They have wrought great harm on two fronts: (1) in the evangelical community, and (2) in the "church-of-the-world," the portion of the Church that adopted the world's methods of knowing truth and thereby undermined people's confidence in the authority of Scripture. Both liberalism and neo-orthodoxy have deliberately attacked Scripture. They have fostered a personal opinion view of Scripture that has encouraged people to feel comfortable professing to accept Scripture as the Word of God and simultaneously ignoring or reinterpreting those parts distasteful to them. People have been encouraged to believe that they can have it both ways—ignore God's truth when it offends them and claim its authority when that suits their purposes. The resulting moral relativism in the Church has greatly reduced its effectiveness in the world.

The evangelical segment of the Church has also suffered much damage in those quarters where God has been portrayed as having a narrow and selected interest in our lives—church activities, not work activities. But God has a strong interest in every area of our lives, including art, music, architecture, drama, business, government, education, family, church, social, athletics, and so on. His Word has application to every area of life. Those who claim God is disinterested in any area of life are encouraging God's children to hide their light under a bushel, and they consequently abandon the area of presumed disinterest to the Devil and his agents.

The final cause for the rise in man-centered thinking in our day grows out of our inborn fallen nature that launches us in life with a self-willed, self-centered, and me-oriented world view. Just as the first two causes for our man-centered thinking continue to encourage practical atheism, more and more moral constraints are jettisoned from the culture, and the worst aspects of our fallen nature are set free to blaspheme God by renouncing His rule, either verbally or behaviorally.

I do not know what the future holds regarding God's plans for giving people over to the resident depravity lurking in their own minds (see Gen. 4:7; Rom. 1:28) or His intentions to constrain human behavior in the areas of advanced technology, but I often reflect on God's statement about mankind's intellectual ability at the tower of Babel when He said, "Nothing which they purpose to do will be impossible for them" (Gen. 11:6). As we continue to explore the genetic and biotechnology fields, for example, the opportunities to cause evil and do good will be astronomical. May God be pleased to pour out His Spirit on us through another reformation or revival on a grand scale, so the Church will be enabled to be salt and light in the world. Without such help, the future prospects for godly moral constraints in the fields of medical technology, information technology, biotechnology, and any other frontier of knowledge are not very promising.

PART X

BANKING AXIOMS
AND BIBLICAL PRINCIPLES

We have to maximize our profits so we can do more good things with the additional money we make. The big problem with that assertion, however, is that we almost never have enough money or profits under such a premise because the goal of making more money usually supplants the purpose of serving the need. It is like asking God to step aside while you make the money you feel you need in order to serve Him better. I have not found a biblical principle anywhere that supports this premise. (emphasis added)

The chapter before us is laced with insights like the one above. Robert Lavelle, its author, presents us with a world view of banking that accepts a good proportion of the logic and prudence of most banking axioms, yet he finds these same operating principles offer bankers a ready rationale for ignoring, overlooking, or rejecting many of God's expressed concerns for the oppressed, widows, needy, and other deprived people.

The chapter is convicting, but not judgmental. It is in part the autobiography of a man's journey from self-righteousness to the faithful acceptance that Christ alone is capable of accomplishing in and through us what is glorifying to His name. It is an account of a man's surrender to God's will as it is expressed in Scripture. It is, perhaps above all else, the telling of a man's acceptance of God's Word *at its face value* and his desire to obey it in the marketplace before the watching world, even when others found his perceptions peculiar. In fact, rather than shrinking from or trying to disguise his beliefs and behavior, Robert Lavelle has used the world's startled reactions as the opportunity to explain that Christ expects such unorthodox (from the world's perspective) behavior.

187

Earlier, it was noted that two chapters in this book would be fundamentally experiential, not topical or functional. Chapter 10 is the second one. The contents, while not ignoring banking at all, really illumine how a man's passion to help those in financial need was neither molded by the conventions of the financial world nor diverted from helping the needy by allowing prevailing notions of prudence to outweigh the simple prescriptions of Scripture.

A careful reading of this material will reveal an enormous amount of wisdom in action. Robert Lavelle was not imprudent in his banking practices. He simply remained compassionate and Christ-centered as he labored to overcome the obstacles in the lives of those who sought to borrow money from his institution when the world had long ago branded them unacceptable credit risks. His patience, caring instructions, and leadership were used to redeem rather than to judge. Numerous lessons in this chapter transcend the bounds of banking.

CHAPTER 10

BIBLICAL PRINCIPLES APPLIED TO BANKING
Robert R. Lavelle

Robert R. Lavelle is the original force and principal architect behind Dwelling House Savings and Loan in Pittsburgh, Pennsylvania—an institution dedicated to meeting, as he states, "the economic needs of the poor, Black, and otherwise deprived people of the Pittsburgh area, so that when they ask why we do what we do [accept loan applications with below standard qualifications and charge interest that is at or below the prevailing market rates] we can tell them about Jesus the Christ!" Mr. Lavelle is also the President of Lavelle Real Estate, Inc., and he and his wife, Adah, still work together in caring for the personnel needs of both organizations. Their two sons, Robert and John, also share in the family ideals of Christian responsibility and stewardship—Robert is now the Chief Operating Officer of Dwelling House Savings and Loan, and John is construction foreman for Breachmenders, a Christian housing firm in Pittsburgh. Mr. Lavelle received his bachelor of science and master's degrees from the University of Pittsburgh and serves today on the Board of Visitors of the Katz Graduate School of Business. He is also a member of the Pittsburgh Symphony Board and is a Director Emeritus of the Board of the Pittsburgh Theological Seminary. These are just a few of the sixteen boards on which he has served.

Blessed is he who has regard for the weak;
    the LORD delivers him in times of trouble.
The LORD will protect him and preserve his life;
    he will bless him in the land
    and not surrender him to the desire of his foes.
The LORD will sustain him on his sickbed
    and restore him from his bed of illness. (Ps. 41:1-3)

Blessed is the man who fears the LORD,
> who finds great delight in his commands. . . .

Wealth and riches are in his house,
> and his righteousness endures forever. . . .

Good will come to him who is generous and lends freely,
> who conducts his affairs with justice. . . .

He will have no fear of bad news;
> his heart is steadfast, trusting in the LORD. (Ps. 112:1, 3, 5, 7)

Trust in the LORD with all your heart
> and lean not on your own understanding;

in all your ways acknowledge him,
> and he will make your paths straight. (Prov. 3:5-6)

He who is kind to the poor lends to the LORD,
> and he will reward him for what he has done. (Prov. 19:17)

"So do not worry, saying, 'What shall we eat?' or 'What shall we drink?'
or 'What shall we wear?' For the pagans run after all these things, and
your heavenly Father knows that you need them. But seek first his kingdom and his righteousness, and all these things will be given to you as
well." (Matt. 6:31-33)

"For whoever wants to save his life will lose it, but whoever loses his life
for me will find it." (Matt. 16:25)

"Teacher, which is the greatest commandment in the Law?" Jesus
replied: "'Love the Lord your God with all your heart and with all your
soul and with all your mind.' This is the first and greatest commandment.
And the second is like it: 'Love your neighbor as yourself.' All the Law
and the Prophets hang on these two commandments." (Matt. 22:36-40)

"My prayer is not that you take them out of the world but that you
protect them from the evil one. They are not of the world, even as I am
not of it. Sanctify them by the truth; your word is truth. As you sent me
into the world, I have sent them into the world. For them I sanctify
myself, that they too may be truly sanctified." (John 17:15-19)

A strange thing happened to me while I was on my way toward trying to corner the real estate market in Pittsburgh with Lavelle Real Estate, Inc., and striving to make state-chartered, uninsured mutual savings institution Dwelling House Building and Loan Association of $67,000 total assets into an insured, competitive savings institution that would help make it possible for Black and poor people to own the homes they lived in and eventually become so big that we would not only get respect but become feared!

I really wanted to show them. I wanted to redress every wrong. I was on sixteen boards and committees trying to do good. I was the first vice president of both the NAACP and the Urban League branches in Pittsburgh. I tried to help everybody. I tried to be morally good, cleaned up my life, stopped doing all the things you stop. I achieved a lot of recognition.

For some reason it was not sufficient. I was always fearful of losing money or my reputation or of receiving bodily harm during holdups. I was always resentful when someone else got credit for something I thought I had done better; I was always jealous of those who had more than I or seemed more adequate than I was in social and business situations and on and on. Then the strange happening was . . . I met the Lord Jesus!

I did not have a dramatic conversion experience like the Apostle Paul did, but I received Jesus as Savior. I continue each day to try to make Him Lord of my life as He permits me to continue to live and move and have my being. The aspect of being "in the world, yet not of the world" makes for a very exciting, yet frightening lifestyle. Trying to stand on His promises daily and to be obedient to His Word requires that I attempt to use whatever talent I have been given to help others know Jesus Christ as Lord and Savior, also. The requirement to have this mind in me that is in Christ Jesus (see Phil. 2:5) at times permits me to see things from God's perspective through the Holy Spirit indwelling.

1. We all know that inexorable banking rule: You will lend at the highest rate you can get, at the lowest risk you can take. This rule is basic for all banking institutions in the world.
2. I have always heard the statement, "Business is business." Does that allow us to be different Monday through Saturday from what we are on Sunday?
3. There is a concept that the only function of a for-profit corporation is to make a profit for its shareholders.
4. We all have to be prudent (i.e., be practical, use common sense, exercise good judgment)!
5. We must maximize our profits so we can do more good for others!

How do these concepts affect the Christian who is a banker? What should the banker do about them?

A DIFFERENT WAY

I was recently (November 2, 1988) asked to speak to a group of graduate students at Carnegie Mellon University. Since the talk was sponsored by the Graduate School of Industrial Administration Bible Discussion Group, I felt free to tell them of my reaction, as a Christian, to these concepts I have listed. I tried to tell them how that affects what Dwelling House Savings and Loan does with the depositors' money.

The depositors live in forty-five states and in eleven foreign countries. Most have never been in the place physically. Many send notes with their deposits or withdrawals saying, "Thank God there is an institution where I can bank that is insured and uses my money to help poor people." Many savers are prisoners who express thanks for the hope they have for respect. Of the approximate four thousands savers, about twenty-five percent have less than twenty-five dollars in their savings accounts. There is no charge for savings, no penalty for low account balances. All savings accounts—passbook, statement, or certificate—are demand accounts. All pay the same rate of 5.5 percent compounded daily, which makes an effective 5.73 percent yearly.

The savings are mostly loaned to poor, Black, and otherwise deprived people. We also lend to the regular market. Our loan rates are mostly below the market. The welfare mother or others in similar need will get our lowest rate of 7.5 percent. We have never made a mortgage loan for more than twelve percent. At times we have paid the Federal Home Loan Bank twenty-one percent for advance money. We no longer borrow in the market. Our savers have withdrawn because of our 5.5 percent rate when the market was 17.5 percent. My IRA at age seventy-three has always been in Dwelling House Savings and Loan Association at 5.5 percent. People say we cannot stay in business and certainly cannot grow with our policies.

In 1957 Dwelling House Savings and Loan Association was $67,000 uninsured. We became insured in 1970 with $154,000 assets and pledged savings accounts of $1,000,000 when insured. Dwelling House Savings and Loan Association assets as of October 31, 1989, were $13,411,000. We think history will measure success. God sees today.

The Carnegie Mellon University talk was to be for forty-five minutes with another forty-five minutes for questions. Our discussion was interrupted after two hours because we were interfering with another group's use of that auditorium. Much of the time was spent trying to answer the question: "How can you expect me to save with Dwelling House when I can get more for my money elsewhere?" It is a good question—and one I hear all the time. The student and most people who ask it base the question on today's inflation rate, projections for the future based on the $2.6 trillion national debt, and the continuing deficits each year that threaten our whole financial existence. I think the student and people generally are aware of no real effort by anyone in power to correct the situation. In 1988 people considered presidential candidate George Bush's pledge of no new taxes to mean a continuation of the deficit spending that saw our national debt, which took two hundred years of our country's existence to reach $900 billion, almost triple itself in eight years of Reagan policies. These same policies in 1980 were labeled by then presidential candidate Bush as "voodoo economics."

The banking rule is to lend high at low risk. Banks everywhere adhere to this rule. But following this rule means disobeying God's command to love others as oneself (see Luke 10:25-37). It makes one fearful of the Judgment story (see Matt. 25:31-46). Each illustration by Jesus convicts the lender who abides by this rule. The poor, Black, and otherwise deprived people are the highest risk; they represent the lowest return. Lending to them violates this basic banking rule.

In Luke 10:25-37 Jesus answers the lawyer's question about who his neighbor is by telling of the man beaten by robbers and left for dead by the roadside. A priest came along, saw him, and passed on the other side. A Levite, when he came to the place, did the same thing. But a Samaritan had compassion on the man, took the risk of stopping to help him, and gave up the precious commodity of time and the applied economic goods of bandages, oil, and wine. He put the man on his donkey, took him to an inn, and cared for him. The next day the Samaritan had to leave, so he gave the innkeeper money to look after the man. He promised to pay any additional sums that might be incurred on the man's behalf. That constituted giving the innkeeper a blank check! He did not know the man. He owed him nothing. He just saw a person in need. He helped with what he had. Jesus said we are to go and do likewise. We are to have eyes open to see the need and try to fill it. We work for God (see Eph. 6:5-8; Col. 3:22-25).

How can you help the poor when you lend at the highest rates? You cannot. So you say, that is a job for government. Can the government really help the poor? This country's effort has alleviated harsh conditions somewhat through the War on Poverty, but endeavors to help the poor help themselves—which is the only real help anyone can give another—have been sadly lacking. You cannot pay people to have concern for others. Jesus' illustration of the hired shepherd who ran away and left the sheep makes the point (see John 10:12-13). Do not misunderstand. Government is needed to offer assistance to the poor. However, the record shows that unregenerate politicians serve themselves. They bloat their payrolls to advance their chances for reelection. They give themselves raises regardless of the state of the economy for which they have responsibility. The Pennsylvania State Legislature in 1987 gave itself a thirty-four percent raise. The rise in the national debt to $2.6 trillion, $1.7 trillion coming in the 1980-1988 period alone, occurred at a time of unprecedented poverty in American cities.

We return to the question: "How can you expect me to save with Dwelling House when I can get more for my money elsewhere?" If a poor person is helped, someone has to provide the money at a price the poor person can afford. Who is to do that if the Christian does not? He is the only one who can walk the second mile Jesus spoke about (see Matt. 5:41). He is the only one who can do what needs to be done without being required by laws, customs, and traditions. His eyes are open to see the need, and he meets it.

HELPING THOSE WHO NEED HELP

In 1983 a young welfare widow, mother of five children, was renting a house in the Hill District of Pittsburgh. The house was owned by an estate that wanted to sell it for $12,000. The widow was distraught. She had been forced to move twice before because the places were sold. The modest house was in a good school district and a nice neighborhood. Her children, seven to seventeen, were happy there. In despair she asked me to help her find a place. I asked her if she would like to buy it. Yes, indeed, she said, but how since she was on public assistance? She had $500, and made an offer to purchase the house, subject to Federal Housing Administration approval. Dwelling House Savings and Loan took the application, noting that her welfare check income would permit a mortgage of $11,600 on a $11,900 sale price if the interest rate was 7.5 percent. The market FHA rate at the time was above sixteen percent.

The FHA appraiser said the property was worth $11,900 if a new porch was put on, other repairs to roof and facia made, plumbing, electrical, and heating certifications obtained, and the house painted. A compassionate contractor was obtained, the sellers agreed to pay some of the costs of repairs, and the Christian Compassionate Fund and Dwelling House contributed the balance needed. The FHA rejected the application again, saying the utility bills would be too high for the buyer. We got the light and gas companies to agree to a special rate for low-income people, and the city winterized the house through its weatherization program with insulation, storm doors, and windows.

During this four-month process, we prayed with the mother several times. When the FHA finally approved the mortgage on the third submission, the widow had a twelve-year mortgage on a house in good repair. Her rent on the house during her two years' occupancy up to purchase had been $175 a month.

Her new mortgage payment as owner was $162 a month including principal, interest, taxes, and insurance. She has never missed a payment.

In the early eighties when interest rates were spiraling upward, the calls were frequent. One irate caller asked, "How can you expect me to keep my money in Dwelling House at 5.5 percent when I can get fifteen percent on it?" I told him if he needed his money, he should take it. He replied, "Why do I have to need it?" I told him I thought people understood why we did not pay higher rates. Being called fools was one of the kinder things said about us during the period. The caller took his money out, as did a lot of other people. Our board had many discussions about our policy. We tried to think of ways to resolve our purpose with our policy. In the meantime, money still came in from savers, and we got new accounts from throughout the country. One saver, a person in economics, wrote a note with his large deposit, saying, "I think you will need this in the light of what is happening to interest rates."

Christianity Today had me on its cover in April 1982 under the title "Putting God to Work in Pittsburgh." We receive a lot of publicity because we resist normal banking rules.

In taking high-risk applicants for loans, we have to try to determine if the persons understand they are being given a chance to make a new start in life. They have to learn from past mistakes in the instance of recent bankruptcy or foreclosure or just plain slow or bad credit through lack of understanding or ability to discipline themselves. They need counseling in terms of budgeting.

The ideal budget is set up to pay God first. If that is ten percent of income, you have ninety percent left. Pay yourself second. If that is ten percent, you have eighty percent left. That eighty percent is what you pay your bills with, and you do not make any bills in excess of the eighty cents left in each dollar you earn. If someone already has debts in excess of one-hundred percent of income, the person has to do some belt tightening, get additional work, and make the disciplined sacrifices necessary to bring debt to its proper level. The person is able then to return to God (others in need) what is owed, have money for self in times of adversity, and still meet obligations at all times. Governments should exercise this same budget.

Correcting the high-risk applicant's habits to those of non-high-risk society will correct many of our most glaring ills of the so-called ghetto underclass. An article in an Association for Public Justice report (November 1988) defines this class as a people with low-level jobs, high unemployment, very high instances of female head of households, very high numbers of teenage pregnancies, high rates of crime and drug activity and, I would add, excessive health problems.

The people in these poor areas are "red lined." This old term defines off-limit areas for sound investments. Red lining is now illegal. Yet it is still practiced by the rule of lend high at low risk. People are poor because they have not had opportunity to learn the system.

Early in Dwelling House experience as an insured institution, I met the federal and state examiners outside the office at 8:00 a.m. one Monday. One examiner said, "What are you doing here? This is a terrible location." I said, "This is where the people are that we serve." The examiner responded, "These people don't have any money!" I said, "True, that's what we are trying to change." The examiner looked at me as if I were crazy or at least did not understand how to run a banking institution.

We try hard to attract the "good" loan applicants, but they usually get their loans through the larger majority lenders. Because of our reputation, we get marginal and submarginal borrowers most of the time. As I stated, we try to take the time to "qualify" someone before taking an application. We take the questionable ones if they show the slightest understanding of what we are trying to do. We also tell them why we are trying to do it. This explanation takes various forms, but I have found there is no substitute for telling them it is because of Christ. He has helped us. We have to help others in His name, through His strength.

A couple were buying a new home in a redeveloping area. The schools showed evidence of neglect; no businesses were in the same cleared area. Dwelling House was the mortgagee. At the closing in the title company, the builder remarked to the buyers that Dwelling House had made a below-market interest loan to them. The man said, "Thanks." The builder continued, "That probably saves you about $15 a month on your mortgage payment." I said, "It saves them $22 a month." The young man again said, "Thanks. Why did you do it?" I explained the FHA would not have approved them at the 9.5 percent rate because his income was not sufficient. We made the rate an affordable 8.5 percent so he could buy the house and have the income tax deduction for interest and taxes that could be the equivalent of having three or four children for income tax deductions. The young man was really impressed at that point and exclaimed, "Yes, but why did you do it?" That was when I had the opportunity to tell him about Christ, right in the Union Title Co. downtown office. Praise God!

Taking the risks and offering lower rates do not make an assured economic success formula. The intent always is to make a loan so that both parties live up to the agreement. Few people can make the change from bad credit habits to good ones in one leap. Dwelling House delinquencies are the worst in the III Region. The examiners cannot find anything to fault us for, except our delinquencies. We follow all the required rules and recommendations for collection. In addition, we call the borrowers, see them in their homes, write personal letters to them, and when they permit, pray with them. We take all these steps before we report them to the credit bureau. We have a policy of not giving up on them until they give up. Our effort is always to appeal to their self-respect. Although our delinquencies are high, our foreclosures are among the lowest. How do we stay in business? We have reserves of eleven percent of our assets, more than enough to cover every delinquent loan. If all were to go completely bad, we would still have positive reserves.

TO WHOM ARE WE TO CONFORM?

Can we separate our economic soul from our spiritual one? Are we different Monday through Saturday from what we are on Sunday?

You have heard the expression, "Business is business." It is often used by executives in boardrooms, by managers at business luncheons, and by the public in general conversation. It usually is said in the context of conformity. When it is used, it follows the patterns society measures as success, which usually does not follow God's mandates for our lives. God's values are used partially or paid only lip service.

When Jimmy Carter was running for president in 1976, the *Wall Street Journal* ran a series of articles on born-again people because he said he was a born-again Christian. One article I read with great interest. It was the last one and told about a born-again businessman. It told of this honest, upright, impeccable businessman who did all the good things in society and supported all the good causes. The article ended with the statement that this born-again businessman did business like everyone else. If that is true, should it be?

The issue of conformity assumes that is the only way to succeed, just do it a little better. It is not uncommon in Dwelling House Board meetings for the statement "We have to do things right" to come up. Someone makes the remark when we are trying to follow biblical principles instead of doing what other savings institutions are doing, usually during loan application approval discussions. To try to help the borderline person being considered—when we have just finished painfully reviewing our increasing delinquency ratios—is always a test of our resolve to help that person. To hold interest rates down when the market calls for more and the person seems capable of paying more is always cause for long deliberations about how to be consistent in our obedience so as not to dilute our effort.

People often act as if we do not understand the laws of supply and demand, diminishing returns, and other economic laws because of our "different policies." Investment bankers cannot understand why I will not consider arbitrating to make additional basis points on our investments. Dwelling House walks the line, which is often blurred by what is God's way as contrasted to man's. To recognize that God's values are different from man's means you have to search the Scriptures for the contrasts. Now we see through a glass darkly (see 1 Cor. 13).

The concept of business is business often results in calamitous situations. The greed and practices of some savings institutions have seriously affected the FSLIC fund (Federal Savings and Loan Insurance Corporation). Up to this point savings and loans have paid special assessments to support the fund. Some relevant data follows:

Data from United States League of Savings Institutions Task Force on Deposit Insurance, November, 1988, Reporting on the 3020 Savings & Loans

August 1988   62.2% of total assets in mortgage loans and mortgage
Savings & Loans   backed securities as of 8-3-88

45% to 55% single family mortgage loans originations 1983-88

8.6% in commercial real estate loans

4.6% in consumer loans

1.9% in commercial and industrial loans

13.8% in investment securities

9.1% in other assets

December 1982   71.8% of total assets in mortgage loans and securities
Savings & Loans

Of 495 GAAP—insolvent institutions, 216 were responsible for 88.9% of the total negative net worth institutions. These few institutions had only 40.1% of their assets in mortgage related assets in mid-1988.

25% of the negative net worth of all 495 GAAP—insolvent institutions was concentrated in only (6) six institutions as of mid-1988. One-third of all negative net worth was in a mere 10 institutions and one-half was accounted for by 24 institutions.

The United States League concludes that the FSLIC's problems are not caused by the vast majority of savings institutions, which have stuck to their basic housing mission and been governed by prudent management practices.

New concepts are being suggested by Congress, regulators, and supervisors to help prevent another crisis like the FSLIC's present situation (1988). Ways of requiring greater capitalized institutions representing a larger minimum number of incorporators for new institutions, tightening up loan standards, appraisal standards and other disciplines are being explored. At this writing, Congress is considering how to stop the losses of the FSLIC at this point, while it determines who is to pay the bill for the losses now estimated to range up to $50 billion.

The concept of layered costs that make the product or service so expensive is expressed in the leveraged buyout situations occurring regularly. The RJR Nabisco buyout, according to the *Wall Street Journal*, will result in $300 million fees to the lawyers and financiers. Who is to pay for this? Who has set the value of the products involved? Why are bankruptcies and business failures increasing? Those who try to look ahead and act honestly in terms of helping others with their product or service are thought to be relegating themselves to a small business position as a goal.

Irresponsible operators in both savings institutions and investment banking circles exploit the federal deposit insurance system. Should not the general public take some responsibility for the greed factor of not inquiring about how the large yields are obtained? Our financial markets continue to permit and increase the layered additional costs of money manipulators who produce nothing. This financial reality adds to the burden of those who try to produce goods and services and try to live in the world but not be of the world (see John 17:15-16). Yet we who judge others are judged by the same word from the One who said, "I am the way and the truth and the life" (John 14:6) and "Judge not, that you be not judged" (Matt. 7:1, RSV).

In 1960 Dwelling House Savings and Loan had $68,000 total assets. It was uninsured; it was, and still is, in the heart of the Pittsburgh Hill District, a poor red-lined area, whose ethnic white population had almost completely moved away. The city declared much of it a zone for demolition and removal of the citizens.

A city demographic study at the time showed the following comparison between the Hill District and Squirrel Hill—an adjacent community two miles southeast of it—as to income, schooling, and home ownership of its inhabitants:

	Income	Schooling	Home Ownership
Squirrel Hill	$23,000	Graduate Level	87%
Hill District	$ 4,800	8th Grade	12%

Since home ownership plays a major part in the economic development of a community, the effort to earn a living became coupled with a desire to see the lives of the other people improved in the process. Would loving God and others as self bring about a banking entity that lends to the community? The community returns more to the bank who lends more to the community. The excess money is put into selected regular markets when not in use in the community.

I do not say that Dwelling House was the only factor in the improvement of the area. In 1988 we are a long way from where we should be economically. Recent figures from the Pittsburgh Urban League indicated that the median income for Black people in Pittsburgh is now $17,100 a year. A demographic study by the city in 1987 also showed that twenty-seven percent now own their homes in the Hill District and that sixty-four percent own their homes on the Upper Hill.

These figures are significant when you consider the impact of home ownership on a community. It means that there will be good schools because property taxes sustain the school systems, teachers can teach instead of just keep order, and kids have incentive to study and stay in school. There will be good city services; the police can protect instead of, at times, exploit, and regular garbage collection contributes to the enhanced image of the area. Businesses will be attracted because of stable community people with something to protect. And there will be jobs.

Serving poor, Black, and deprived people in accordance with Luke 10:25-37 and Matthew 25:31-46 means working with persons who exhibit a desire to have a new start, even though they have been bankrupt. We talk with them about what that means in terms of having denied their responsibilities, thus compromising their self-respect. We take the person who has had a foreclosure, again counseling as to why it happened, and the person who has had bad credit but desires to start anew. We try to teach the basic budgeting principle of paying God first, then paying self second. If that is ten percent, they have eighty cents out of every dollar they earn to pay their bills and they are not to make any bills in excess of that eighty percent.

The one and only function of a corporation is to make a profit for its shareholders. This statement has been made and accepted as fact. The thought seems to be that the legal entity can do anything within the parameters of its charter and purpose that is legal.

Early banking principles were laid out in the Bible. That the good economic things belong to God and to us, who are to be faithful stewards, is indicated in Psalm 24:1 and clearly stated in Genesis 1:26-30. God gave man and woman dominion over all the fish of the sea, the birds of the air, every living creature that moves on the ground, and every seed-bearing plant on the face of the earth.

Man's attempt to be faithful to this mandate, since he is plagued by sin from the Fall, is outlined throughout the Old Testament. Early bankers, who kept money belonging to others for safekeeping, would lend the money and charge interest for its use depending on the time used, just as we do today. They were not to charge interest to a brother (see Exod. 22:25-27) or keep his collateral overnight (see Lev. 25:35-37). The Lord stated that the land belonged to Him, the people were His tenants, it must not be sold permanently, and they must provide for the redemption of the land (see Lev. 25:23-24). Land was to be bought and sold according to the number of years until the Jubilee Year, the fiftieth year. The price of land was to be increased in proportion to the number of years remaining if many or reduced if few. This principle of proration is standard in banking procedures today. Deuteronomy 23:19-20 repeats the admonition not to charge a brother interest but grants permission to charge a foreigner. Deuteronomy 25:14-15 warns people not to have two differing measures, one large and one small; they must have honest weights and measures. In New Testament writings the interest amount is determined by motive (see 1 Tim. 6:10).

This Old Testament principle, "He that hath pity upon the poor lendeth unto the LORD; and that which he hath given will he pay him again" (Prov. 19:17, KJV), is carried forward to the New Testament in an illustration of Jesus (see Matt. 25:31-46). In this illustration those who saw Him in all the conditions of poverty and need and served His needs were repaid with eternal life. Those who did nothing for Him or were against Him or just did not see or supply need were cast into eternal damnation at Judgment Day. Jesus endorsed the same principle in the story of the rich man and the beggar Lazarus (see Luke 16:19-31). The rich man did nothing for or against the beggar; he simply ignored him. That was the sin, passing by the need. So, the rich man went into eternal damnation while the poor beggar went to Heaven.

We might say that has to do with personal responsibility. The corporation is not personal; it is just a legal entity! The corporate executives do their good personally; they are tithers in their churches; they head all the do-good committees in town. They are good husbands and fathers. They use the good sense God gave them to run their corporations successfully. Is it true that the corporation is separate from the management in God's eyes? Is the principle that we are accountable to God reserved for personal piety only? Are we not to use everything we have been given to glorify God and enjoy Him forever? Is it not possible that loving God and others as self (see Matt. 22:36-40) might conflict with the customs, traditions, and culture of the day? Are we not always in danger of justifying ourselves (see Jer. 17:9) and not walking the narrow path (see Matt. 7:13-14), for there is a way that seems right to man but ends in destruction (see Prov. 14:12; 16:25)?

THE PRINCIPLES OF OBEDIENCE

The principle of being obedient to God runs throughout the Bible: "To obey is better than sacrifice" (1 Sam. 15:22). But the often-heard statement, "We have to be prudent," is the rule by which business procedures are considered. It means we are to be practical, exert common sense, and use good judgment.

We are to trust God and not our own understanding, in all our ways acknowledge Him, and He will direct our paths (see Prov. 3:5-6). That seems to be the opposite of using our own good judgment. We always seem to run up against that absolute *all* appearing so frequently in God's Word: "Seek first his kingdom and his righteousness, and *all* things will be given to you as well" (Matt. 6:33, emphasis added). The emphasis on obedience to God's commands seems to make it mandatory on our part to pay attention. Jesus stressed the losing of one's life in order to find life (see Matt. 16:25; Mark 8:35; Luke 9:24; John 12:25); that seems to be a prerequisite to having the ability to see and to do in accordance with the insight needed, regardless of the circumstances or cultural situation.

Jeremiah was confined while the army of the king of Babylon besieged Jerusalem. While he was in prison, the word of the Lord came to him to buy his cousin's field. He obeyed, knowing the city would fall to the Babylonians. He paid the seventeen shekels of silver, signed, sealed, and had witnessed the deed, and had all documents placed in a clay jar for safekeeping. Then he said, "Ah, Sovereign LORD, you have made the heavens and the earth by your great power and outstretched arm. Nothing is too hard for you" (Jer. 32:17).

How do we attempt to work out our obedience in a prudent way? We usually try to do it by doing good things acceptable to us, such as serving on United Way boards and committees, being involved in the affairs of our respective community's needs, working for political causes for reform, and so forth. All these are good and certainly necessary. They always seem to help the outward man. However, things do not get better. Man remains the same. There is no inward change. No knowledge is conveyed about the Bread of Life, or the Living Water that will well up to eternal life.

There is no guarantee of physical profit from being obedient to God. Yet there is the guarantee that you will be sustained in whatever you do, when it is done for God:

> I have never seen the righteous forsaken
>   or their children begging bread.
> They are always generous and lend freely;
>   their children will be blessed. (Ps. 37:25-26)

Just as individuals refuse to save in Dwelling House because we will not pay the high market rates, the government will not do it, either. The federal government is required by constitutional mandate to promote the general welfare. That means to help all its citizens equally. The federal government agencies refuse to deposit money in Dwelling House Savings and Loan because our rates are not competitive. My letters and appeals stating that we are trying to do what the government is supposed to do make no difference.

In 1974, I introduced a resolution at the U.S. League of Savings Institutions Convention in San Francisco that was passed and sent to our legislative committee to present to Congress for enactment. The resolution called for the federal Treasury Department to make deposits into any banking institutions in the country that would take the money for the purpose of lending to poor, Black, and otherwise needy people. The money would be earmarked by the institutions to lend according to need-agreed-on guidelines at, say, three percent interest to low-income people whose ability to pay matched that rate. The people who could pay four percent would pay that, and so on as incomes increased. The institution would maintain a two percent spread for itself and pay the government the difference in interest. The government would be earning money with its tax dollar revenue to be used to help retire its debt and put into other social programs. No new bureaus would have to be set up to provide decent, safe, and sanitary housing for poor people under this plan. Its enforcement would be carried out by federal examiners in their yearly examinations of the books of the institutions that received the deposits. Can anyone see why such a proposal did not get off the ground?

I sent this same proposal to President Nixon in 1972 and received commendatory letters from Secretary of Housing and Urban Development Romney, Secretary of Commerce Stans, and Federal Home Loan Bank Chairman Hal Kamp, all saying that it was a good idea but unfortunately there were no laws to bring it about. I thought that was why I wrote the letter!

As it stands today, federal agencies send Dwelling House proposals for bids on use of their deposits. They expect the highest market rates, just as the business financial world. They do not seem to realize the government is supposed to complete, not compete.

Former Pennsylvania State Treasurer Dwyer's office called Dwelling House from Harrisburg to tell us they were wiring $100,000 of state money to us. When I asked what rate they expected, they said the highest market rate available at the time, of course. When I explained that we could not meet those rates because they were higher than some of the mortgages we were currently making, they said they were required by law to get the market rates. I tried to get them to see that Dwelling House was trying to do what government should.

I suggested that the administration petition the legislature to recognize this and consider laws to meet it. I received a very nice letter from Secretary Dwyer commending Dwelling House on what we were trying to do, but Dwelling House did not get the deposit. Can we say the government is not required to look at things from God's point of view?

Many years ago, the *Guinness Book of World Records* stated there were 1,176,000 laws in this country. Surely there are thousands more now. But the Christian has to remember only two laws: loving God with all the heart, soul, and mind and one's neighbor as oneself. Jesus said if we do these, we fulfill all the laws and what the prophets predicted.

Efforts to bring ethical considerations into the picture are tolerated as long as they do not interfere with the perceived purposes of making profit. The concept that profit comes as a result of serving the need of people with the product or service is considered idealism.

We have to maximize our profits so we can do more good things with the additional money we make. The big problem with that assertion, however, is that we almost never have enough money or profits under such a premise because the goal of making more money usually supplants the purpose of serving the need. It is like asking God to step aside while you make the money you feel you need in order to serve Him better. I have not found a biblical principle anywhere that supports this premise.

Our present system of economic distribution lends itself to this concept. The general theory that man will do the most good for others when he looks out for himself first (was it Adam Smith's proposition?) has evolved into today's "trickle down" theory in the American economy. How does this meet Jesus' requirement, expressed in all four gospels, of our need to lose our lives if we are to find them or follow the servanthood Jesus exhibited when He washed His disciples' feet (see John 13:5)?

The government uses the same theory for raising taxes. It never has enough money. The requirements to raise taxes result in the profligacy we see in government. The motive to maximize money profits is transferred to our desire for power and the good life that brings. We see the same syndrome in nonprofit and some charitable corporations. The term is not profit by law, but the same needs for money result. This same syndrome applies to Dwelling House Savings and Loan and myself in my own strength. I cannot be different from anyone else by my own resolve to be so. If I exhibit any differences at any time, it is the result of the Holy Spirit indwelling me and making it possible. He will dwell in us and do this if we ask Him to, as Jesus told us (see Luke 11:13).

Money is to be earned biblically and used the same way. The measuring rod is the motive behind each activity. Jesus said that we cannot serve God and mammon (money, world; Matt. 6:24). To have pure motives, we need the new heart the born-again believer is promised ("a new heart" and "a new spirit" [Ezek. 36:26]; "the old has gone, the new has come" [2 Cor. 5:17]; "I have been crucified with Christ . . . I live by faith in the Son of God, who loved me and gave himself for me" [Gal. 2:20]). As God's children, we "participate in the divine nature" (2 Pet. 1:4).

At Dwelling House we take seriously Jesus' command, "Give to the one who asks you, and do not turn away from the one who wants to borrow from you" (Matt. 5:42).

We often get requests for loans that we know at the beginning cannot or should not be made. Much time is spent in respectfully responding to these requests. We usually ask applicants some questions, and their answers reveal to them the answers to their requests. For example, a man wanted to borrow on some property for the purpose of buying another piece of property. As he explained his request, I could see it was not a good thing for him to do. I asked him if he was sure he wanted to do this. When he assured me he did, I asked him for the usual financial statements for the last three years. He returned with them, and we went over them, looking at the good features and the questionable ones. He still wanted to apply for the loan. I asked him to check on the conditions in the present market for that type of investment as to comparable sales, neighborhood trends, projected future value, and so on. He came back with the information, shook my hand, and said, "Thanks, Mr. Lavelle, I don't think I should ask for that loan." Praise God!

People regularly ask for some type of money assistance. We try to be helpful. We permit the high-activity, low-balance accounts that are costly to maintain. In the process of doing this, we attempt to teach customers why we do it without demeaning them or discouraging them from saving. A retired Presbyterian minister started a Christian Compassionate Fund in Dwelling House. The account is replenished from time to time by savers who know about it, and those who have been recipients of funds in times of mortgage payment or other needs. This is all in accordance, we hope, with the principles throughout the Bible of helping the poor to help themselves, the principle of forgiveness, and the principle of restoration.

EDITOR'S PERSPECTIVE

The beauty of a testimony like Robert Lavelle's is that it illustrates how the Holy Spirit can work in someone's life so that he or she, with childlike faith and devotion to Christ, is enabled to bring into focus God's intentions regarding ministry to the deprived people of the world in the midst of circumstances that logic and general prudence (not *love*-guided prudence) tell us to avoid. Such testimony should cause us to ask ourselves if we are as sensitive as we ought to be to the leading of the Holy Spirit as He calls us to follow Christ in the market-place. Am I resisting the Spirit's call in Scripture by rationalizing why the scriptural testimony to God's desires does not apply at this time and in this circumstance rather than simply obeying its call and trusting God to accomplish His will through my obedience? Robert Lavelle believed, trusted, and obeyed God. Am I as trusting and obedient?

Part of the power of Bob Lavelle's testimony, though, is felt because he did not tell us that we ought to try to do what he has done at Dwelling House Savings and Loan. If he had done that, we could too easily find reasons that would justify not following his example (we serve a different clientele; we are not in the mortgage industry; and so on). No, his account insists on a far deeper self-examination. I am compelled to look at my attitudes and heart's sensitivity (or lack of it) when I read the account of how he put his love for hurting people ahead of his good business sense. He was, in fact, very wise in the way he helped people learn how to help themselves. Somehow, his story elevates the biblical teaching of love to a high and exalted position, and I suspect (know) that my heart is not as soft and sensitive and responsive to many of my neighbors as it should be.

Philosophers and theologians are prone to talk about people choosing the

206

lesser good or sinning, but we are given few lessons in choosing the *greater good*, except as illustrated in choosing good over evil (do not be conformed to the world by lying, stealing, murdering, etc.). But I do not ever remember hearing a sermon on choosing a greater good over a lesser good. And the vast majority of decisions we make in the marketplace are precisely in this area—choosing between competing "goods."

It would not have been wrong for Mr. Lavelle to have run a traditional savings and loan business. He would not have been sinning if he had chosen to stick to the banking axioms regarding people's qualifications to be extended credit. He would not have violated a moral law if he had always charged market rates of interest (provided they were not usurious). But neither would he have been as loving and Christlike as he was.

God does not call us to simply be moral (keep our noses clean) in the marketplace. We are called to be imitators of Christ and to love our neighbors in the marketplace. The difference between being morally correct and being loving can be subtle, but the difference is as sharp as the distinction between a hot breeze in the summer and a breath of cool air. I am afraid the Church has too frequently limited its teaching on obedience to personal pietism and positive moral standards of conduct—which do need emphasizing—to the virtual exclusion of any teaching on the need for a truly caring and loving heart in the marketplace.

Moral conduct and biblical love are clearly compatible ideals, but they are not synonymous in their content. Moral conduct is measured only on the behavioral and consequential planes, while love embodies these appropriate qualities in a heart concerned for the greatest good for the people affected. Putting it another way, moral conduct may be placed on a continuum of conduct that runs from being immoral through points of acceptable or minimal morality on up the scale to levels of sacrificial love. Love is by nature concerned for the very best for others. Love embodies caring along with its propensity for moral correctness. Pietism is all too frequently presented to the Church in terms of personal holiness instead of relational holiness, which Dr. Packer so ably talks about in the opening chapter. This one-sided form of pietism can easily degenerate into a self-protective and self-justifying perception of the world that allows people to do minimal things for their neighbors rather than the greater and best things for them. Robert Lavelle has traveled the higher road.

The cure for this condition of the human heart—letting "acceptable" moral conduct be a substitute for concerned love—is not to be found through reading more or even through better teaching. These can only point us to Christ, the source of any true cure for an immature heart. We are to grow in the likeness of Christ, which must be brought about by the Holy Spirit's renovating work.

Only He can create a truly loving heart, and He effects this by orchestrating and balancing two essential experiences: (1) empowering us to be obedient to God's revealed will, and (2) opening the heart to recognize Christ's further self-revelation. To the degree that Christ has revealed Himself to the heart of a believer, the believer must then respond to that truth before Christ will continue to further reveal Himself (see John 14:15-24; 15:9-10; 1 John 2:3-6). This is not a doctrine of works or a tit-for-tat philosophy, but an essential part of the doctrine of growth and sanctification. The process could be described as follows: Christ first takes the initiative and reveals Himself and His love to us; being loved strengthens us and enables us to respond to and obey what we have come to know; Christ will then reveal *more* of His grace and will to us as we respond in faith to what we already know; and we are then further enabled to grow in our commitment to doing His will as our fellowship with Him matures. This process is intended to be ever growing and expanding.

> The strangest part of this whole paradox—more true knowledge of Christ requires a growing obedience to Him—is the fact that our outward conduct is the easiest part of the human struggle (between our old nature and our new nature) to effect a change in—from the human side of the God and man relationship. We cannot of our own volition change our own spirits—attitudes, motives, and thoughts that bubble up into our consciousness from the heart of our being. We can take such thoughts captive to Christ (2 Cor. 10:5), but we cannot change our heart.
>
> It is the "seeing" of Christ that transforms our innermost being—heart, character, thoughts, etc. (1 John 3:2; 2 Cor. 3:18; Eph. 1:18). And this "seeing" is absolutely under the power and control of God, not ourselves. At the same time, however, "if [we] seek Him, He will let [us] find Him" (2 Chron. 15:2). We are told that if we will draw near to Him, He will draw near to us (James 4:8). But our innermost transformation (actual change in character) is a transforming work done by the personal and present Spirit of Christ.[1]

May God grant us the grace to receive the truth of Scripture and unite it with genuine faith (see Heb. 4:2) so that we will be enabled to respond in love to His expressed will and become effective salt and light in the world. Self-protective prudence must not be substituted for loving prudence that will seek a way to truly love our neighbors. Minimal morality must not be allowed to satisfy our thirst for true righteousness. We are to become like Christ in our love for our neighbors (see Matt. 10:25; Luke 6:40; John 13:13-17; 1 John 3:2).

PART XI

TAKING REFUGE FROM RISKS

A difficult dilemma for Christians concerns the extent to which we should seek to control life's outcomes by our personal efforts and the extent to which we should look to God to work out the ends for us. In the first case we run the risk of exhibiting too little faith, and in the other case we run the risk of testing God. This tension becomes evident when we encounter known risks: Do we act in an effort to try to control the risk, or do we accept the risk and trust in God's providential provisions? People face these decisions when they decide whether to protect themselves against the financial consequences of risk or to assume it.

We are all engaged in some kind of risk management, whether or not we think of it as such. We are involved with risk management every time we drive an automobile, walk across a busy street, or select foods that are compatible or incompatible with our personal physiology. We give little thought to these, but as the risks rise, and the potential consequences to life and property are enlarged, we generally seek ways to limit the risks or justify assuming them.

Risk management has taken on new forms, though, during the past hundred years as the hazards of technology have multiplied and placed us at risk as we use our automobiles, airplanes, medical technology, chemicals, and hundreds of other modern inventions. Natural risks—storms, health, and so forth—have been joined by many man-created risks. This growth in the assumption of risks has been accompanied by a growth in urbanization, which has seen a large portion of people's assets converted from natural wealth (land, animals, vegetation) to forms of monetary wealth subject to a wider variety of new risks. The result is a heightened awareness of what we call *financial risks*. These new risks have accelerated our demands for opportunities to pool and spread them, which in turn have given rise to the insurance industry.

Many Christians wrestle with questions about what they should insure (life, health, property, liability) and how much coverage they should have. Many people have asked me if taking out life insurance shows a lack of trust in God. No, for there is *no necessary* relationship between the purchase of life insurance and one's trust in God's general providence regarding the care of a family. There are numerous other issues as well. At what age should one buy life insurance? What kind of life insurance is best? What should one's family status be when considering such insurance? How much should be purchased? What size should the premium be? However, the real question that needs answering is this: Who should bear the financial burdens if the primary provider for the family dies—the spouse, the Church, the state?

The church has a responsibility for widows (under certain conditions; see 1 Tim. 5:3-16), orphans, and others in distress, but Scripture first holds the family responsible for the care of its own. Others are called on to assume such burdens only after the first line of responsibility has been exhausted. My failure to discharge my personal responsibilities toward my family or my resolve to "live by faith" in a way that looks to God to keep me from an early death or that expects the Church to care for my dependents should I die, when I was capable of doing so, is a misunderstanding and misappropriation of faith. We have no biblical warrant to look to God to do for us what He has given us to do—care for our families as responsibly as possible.

There is nothing wrong, however, with a group of Christians covenanting to care for one another without the use of insurance. They become a special "pooling of risks" group that will, if you like, practice a form of self-insurance or a form of mutual insurance without the payment of prior premiums. God Himself recognized the need for pooled and shared risk management when He instructed Israel, and then the Church, about the care of widows and orphans. But He never implied that community care was the only acceptable way of discharging the responsibilities for surviving dependents when an untimely death of the primary breadwinner should occur.

Fred Potter gives us a good overview of the development of the concept of insurance. He cites historical illustrations of church ministers deeply involved in its early development as they sought ways to discharge the responsibilities God assigned His people. The main thrust of Mr. Potter's work, though, provides a clear integration of scriptural principles with the biblically assigned personal and collective responsibilities: stewardship obligations regarding the care of property (property and casualty insurance), duties to make restitution for the damage or losses we bring about on another's property (liability insurance), the need for wisdom regarding the purchase of prepaid benefits (health, dental, legal insurance), and the appropriate use of life and disability insurance.

CHAPTER 11

BIBLICAL PRINCIPLES APPLIED TO INSURANCE

Fred L. Potter

Fred L. Potter lives in Concord, New Hampshire, with his wife, Mertie, and their three children. He is active in the leadership and teaching ministry of their local church. An honors graduate of Harvard College, Harvard Business School, and the University of Michigan Law School, he began his career as an attorney focusing on commercial law. Shortly after being elected to partnership in his legal practice, he joined Christian Mutual Life Insurance Company to serve as its President. He has also been President of the New Hampshire Bar Association, and he is a member of the Christian Legal Society. He is on the boards at New Hampshire Savings Bank Corporation and Gordon Conwell Theological Seminary.

In 1896, when there were four automobiles in the United States, two were in St. Louis. They collided. Both drivers were hurt, one seriously.
—Andrew Tobias, *The Invisible Bankers*

in·sur·ance/in-'shur-en(t)s/*n*(1651)—coverage by contract whereby one party undertakes to indemnify or guarantee another against loss by a specified contingency or peril.
—*Webster's Ninth New Collegiate Dictionary*

B y the 1980s the business of insurance in the United States had grown to more than $400 billion in annual premium income divided among nearly six thousand insurance companies. These companies controlled nearly $1.5 trillion in assets and employed more than two million individuals. Remarkably, these industry statistics are exclusive of the government sector. Annually, through taxes, an amount in excess of $300 billion is collected for mandatory government programs such as social security and unemployment compensation, which perform functions similar to private insurance.

The enormous size of this industry does not indicate its moral content, either good or bad. Nevertheless, the broad involvement of Christians who work, drive an automobile, own a home, and so on in one form of insurance or another provides good reason to examine scriptural insights to guide that involvement. Nearly two percent of the American working population is employed directly or indirectly by the insurance industry. We, as Christians, should seek ways to be salt and light in the workplace to influence this industry for the cause of Jesus Christ. Also, we need to examine how we, as Christian consumers of insurance products, can best apply scriptural principles in our purchasing decisions.

The first known written use of the word *insurance* was in the seventeenth century. Historians believe that the commercial practice of life insurance began sometime in the sixteenth century. Accordingly, exposition on the subject cannot be expected in the original biblical manuscripts. Nevertheless, the scriptural mandate for the wise steward to anticipate and prepare for future risks is evident:

A prudent man sees danger and takes refuge,
but the simple keep going and suffer for it. (Prov. 22:3; see 27:12)

"Therefore everyone who hears these words of mine and puts them into practice is like a wise man who builds his house on the rock. The rain came down, the streams rose, and the winds blew and beat against that house; yet it did not fall, because it had its foundation on the rock. But everyone who hears these words of mine and does not put them into practice is like a foolish man who built his house on sand. The rain came down, the streams rose, and the winds blew and beat against that house, and it fell with a great crash." (Matt. 7:24-27)

This renunciation of head-in-the-sand (and house-on-the-sand) living encourages Christians to anticipate and prepare in advance for future risks.

Jesus commends as "wise" the man who protected his house against the perils of excessive rains. This illustration points to a tension that often arises in the discussion of insurance among Christians. We know, after all, that "the earth is the LORD's, and everything in it, the world, and all who live in it" (Ps. 24:1). Thus, if our lives, our dependents, and our assets are the Lord's, can we not depend on Him to care for His and His own?

Surely, if this transfer of responsibility were to apply to any of the many perils we face, it would apply to excessive rain. The Scriptures document nearly one hundred circumstances in which God has sent or withheld rain. God uses rain both to bless and to curse:

> Then I will send rain on your land in its season, both autumn and spring rains, so that you may gather in your grain, new wine and oil. (Deut. 11:14)

> "Therefore, this is what the Sovereign LORD says: In my wrath I will unleash a violent wind, and in my anger hailstones and torrents of rain will fall with destructive fury." (Ezek. 13:13)

God has the power—and often in the scriptural records He demonstrated His will—selectively to send and withhold rain:

> "I also withheld rain from you
>   when the harvest was still three months away.
> I sent rain on one town,
>   but withheld it from another.
> One field had rain;
>   another had none and dried up." (Amos 4:7)

God used rain to bring judgment on the evil of mankind and prepare for renewal through His servant Noah (see Gen. 6–9). Under the Lord's direction, Moses brought together thunder, hail, lightning, and rain as one of the plagues on the land of Egypt. The ministries of Samuel and Elijah were confirmed in the minds of the people, in part, through the Lord's response to His servants' prayers concerning rain.

Reading such passages alone, therefore, we might develop the impression that human protection against the peril of flooding is somehow unspiritual. Such protection might reflect a lack of dependence on God or a lack of faith in His ability to control the natural elements.

Further, the scriptural record on God's use of rain for blessing, cursing, and guidance might mean that our precautions reflect a resistance to be under God's direction. Would we thereby resist His desire to enlarge or reduce our assets? Taken to the extreme, such thinking would stop us from building canals and irrigation systems to compensate for lack of rain on the one hand and would inhibit our use of insurance to protect against financial losses from flooding on the other.

However, the whole counsel of Scripture leads us in a more balanced direction. The scriptural examples of rainfall as an instrument of God's direction are clear. Also clear is Jesus' teaching that the distribution of the natural elements may occur with no moral significance: "He causes his sun to rise on the evil and the good, and sends rain on the righteous and the unrighteous" (Matt. 5:45). Thus, Jesus describes as *wise* the man who built his house on the rock to protect against those natural disasters (see Matt. 7).

The scriptural record and modern-day experience offer many illustrations of the miraculous power of our heavenly Father to protect believers from natural disaster. However, both sources (including regular reports in missionary letters) confirm that modern men and women, believers and nonbelievers alike, are not exempt from such perils. In the twenty-year period from 1947 to 1967, for example, over 200 major floods occurred worldwide resulting in documented loss of life in excess of 170,000. The next leading category of natural disasters for that period was wind related (148 major typhoon, hurricane, and cyclone disasters with loss of life in excess of 100,000), followed by earthquakes (eighty-six disasters with loss of life in excess of 56,000). All told, accurate documentation is available on more than 655 natural disasters during that twenty-year period alone, claiming nearly 400,000 lives. Thus, despite our modern advances, mankind has been unable to insulate itself from even the most basic natural disasters.

Moreover, God cannot be restrained from accomplishing His purposes by any manmade wall of protection. Jesus illustrates this point in the parable of the rich fool (see Luke 12). The rich fool had exceeded even his own plans for providing for his present and future pleasures. Preparing for yet another bountiful crop, the rich fool made additional plans to increase his savings and protect more extensively his resources. He said to himself smugly, "You have plenty of good things laid up for many years. Take life easy; eat, drink and be merry" (Luke 12:19). But the omnipotent heavenly Father had different plans: "You fool! This very night your life will be demanded from you. Then who will get what you have prepared for yourself?" (Luke 12:20). Our wisdom in planning for future contingencies must at all points be tempered with humble awareness of God's sovereignty: "Our God is in heaven; he does whatever pleases him" (Ps. 115:3).

Just as balance is needed in considering our role and God's role in protecting against future risks, so must we develop balance in setting the role of insurance in our protection plans. The "prudent man" of the Proverbs and the "wise man" of the gospels were commended for their actions. Since the commercial practice of insurance did not begin until much later, their actions did not involve an application for insurance with Jerusalem Insurance Company. In light of our increasingly heavy reliance on insurance to protect against contingencies, this historic fact should cause us to note other duties in these passages.

The builder did not build his house on the sand and then insure against the risk of flooding (see Matt. 7). Rather, the builder undertook steps to reduce the risk itself. For duties such as providing a safe and productive work environment (see Exod. 21; Prov. 31:15; Eph. 6:9) and caring for our environment (see Gen. 2:15), there may be some proper applications of insurance. Nevertheless, these duties cannot be fully discharged by simply protecting against financial losses from a breach of those duties. Workers' compensation and general liability insurance covering pollution damage are wise protections in a business sense. However, our biblical obligations extend further to take precautions consistent with our duties to care for others.

In addition, an excessive tendency to deal with everything in purely financial terms can cause a breakdown in human relationships and in the insurance system itself. This factor is evidenced from time to time in insurance "crises" when industry segments, or activities, develop particularly adverse experience.

Although insurance is not the sole method of preparing wisely against future hazards, it has become increasingly effective due to changes in societal and economic structures over the past two thousand years. These changes have become more pronounced since the advent of the industrial revolution. Among the major changes still occurring are the following:

Urbanization
As the United States approached the end of the eighteenth century, it remained a nation of farmers with only five percent of the population in urban areas. As late as 1900, only about forty percent of the American population lived in cities. By the 1970s, however, the statistics had nearly reversed from those at the nation's birth. Only five percent of Americans lived on farms. Moreover, by 1985 only half of all employed farm residents reported farming as their primary occupation.

Increased Mobility
Between March 1984 and March 1985, 46.5 million Americans (20.2 percent of the population) moved from one house or apartment to another. While most people did not move far, this high mobility obviously strains the stability of basic human networks.

Increased Information Flow
An average businessperson working for thirty years uses up more than one million sheets of paper weighing 8,500 pounds. More than 120

million checks are cleared daily by the banking system. More than thirty-five billion pieces of paper are processed each year in the United States. Moreover, the rate of this information explosion is increasing. Over seventy-five percent of all information recorded by mankind has been written in the last twenty years. Our addition to this information base is now over seventy-five billion items annually. In 1986 alone, more than forty-two thousand new books were available in United States markets.

These changes have also intensified the depersonalization of society. Thus, when a catastrophic loss occurs, the support available from social and family networks has diminished.

The technological changes accompanying these social and economic changes compound the practical difficulties for the wise twentieth-century steward who seeks to anticipate and prepare for risks. Consider, for example, some headlines of the eighties:

July 18, 1981—Kansas City, Missouri—Hyatt Regency Hotel—two concrete and steel aerial walkways collapse leaving 113 dead, another 186 injured.

December 3, 1984—Bhopal, India—Union Carbide Plant—the toxic gas methyl isocyanate used in pesticide production escapes into the surrounding community killing more than 2,000. Another 150,000 suffer from various degrees of injury.

January 28, 1986—Cape Canaveral, Florida—the *Challenger* space shuttle mission is ended by a tragic explosion less than two minutes after takeoff. All seven crew members, including the nation's first "teacher in space," are killed.

April 16, 1986—Soviet Ukraine—an explosion rocks the Chernobyl Nuclear Reactor Number 4 killing at least 31 and requiring the evacuation of more than 135,000 from the surrounding area. Damage and contamination from the disaster may continue into the twenty-first century.

As illustrated by these examples, the same technology that has contributed to our material prosperity has also increased the complexity and severity of the risks we face. Many times the risks of our industrial society extend to persons who have no association with the activity that gives rise to the hazard (as in the Bhopal and Chernobyl disasters). Insurance, with its uniform monetary base, becomes for such risks the only practical common denominator with which to anticipate and prepare for such losses.

Additionally, with our movement away from an agrarian economy, a larger percentage of our assets being protected are financial in nature. In the Old Testament economy, land was the primary source of sustenance and the major resource in the production process. Then, only an extraordinarily rare disaster, natural or manmade, would produce more than temporary loss in the value of that resource. The Old Testament economic structure placed ownership of land in family groups and provided for its periodic redistribution to overcome the impact of losses due to either mismanagement or external hardship. Terra firma thus provided stability economically as well as physically. Many of today's modern urban dwellers, on the other hand, are far removed from this primary natural resource. Changes from the land-based economy of biblical times are striking. By 1984, farmland (the primary productive asset of the agrarian economy of earlier ages) accounted for less than five percent of our nation's wealth.

With money as the primary means of exchange to support our increasing trade of goods and services, the rise of insurance to provide monetary resources to deal with various perils is understandable. As our society has progressed through the major economic changes outlined above, the purchasing power of monetary insurance settlements has provided an increasingly meaningful substitute for resources lost to life's perils. Further, since data are essential to evaluating and predicting risks, the advent of the Information Age has made application of insurance to more and more endeavors technologically feasible and increasingly efficient.

For our purpose of considering application of insurance, which is consistent with spiritual principles, to financial planning, insurance may be classified into four major areas. The first is *casualty insurance*. Casualty insurance provides a dollar payment in the event of loss of an asset. This type of insurance has the most direct application to natural perils such as the flooding referenced in Jesus' parable (see Matt. 7). In the event of such loss, casualty insurance is designed to provide funds to compensate for the loss or replace the lost asset.

The next broad category is *liability insurance*, which provides for payment to third parties for breach of a legal duty owed them by the insured. Perhaps the most common example is automobile liability insurance.

The underlying legal concept of fairly compensating others for injuries has scriptural roots (see, for example, Exod. 21–22). Regrettably, the complexity of our legal system has grown along with the complexity of our economy. Simple rules of restitution such as those found in Exod. 22:14-15 are no longer the sole controlling legal principles governing legal duties. Additionally, within our mechanized society, the hazards we face have become so diverse that for all but the most wealthy, insurance is the only realistic way to prepare wisely for such foreseeable dangers.

The operation of liability insurance in relationship to the American legal system produces a conflict with scriptural principles for which a solution is not yet widely available. Many liability coverages provide for the costs of legal defense as well as indemnification against the potential claim itself. A common covenant in such coverage, however, is the agreement of the insured to allow the insurance company to control the course of litigation. And casualty insurance policies often contain mandatory provisions that the insured permit the insurer to have the rights to sue others on account of any losses incurred (i.e., "subrogation rights"). That insurance may cause an individual to lose control of his or her claim runs the risk of violating the scriptural guidelines in Matthew 18 and 1 Corinthians 6 for resolution of disputes among believers.

Happily, arbitration and similar procedures are gaining favor within the insurance community. With the effort of the Christian Legal Society and other organizations to offer a biblical means of resolving disputes among believers, there may be opportunity to find alternatives more consistent with the scriptural pattern. Nevertheless, with the common contractual obligation to allow the insurance company to control the course of defense or subrogation matters in litigation, scriptural considerations may create conflicts for believers, particularly where other Christians are involved in the dispute.

Automobile liability insurance illustrates an additional factor to be considered by the Christian in making personal decisions under the guidance of scriptural principles. Often our decision-making alternatives for insurance are limited as a result of other choices. Many states, for example, have financial responsibility laws, which require threshold coverages as a condition for lawful operation of a vehicle. The Christian who chooses to own and operate a vehicle may be duty-bound to maintain the requisite insurance in order to maintain proper obedience to legitimate governmental authority.

Similarly, in connection with lending transactions (for example, the mortgage on a residence or business property) an agreement to maintain one or more types of insurance coverage is part of standard loan documentation. Thus, the wise scriptural observation that the "borrower is servant to the lender" (Prov. 22:7) is at work. The Christian, having entered into the loan transaction, is required to keep commitments made to secure the loan (see, for example, Gal. 3:15).

Obligations of mandatory coverage extend to many relationships in our society (e.g., workers' compensation in employment, fire and extended hazard insurance in real estate mortgages, and automobile liability insurance in transportation). These factors are not altogether negative since many times believers as well as nonbelievers are helped to make wise decisions by such external discipline.

The third broad category of insurance protection consists of *prepaid benefit plans*. Many health insurance programs can be placed in this category as well as plans that carry the label "prepaid," such as prepaid legal services programs. Next to retirement spending, health expenditures constitute the largest single component of private and governmental expenditure on personal financial security. More than $300 billion was spent for this purpose in 1986, and the rate of growth in this segment has been very high due to the effects of inflation and the expanding technological alternatives available for health care. The expansion of health care options and the corresponding increase in costs have been dramatic in the last fifty years. As late as 1942, expenditures for funeral observances in the United States outstripped those for hospitals and sanitariums. By 1986, however, annual per capita health care costs exceeded $1,620.

Health insurance provides the tool to manage the fluctuations in health care costs, which otherwise might wreak havoc with an individual's or a family's budgeting effort. It also applies general principles of risk pooling (which are common to all insurance plans) to this aspect of planning to meet the needs of dependents. The positive feature of risk pooling through insurance will be discussed in greater detail below.

With the rise of third-party payment through insurance, sobering questions of medical ethics and quality of life become intertwined with the economic aspects of health insurance. Health insurance can relieve the family from having to make cruel choices about care for medical needs based on economic factors. At the same time, this uncoupling of purchasing and spending decisions may contribute to unproductive waste in the health care system. Finally, in the later stages of life, Christians must wrestle with issues about the frailty of life and the practical twentieth-century dilemma medical care presents in light of Paul's exclamation: "For to me, to live is Christ and to die is gain" (Phil. 1:21). Here insurance may be helpful in drawing the focus away from financial considerations so that clearer moral choices can be made about extraordinary life support efforts.

Life insurance and *disability insurance* represent the fourth major category of coverage. These coverages generally are designed to protect against the disruption to the family from loss of income in the event of a wage earner's death or disability. The concept of provision for basic family living needs is central to several themes of Scripture. Thus, these coverages embrace additional scriptural principles.

On January 11, 1759, a business was started by two Presbyterian preachers from Ireland and a Philadelphian judge. They received a charter from the Commonwealth of Pennsylvania for "The Corporation for the Relief of Poor and Distressed Presbyterian Ministers and of the Poor and Distressed Widows and Children of Presbyterian Ministers." The granting of this corporate charter marked the formation of the nation's oldest life insurance company, now the Presbyterian Ministers Fund. The founders sought application of more disciplined business principles to a heartfelt desire to respond practically to the scriptural injunction: "Bear ye one another's burdens, and so fulfill the law of Christ" (Gal. 6:2, KJV).

Similar scriptural motivation lay behind the formation in 1885 of the Christian Burden Bearers Association, which subsequently evolved into Christian Mutual Life. Christian Burden Bearers began with a minister who encountered a unanimous affirmative response from fifty fellow pastors to contribute one dollar to provide for burial of their colleague in Portsmouth, New Hampshire. The motivation of the Association's founders was evident in the statement of purpose contained in its constitution:

> The object of this Association is to promote unsectarian work on all Gospel lines. . . . This Association institutes Local Branches with which all Christians can consistently unite in a conformity with the laws of God and of man, and at the same time make a systematic and united Christian effort to relieve from financial embarrassment such persons who are legally specified by, and dependent upon its members in the event of their death.

This Christian focus was evident in the formation of several life insurance companies in the eighteenth and nineteenth centuries. Founders of these organizations often were engaged in other business enterprises. At times, the life insurance activity was conducted as a part-time business on a not-for-profit basis or as a fraternal benefit related to other charitable work. Today we ask the question of how scriptural principles can guide our involvement in life insurance. These industry pioneers found in the risk-sharing principles of insurance an application to help the Church respond to its scriptural duties of provision in an orderly way.

The concept of pooling of risks, of course, is the central principle of insurance. Risk pooling provides that, through common enterprise, all will share to a small extent in the burden of major losses. Thereby, the small number of individuals actually affected by the losses that will occur can be afforded some method of protection.

Risk pooling in this generic fashion was present in many cultures long before the beginning of the commercial practice of insurance. As early as three thousand years before the birth of Christ, for example, the Chinese shared river transportation risks. Before passing the dangerous Yangtze River rapids, merchant shippers would spread the chance of loss. Instead of having each merchant concentrate goods in one or two boats, they would break the cargo into smaller packets and distribute a small portion of each merchant's cargo ahead of the rapids and then recover the bulk of the shipment that successfully passed through the hazard as the boats were again assembled downstream. The practical wisdom of spreading risks is reflected in the inspired writings of King Solomon: "Give portions to seven, yes to eight, for you do not know what disaster may come upon the land" (Eccles. 11:2).

The intense sense of community prevalent among the early Christians caused them to extend their sharing beyond obvious short-term risks like those facing the Chinese shippers. The early Church responded to help one another meet life's needs broadly:

> All the believers were one in heart and mind. No one claimed that any of his possessions were his own, but they shared everything they had. . . . There were no needy persons among them. For from time to time those who owned lands or houses sold them, brought the money from the sales and put it at the apostles' feet and it was distributed to anyone as he had need. (Acts 4:32-35)

It is evident from Jesus' extensive teaching on finances that the attitude toward money reflects the heart's condition toward God. Thus, as encouraging as was the generous example of Barnabas in selling a field he owned and bringing the money for distribution by the apostles (see Acts 4:36-37), the spontaneous exercise of this type of economic sharing posed risk to the early Church. Acts 5 reports the tragedy of the deceit of Ananias and Sapphira. Peter confirmed that they were under no obligation to follow Barnabas's example. Their deceit in holding back a portion of the price revealed their unspiritual attitude toward God. Their deception, if unchecked, could have undermined the financial base and also drained spiritual strength from the early Church community.

The mandate of Galatians 6:2 to "bear ye one another's burdens, and so fulfill the law of Christ" (KJV) is echoed in numerous passages of Scripture. Jesus' teaching concerning separation of the sheep and the goats emphasizes the importance of our sensitivity to the basic material needs of others (see Matt. 25:31-46). James's sharp rebuke reminds us that ignoring the physical needs of others is evidence of a dead faith:

Suppose a brother or sister is without clothes and daily food. If one of you says to him, "Go, I wish you well; keep warm and well fed," but does nothing about his physical needs, what good is it? In the same way, faith by itself, if it is not accompanied by action, is dead. (James 2:15-17)

Our duty to assist one another is especially strong with respect to fellow believers: "Therefore, as we have opportunity, let us do good to all people, especially to those who belong to the family of believers" (Gal. 6:10). Moreover, this care for the physical needs of others is of particular spiritual significance when directed toward orphans and widows: "Religion that God our Father accepts as pure and faultless is this: to look after orphans and widows in their distress and to keep oneself from being polluted by the world" (James 1:27).

Jesus' own life example forcefully brings home to us this point. As He approached the climax of His redemptive work at Calvary, our Lord turned to His beloved disciple John to make sure that John would take responsibility for the needs of Jesus' mother:

When Jesus saw his mother there, and the disciple whom he loved standing nearby, he said to his mother, "Dear woman, here is your son," and to the disciple, "Here is your mother." From that time on, this disciple took her into his home. (John 19:26-27)

Indeed, the Scriptures are replete with passages emphasizing God's special concern for widows and orphans and the value of our being available to minister to them:

Exod. 22:22-24	Deut. 26:12	Ps. 68:5	Jer. 22:3
Lev. 22:13	Deut. 27:19	Ps. 82:3	Jer. 49:11
Deut. 10:18	Job 24:9	Ps. 146:9	Mal. 3:5
Deut. 14:29	Job 29:12	Prov. 15:25	Luke 20:47
Deut. 24:17	Job 31:16-21	Prov. 23:10	James 1:27
Deut. 24:19-21	Ps. 10:14	Isa. 1:17-23	
Deut. 25:5	Ps. 10:18	Jer. 7:6	

Practical implementation of care for widows and orphans, however, can be marred by administrative difficulties. Following the report of Ananias and Sapphira in Acts is the record of murmuring related to the discord between the Grecian and the Hebraic Jews concerning the daily distribution of food to widows. The matter had become so serious that the apostles perceived their attention to the ministry of the Word of God to be in jeopardy (see Acts 6:2).

Proper balance in meeting the needs of widows was of such importance that Paul devoted a substantial portion of his first letter of instruction to Timothy to this topic. Paul strongly stated that the primary responsibility for such provision is with the immediate family: "If anyone does not provide for his relatives, and especially for his immediate family, he has denied the faith and is worse than an unbeliever" (1 Tim. 5:8).

Despite the duties of the Church to provide a caring network to support the physical as well as the spiritual needs of those within the community of believers, we as Christian individuals carry a special burden with respect to our family members. As is evident by the context of 1 Timothy 5, this is not just because of the believer's natural affection and obligation for those in his or her care. Individual action relieves the broader community of believers from having to pick up responsibilities for those who have mismanaged their funds. The Church's efforts can concentrate on those who are "really in need" (1 Tim. 5:5).

The word *provide* in 1 Timothy 5:8 encompasses continuing duties, which may extend beyond one's lifetime. Life insurance, of course, provides an ideal vehicle for discharge of this individual responsibility. It accomplishes the pooling of assets in the spirit of Acts 4. By sharing the burden (see Gal. 6:2), every person can assist the few for whom death creates hardship from the loss of income of the breadwinner. It also provides a ready vehicle for responsible individual action to discharge the scriptural duty of 1 Timothy 5:8. By operating under orderly administration with sound business principles, it can lessen the financial disputes surrounding the care for widows and orphans so that the other ministries of the Church will not be impaired.

We also need to be sure that other "religious" activity does not stand in the way of the discharge of this duty (see Matt. 15:3-9). The Old Testament economic order made provision for widows, orphans, and others similarly in need by consciously leaving something from the harvest in the fields (see Deut. 24:19-21). In view of economic and social changes of the last two centuries, such a method is no longer adequate. Life insurance provides a meaningful substitute for the agrarian plan of Deuteronomy consistent with our current money-based urbanized economic culture. It is little wonder, then, that godly church leaders at the start of the industrial revolution looked to the principles of insurance to help the church and its members meet this obligation.

The response of twentieth-century believers to our obligation "to provide" again requires a balanced understanding of the division of responsibilities between ourselves and our heavenly Father. Jesus teaches that matters of material provision for basic needs should not cause us to worry about the future:

"Therefore I tell you, do not worry about your life, what you will eat or drink; or about your body, what you will wear. Is not life more important than food, and the body more important than clothes? Look at the birds of the air; they do not sow or reap or store away in barns, and yet your heavenly Father feeds them. Are you not much more valuable than they? Who of you by worrying can add a single hour to his life?

"And why do you worry about clothes? See how the lilies of the field grow. They do not labor or spin. Yet I tell you that not even Solomon in all his splendor was dressed like one of these. If that is how God clothes the grass of the field, which is here today and tomorrow is thrown into the fire, will he not much more clothe you, O you of little faith? So do not worry, saying, 'What shall we eat?' or 'What shall we drink?' or 'What shall we wear?' For the pagans run after all these things, and your heavenly Father knows that you need them. But seek first his kingdom and his righteousness, and all these things will be given to you as well. Therefore do not worry about tomorrow, for tomorrow will worry about itself. Each day has enough trouble of its own." (Matt. 6:25-34)

Material things should not become the focus of our life's energy and devotion. Rather, our first priority must be to serve God. This focus, however, does not remove our responsibility to use our God-given strengths, abilities, and resources to provide for our needs. Paul summarized this principle for the benefit of the Church (and for the benefit of those employable individuals who would presume upon God or His Church for their sustenance): "For even when we were with you, we gave you this rule: 'If man will not work, he shall not eat'" (2 Thess. 3:10).

Further, the availability of life insurance to enable persons with dependents to meet these continuing obligations has added significance in light of the increasing affluence that has accompanied the industrialization of America. Tragically, despite our rising affluence, the personal savings rate of Americans has been steadily declining to one of the lowest in the industrialized world. Our consumption-oriented culture encourages us to spend *all* (and—through credit card and other debt—more than *all*) we earn on current consumption. Yet, Scripture teaches that resources beyond our basic current needs may be given to us for other purposes. First, we may be simply a conduit through which resources are made available to meet the needs of others. Second, present resources may be entrusted to us to meet future needs of ourselves and our dependents.

In Proverbs 6:6-8 we are given the simple but powerful example of the ant from nature:

Go to the ant, you sluggard;
    consider its ways and be wise!
It has no commander,
    no overseer or ruler,
yet it stores its provisions in summer
    and gathers its food at harvest.

The ant's setting aside small sums during the productive season to meet the needs of a later unproductive season illustrates the basic principle of financial planning. In Genesis 41, this example is repeated for us on a grand scale. There the wisdom of God is revealed to Pharaoh through God's servant Joseph. The abundance of Egypt during the seven years of bountiful harvest was systematically saved and preserved for the seven years of need that followed.

Life insurance applies the Proverbs 6 and Genesis 41 principles in monetary terms to respond to other scriptural exhortations. It enables an individual to anticipate the risks of death, take small amounts from excess resources beyond those required to meet basic needs during the years of good health and productive earnings, and set them aside to meet the obligations of 1 Timothy 5:8. In this way, a breadwinner can provide continuing care for the family should his or her earned income be disrupted by death or disability. Particularly for young families, it is often the only practical means in our current money-based economic system to meet such needs.

Lessons from the ant and the godly plan implemented through Joseph also have direct bearing on another focus of financial planning: retirement. One can well debate whether the American concept of retirement is consistent with the scriptural view of old age. Nevertheless, our current economic structure, for most Americans, presents fewer income opportunities for those of retirement age. Accordingly, these biblical principles need to be implemented to prepare for the economic impact of retirement.

Life insurance is only one of many savings vehicles that can be used to prepare for retirement needs. As such, it should be evaluated along with other investment alternatives in order to develop a balanced plan. Through annuity contracts, insurance companies provide a means of investing and disbursing retirement benefits to help clients protect against other risks. Guaranteed lifetime incomes can protect against retirement income losses and also against the financial risk of "living too long." By guaranteeing income for life, such contracts reduce financial risk at a stage in life when many individuals have a strong motivation to minimize risk taking. Often, annuity programs are sponsored by Christian organizations. They can be combined with charitable giving plans not only to care for the income needs of the retiree but also to further the retiree's lifetime interests by careful preservation of any remaining funds for ministry purposes.

Thus, we can see clear scriptural guidance to encourage prudent application of insurance in response to scriptural mandates (1) to anticipate and prepare for future risks and (2) to provide for the needs of our dependents, particularly widows and orphans. Many individuals have difficulty confronting the reality of these needs, particularly as they relate to their own mortality. As believers, we can more readily embrace the uncertainty of this life given the counsel of Scripture:

> Do not boast about tomorrow,
>   for you do not know what a day may bring forth. (Prov. 27:1)

> Why, you do not even know what will happen tomorrow. What is your life? You are a mist that appears for a little while and then vanishes. (James 4:14)

We can humbly prepare for the future while remaining safely under the protection of our heavenly Father who controls the universe.

In addition to the broad themes of Scripture considered above in their application to insurance, numerous specific concepts may be helpful in maximizing the spiritual effectiveness of our insurance programs. Because of budget pressures on young families, low price often becomes a major consideration in life insurance purchasing decisions, particularly during the family's early child-bearing years. The heavy weight given to cost at that time makes sense in light of the large insurance amounts needed to provide for income for a long period of potential dependence of newborn children. Industry statistics show, however, that more than ninety percent of claims paid on adults are paid on individuals above age fifty-five. Nearly eighty percent of claims are for deaths that occur over age sixty-five, and fifty percent over age seventy-five. Rates are low at early ages for term insurance because few claims are paid on those policies. Indeed, because of increasing cost of coverage, term policies generally are discontinued well before they reach the point where payments are likely to be made. We know, except for those of us who may greet the Lord at His return, that "it is appointed unto men once to die" (Heb. 9:27, KJV). We should take into account provisions for proper burial:

> A man may have a hundred children and live many years; yet no matter how long he lives, if he cannot enjoy his prosperity and does not receive proper burial, I say that a stillborn child is better off than he. (Eccles. 6:3)

Statistics show that very few of our elderly carry meaningful cash reserves into retirement. Accordingly, in anticipation of this known risk that carries a 100 percent probability of occurring (only the time is unknown), it makes sense to have at least a portion of an individual's insurance plan in permanent insurance, which will be available for burial and short-term cash needs at the time of death.

Although modest lump-sum cash reserves for final expenses are a sound part of wise planning, a large lump-sum insurance settlement intended to provide for basic needs of food, clothing, and shelter over a long period of time can instead become a snare:

> An inheritance quickly gained at the beginning
> will not be blessed at the end. (Prov. 20:21)

> Godliness with contentment is great gain. . . . But if we have food and clothing, we will be content with that. People who want to get rich fall into temptation and a trap and into many foolish and harmful desires that plunge men into ruin and destruction. For the love of money is a root of all kinds of evil. Some people, eager for money, have wandered from the faith and pierced themselves with many griefs. (1 Tim. 6:6, 8-10)

It would be a tragedy if an individual seeking to meet family obligations in accordance with 1 Timothy 5:8 produced the unwanted negative spiritual effect of laying a trap for his or her family. Regrettably, that seems to be exactly what happens in many cases. Although income replacement is a primary need motivating insurance purchases for young families, less than eight percent of all benefits are paid out in regular income payments. Over ninety percent of benefits intended to meet basic long-term living needs of dependents are instead paid as a large lump-sum amount.

The parable of the prodigal son (see Luke 15:11-32), though not directed to this point, illustrates forcefully the danger of the common practice of paying out large income protection settlements in lump sums. The immature son's early receipt of his inheritance led to wasteful dissipation of the fruit of his father's labor (and to the son's rapid degeneration to a keeper of pigs). Therefore, the individual who loves his or her family and prudently prepares for the risk of death would be well advised to prepare also for the contingencies of creditor claims and the temptation and demands that large lump-sum settlements may place on that family. These strains are often most intense around the time of death, when judgment of the survivors is clouded by their grief. Insurance planning can easily accomplish, at little or no additional expense, a structuring of the benefits or protection of the proceeds through a trust or similar device.

Benefits can be disbursed in small increments to meet the basic living needs of family members over the intended period of time.

One other aspect of good stewardship in insurance is somewhat disguised as a result of the nature of the insurance business. Insurance involves implicit investment programs, particularly where savings elements such as retirement planning are involved. In 1987, for example, net investments by United States life insurance companies totaled approximately $100 billion. This was the third largest source, among private domestic institutions, of funds for United States capital markets.

The Scriptures teach us to be consistent and thorough in our practice: "And whatever you do, whether in word or deed, do it all in the name of the Lord Jesus, giving thanks to God the Father through him" (Col. 3:17). Since our resources are being used to support various industries through our insurance programs, we should seek, wherever possible, companies whose investment practices are consistent with our beliefs. Just as we would not invest directly in a company, for example, that produces child pornography, we would not want to support indirectly such an industry through investments backing our insurance programs.

Our analysis to this point has focused on how scriptural understanding can guide insurance decisions. An interesting byproduct of the growth of the insurance industry is the development of detailed mortality information, which affirms the wisdom of Scripture. Although many life insurance companies in the United States had their origin in a response to the New Testament command to bear one another's burdens, few companies have retained their Christian distinctives. All of these distinctly Christian companies, however, have maintained favorable mortality rates. The statistics confirm God's promise in Psalm 91:

> "Because he loves me," says the LORD, "I will rescue him;
>   I will protect him, for he acknowledges my name.
> He will call upon me, and I will answer him;
>   I will be with him in trouble,
>   I will deliver him and honor him.
> With long life will I satisfy him
>   and show him my salvation." (vv. 14-16)

Practicing Christians seem to enjoy noticeably superior mortality experience.

Increasing medical understanding has heightened our awareness of the Christian lifestyle's contribution to longevity. Because of scriptural instructions concerning the body as the temple of the Holy Spirit and strong admonitions against drunkenness, many Christians have avoided the use of tobacco products and restricted the use of alcoholic beverages to moderation or total abstinence. Insurance industry statistics demonstrate the strong positive impact those practices have on mortality.

Medical science has discovered more about the effect of stress on aggravating or precipitating many chronic diseases. Believers who understand promises of Scripture such as the following have the benefit of much lower stress levels in daily life:

And we know that in all things God works for the good of those who love him, who have been called according to his purpose. (Rom. 8:28)

Cast all your anxiety on him because he cares for you. (1 Pet. 5:7)

Moreover, support through the community of believers reinforces these truths. A University of California study in the 1970s reported that it provides the first strong scientific evidence to link social and community ties to mortality rates and perhaps to an overall resistance to disease. In short, the study found that people live longer and are healthier if they enjoy good social ties attendant to social and religious groups. What a wonderful byproduct of active involvement in a caring local church!

One way support from a caring local church body helps is through the intercessory prayers of fellow believers to speed recovery from acute medical problems. In the July 1988 *Southern Medical Journal*, Dr. Randolph C. Byrd reported on the effects of prayer on recovery of coronary care unit patients. Using a controlled double-blind randomized protocol, he studied the differences in treatment course for patients who received intercessory prayer from believers. Those patients had a significantly lower severity score for their hospital course than patients who did not receive the added prayer support. According to Dr. Byrd, the prayed-for patients "had less congestive heart failure, required less diuretic and antibiotic therapy, had fewer episodes of pneumonia, had fewer cardiac arrests, and were less frequently intubated and ventilated." His study further evidences the important role that the local church can play to help believers avoid difficulties and also to assist believers through hard times.

Finally, a recent study of twenty-seven thousand Seventh-Day Adventists found dramatically superior mortality statistics, which confirmed the positive effect of combining moderate dietary habits with a conservative lifestyle. The average thirty-five-year-old male Adventist had a life expectancy of eighty-two, or nine years more than the average Californian generally. For females, life expectancy of the church group was 7.6 years longer. Researchers attributed these significant differences to the healthy lifestyle encouraged by efforts to apply scriptural principles to daily living practices.

The growth of insurance has paralleled the growth in monetary assets in our economy because the two factors are related. As more and more economic activity became money based, the need for monetary protection against risks that accompanied industrialization increased. The wisdom of Scripture is evident as we see how it gives balance to today's insurance decisions, which clearly were not considered by the human instruments of God's written revelation.

Insurance is but one means whereby we can respond to scriptural mandates to anticipate and prepare for future risks and to provide for our families. With all the information available to assess risk, insurance has become an increasingly efficient means for spreading those risks. Insurance permits us to address well the financial aspects of loss. When this care is directed toward our dependents, it reflects a loving choice in favor of *their* future needs over *our* current consumption.

A sound insurance program established by wise individual choices can also help the broader Christian community. In relieving the Church of economic burdens for those with adequate family resources, we must not lose sight of those who do not have such resources. At the same time, even when the financial aspect of loss has been adequately compensated, the ministry of the Church in supporting individuals through the grief process and caring for nonmaterial needs should not be forgotten. In light of the scriptural teaching and the pattern of the early Church, our increasing effectiveness in buffering financial risks should not cause us to place greater value on the financial aspects of life. Rather, it should enable us to channel more of our energies into the service of our heavenly Father, fellow believers, and others.

Applying the wisdom of Scripture to personal insurance decisions, therefore, can have a meaningful spiritual dimension in strengthening and focusing the ministry of the Body of Christ. We need to apply the counsel of Scripture with a servant's attitude cultivated by a daily walk with our heavenly Father. This is one way in which we can more fully seek the Lord's best will for us:

> He showed you, O man, what is good.
>   And what does the LORD require of you?
> To act justly and to love mercy
>   and to walk humbly with your God. (Mic. 6:8)

EDITOR'S PERSPECTIVE

Fred Potter mentioned two problems in the insurance industry that have become quite troublesome (litigation with regard to liability claims, and third-party payments for prepaid health benefits), but since developing a discussion of them was not his assignment, he left this task to me. We need to be sensitized to them so that we can act in ways pleasing to our Lord when we encounter them.

The biblical concept of liability is closely tied to the notion that there must be an identifiable person who *deserves to be blamed* or held responsible for a specific personal or property loss before that loss can be assigned to anybody. If there is no such identifiable party, the injured person must suffer the loss. While it may be argued that this is still generally the case (on the law books), few will argue with the fact that the legal profession and sympathetic juries have expanded the biblical notion of liability to include one's ability to pay (having "deep pockets"), independent of one's culpability. (Dr. John Sparks has a good discussion of this very point in chapter 13.)

The fear of having to pay unjust claims has greatly expanded the market's demand for higher limits for liability insurance and added significantly to the cost of such insurance. For example, many citizens now purchase "umbrella liability" coverage so that should the upper limits of their basic coverage be exhausted in a lawsuit, they will still be protected. But Christians can also face serious temptations when they are injured and encouraged to get whatever award the market will bear rather than assess their contribution to the loss or consider what is fair.

For example, some years ago a couple I know received word that their youngest son had broken his neck in an off-highway vehicular accident and was permanently paralyzed from the neck down. Financial reality descended on them all in a hurry. The young man had no personal health or accident insurance—plenty to cover others he might injure, but none on himself. He spent thirty-one days in intensive care in a hospital and underwent two major operations, both requiring bone grafts from his hip and lower leg. Following his hospital stay, he was sent to a specialty rehabilitation hospital for ninety days where the average daily cost of care was $1,100. (The average additional lifetime medical expenses associated with his particular kind of injury exceeds $440,000.)

The owner of the vehicle and the person on whose property the accident occurred had $100,000 of liability coverage. Would a jury award a young quadriplegic $100,000 in such a case? Should the case be taken to court? The truth is, the financial figures and situation outlined above are not even germane to Scripture's primary concern about personal liability—who is at fault? But the information helps us understand the financial pressures that can lead people to rationalize litigation that may not be particularly concerned with upholding the biblical principles of justice. The desire to protect ourselves financially can give birth to a lot of self-protective rationalizing that may cloud our thinking and allow us to justify (to ourselves) our intentions to disassociate ourselves from the blame due us. Adam did this when he blamed God for creating Eve and for giving her to him. Adam also blamed Eve for taking the forbidden fruit. He assumed no voluntary responsibility (see Gen. 3:12).

In the situation just described, there were no threats between the insured and the injured parties and no suits; all involved agreed to a merciful and amiable financial arrangement. But the insurance company revealed, after the agreement was reached, that a great deal of their thinking had been based on the projected legal costs if a suit had been filed and the probability of their being able to convince a jury that their client was not liable under the circumstances. Justice was not at the center of their thinking.

Christians, of course, are found on both sides of such cases. Sometimes we are the injured party; sometimes we are the insured party. God desires justice, though. That is why He has provided us with the culpability requirements so essential to the administration of justice. The world, in our day, is abandoning God's standards once again, and we Christians cannot stick our heads in the sand like ostriches and ignore the potential liability we face in the world. Our stewardship responsibilities require that we act prudently. But neither can we take advantage of the opportunity to "benefit" from the world's perversions when we are the potential recipients of the financial awards. We have an obligation to live by God's standards. We have a responsibility to seek, in a godly way and on godly terms, what is due us when we are due justice. We are not to walk in the ways of the world and seek what is not rightfully ours, even if the system of justice is perverted and will grant us unjust awards.

The second problem disturbing the insurance industry today is in the area of prepaid health benefits coverage where third-party payments have become dominant—employers pay the insurance premiums, insurance companies pay the medical bills, and the person insured ends up with little incentive to be financially cautious regarding medical care. Three troubling issues arise in this area. The first is almost identical to the liability/litigation issue just discussed. The number of malpractice suits being brought against physicians drive them to practice defensive medicine. They run more diagnostic tests, which in turn drives medical costs up substantially. Because third-party payments dominate the health insurance field, patients are less likely to be concerned about escalating costs when their employers are paying the health insurance premiums.

Second, the quality of life issues associated with severe injuries and the irreversible infirmities of the elderly are also exacerbated by fears of malpractice suits and the third-party payment procedures already described. These two forces, combined with the emotional circumstances associated with a serious accident or the illness of an elderly loved one, can assert enormous pressures on people to take every possible step to preserve a person's life, even when the person under treatment would not want "heroic measures" taken. As hard as it may sound, third-party payments for insurance often shield families from the necessity of facing and making some very difficult but morally appropriate decisions. The mere presence of available technology to preserve life is not, in itself, sufficient grounds for using it. The Christian may not take a conscious action to shorten the natural life of anybody, but the medical profession presents us with various ethical knots to untie as we face the issues associated with using or not using the medical technology that can sustain vital body functions long beyond the time the natural body could sustain them on its own. The moral, emotional, and financial pressures are horrendous in this area.

The last issue directly related to the very high medical costs associated with advancing medical technology is the pressure put on medical professionals to become respectors of persons from a utilitarian (financial) point of view. Everyday medical professionals make decisions about service and hospital admittance on the basis of who can pay and who is perceived to have the greatest chance of continuing to make a viable contribution to society. Ability to pay grows in importance as the financial pressures grow to be able to pay for the high-tech medical equipment that includes x-rays, CAT scans, radiation and chemotherapy, and others. For financial reasons, this equipment needs to be fully utilized.

Risk management, as undertaken through the utilization of insurance, is becoming more entangled with moral questions as litigation increases in all areas of business. A whole book could be written solely on product and service liability problems. Christians have an opportunity to make an impact in all these areas, however, if in no other way than by acting in a biblically responsible way when they are directly affected.

PART XII

INVESTING: A PART OF STEWARDSHIP

Almost everyone is an investor. If you save any portion of your income, you are an investor. Putting money in your sock is a form of investing—a negative form to be sure, for all potential earnings on it are forgone. The stewarding of a surplus (any amount that exceeds current needs) requires a management decision—leave the surplus in the checking account to draw interest, transfer the surplus to a savings account, buy a United States treasury note, invest it in real estate, buy common stocks, start a business, and so forth.

Because investing cannot really be avoided by most people, it behooves Christians to take the time to ponder God's instructions regarding the subject. God's help in this area is most often discovered in the wisdom literature where an appeal is made to prudence and good sense more than to specific moral principles. For example, it is unwise to provide surety for someone else's debt (obligate yourself to repay someone else's debt if he or she fails to), but it is not immoral to do so (see Prov. 6:1-5; 11:15; 17:18; 22:26-27).

Prudence—one's ability to act wisely, discreetly, practically, and soundly on the basis of real information—is commended throughout the wisdom literature in Scripture, so we ought to digest its instructions in order to be blessed rather than fleeced by our ignorance or by the deceptions of others who are either well intended or unscrupulous.

There are two great temptations to avoid when making investments. The first is the excessive fear of failure, which can easily cause a person to become imprudently conservative. A good example is the person in the parable of the talents who was given one talent of silver and buried it rather than put it in the bank to earn interest (see Matt. 25:14-30). Jesus used investing in that parable as the vehicle to emphasize our accountability for cultivating the spiritual gifts God

235

gives us. But investing money is the mirror image of this spiritual reality. Those who "bury" their investments either forfeit great opportunities to grow financially or are devastated by inflation (a long-term historic reality) so that the original capital is materially eroded.

The second temptation to be avoided is the belief that one can become rich by multiplying a little money into a great fortune through investing. The practical probability of this occurring, even if the person is knowledgeable about investments, is about one in fifty thousand. The reasons for this low probability are complex and many, but the two major ones are these: (1) forecasting the future is beyond the capacity of anyone, outside the range of prudent extrapolations (see Isa. 44:24-25; Ezek. 13:1-10; James 4:13-16); and (2) the number of times a small investment needs to be multiplied before it can become real wealth are so many that the opportunity to do this on a consistent basis, without some setbacks, mitigates against its being realized.

Great wealth is more normally acquired in one of four ways: (1) by discovering a natural resource (oil, ore, etc.) on land already in the individual's family; (2) by spending a lifetime developing a business to the point that the operations and earnings per share become attractive to others and the original owners can capitalize their earnings by selling the company's common stock for a market price five to ten times earnings; (3) by marrying a wealthy individual; or (4) by inheriting it.

Larry Burkett sets forth ten guides in this chapter that, if followed, will go a long way toward helping a sensible person construct a responsible investment plan. But even following these principles cannot guarantee success. Other factors (such as the *timing* of one's investment purchases and the *judgment* necessary to make specific investment choices) transcend our ability to teach others *when* to buy or *what* to buy. If we could do just these two things successfully, we could all be rich.

CHAPTER 12

BIBLICAL PRINCIPLES GOVERNING PERSONAL INVESTING

Larry Burkett

In 1976 Larry Burkett founded Christian Financial Concepts (CFC), a non-profit, nondenominational ministry dedicated to teaching God's principles of handling money. Its primary goal is training teachers and counselors to minister in their churches and communities through life-changing materials.

Larry has written eleven books on financial topics—his latest ones being The Complete Financial Guide For Young Couples *and* Debt-Free Living. *He also writes "How to Manage Your Money," a monthly Christian economic newsletter.*

One of the strongest tools CFC uses to reach others with God's principles of finance is Larry's daily radio ministry, including the five-minute program, "How to Manage Your Money," heard on almost 800 stations around the world, and "Money Matters," a live, thirty-minute call-in program, heard on more than 250 stations.

Larry and his wife, Judy, have been married for thirty-one years, and they have four grown children and four grandchildren. The Burketts currently live in Dahlonega, Georgia.

The most critical thing to remember about investing is that it is wrong to invest just for the sake of making money. Making money should be a byproduct of God's direction. Peace does not come through the accumulation of material possessions; if it did, the wealthiest people in the world would be the most at peace. Instead, they are often frustrated and miserable. True peace comes only from God. As Jesus said, "Peace I leave with you; My peace I give to you; not as the world gives, do I give to you. Let not your heart be troubled, nor let it be fearful" (John 14:27).

Another essential principle to remember when considering any type of investing is that we are to be stewards, literally, managers of another's property. More specifically, we are the managers of God's property. The Apostle Paul reminds us, "For we have brought nothing into the world, so we cannot take anything out of it either" (1 Tim. 6:7). It is not how much someone can accumulate that is significant, but how the resources are used.

FIND THE RIGHT BALANCE

To allow material assets to erode through bad management is not good stewardship. It is a sign of slothfulness and poor stewardship. But to simply multiply and store them without purpose constitutes hoarding, just as with the rich fool in Luke 12.

Investing is *not* unscriptural. In fact, in the parable of the talents recorded in Matthew 25:14-30, God gave according to each man's ability and directed each to manage his portion well. One was given five talents, one was given three talents, and one was given one talent to invest as God told each of them. Each was rewarded or punished in keeping with his stewardship.

Learning to invest according to God's principles increases the opportunities to help other people. That is the real purpose of investing: to increase our assets so that we can serve God more fully.

PURPOSES OF INVESTING

One legitimate purpose of an investment program is to achieve a greater degree of security, which can include investing to provide for education, an inheritance, retirement, and so forth. But many nonscriptural reasons for investing include greed, indulgence, and covetousness.

No single financial plan will fit every family. However, certain common principles apply to everyone. These have been distilled into ten keys or guidelines, and each one is rooted in financial principles in God's Word.

Key 1: Formulate clear-cut investment goals—No one should invest without having an ultimate purpose for the money. The purpose may be for education or retirement, but each investment should have a clear-cut financial goal.

Retirement goal—There is nothing wrong with retirement planning, provided that it is kept in balance. But in our society today, an eighteen-year-old goes out looking for a job with a good retirement plan. Many people look forward to retirement only because they hate the jobs they are in.

The long-range goal of retirement will vary depending on the age and income of every individual. For a twenty-five-year-old, the perspective should be long-range growth and flexibility (diversity) of investments. The amount needed to be invested each month or year will be significantly less than that required for someone age forty-five.

This same rule is true regardless of the long-range financial goal (retirement, education, etc.). The longer the time period in which to plan, the less initial money it takes. However, different criteria apply to long-range investing, including hedging against inflation, depression, financial collapse, and so forth. Therefore, the actual investments selected for retirement in, say, ten years would be different from those selected for retirement in thirty years.

A United States treasury bill paying seven percent may perfectly fit the retirement plan for a sixty-five-year-old widow and be totally inappropriate for a thirty-year-old attorney. This is true for the investments of any age group.

Proverbs 6:6-8 offers this advice:

Go to the ant, O sluggard,
Observe her ways and be wise,
Which, having no chief,
Officer or ruler,
Prepares her food in the summer,
And gathers her provision in the harvest.

Preservation goal—Someone inheriting $100,000 may desire to preserve those funds for a particular purpose at a later date, perhaps education, retirement, or charitable donation. Thus, someone starting out with $100,000 will have a different plan from a couple starting out from zero.

That is also the case for people who can put away sizable amounts from their current incomes. The majority of money that most high-income earners accumulate is earned through their primary profession. Most of what they lose is through speculative investments. Most high-income earners should focus on the preservation of capital with a reasonable degree of growth to keep the value of their money current. They do not need high-risk investments.

Education goals—Unlike those who are trying to preserve a windfall, an average-income family with the children's education in mind must think more in terms of growth, again depending on the amount available to invest and the duration it can be invested.

Assume, for instance, that a couple puts aside $1,000 a year for the education of their children, who will reach college age in ten years. The $10,000 they can save may not educate one child, much less two or three. So they are going to have to take additional risks to achieve the growth they need.

Income goal—A couple entering retirement and looking for maximum income to live on will likely have this objective. They need income, but they must also be concerned with the preservation of their assets. Once their needed income level is met, other assets can be invested to offset inflation.

Growth goal—Everyone would like to have investments grow. Growth strategy means that there is minimal immediate need for the funds but a sizable future need. Carried to the extreme, this strategy is called get rich quick, in which case it is unscriptural. Proverbs 28:22 warns, "A man with an evil eye hastens after wealth, and does not know that want will come upon him."

A growth goal would normally be the strategy of someone fifty years of age who is able to save $1,000 a year toward retirement. The short period of time (fifteen years) and the limited funds ($1,000 a year) dictate an aggressive growth strategy.

A couple with $10,000 to educate their children also needs an aggressive strategy that leans more toward risk taking than preservation.

Tax shelter goal—The sixth and final goal in investing is tax sheltering, which is very complex. Over the last few years, for all intents and purposes, the federal government's changes in the tax laws have virtually shut down tax shelters, other than depreciation and interest, for the average investor. It is often taught that paying interest is a good tax shelter. That is an old wives' tale. When people pay interest to save income tax, they lose and the lender gains.

However, depreciation and investment tax credits can be legitimate tax shelters. But when income tax is deferred through depreciation, eventually it must be recaptured. Most tax shelters do not really eliminate income tax; they only defer it to a later time.

For instance, money in a retirement plan, such as an IRA (individual retirement account), is an excellent tax shelter. But placing money in an IRA does not avoid the income taxes. They are merely deferred to a time later when the wage earner is in a lower tax category.

One final note about tax shelters. No investment should be selected solely for the tax benefits involved. Any good investment is eventually supposed to make money, and that is the true test of a good investment. Remember the caution of Proverbs 28:20: "A faithful man will abound with blessings, but he who makes haste to be rich will not go unpunished."

Key 2: Avoid personal liability—Most get-rich-quick schemes, as well as most tax shelters, are available only if the investors accept personal liability for a large debt. According to God's Word, we are to avoid surety, which means never accept personal liability for any indebtedness. For example, let us say that an investor was going to buy a $10,000 piece of property, but had only $2,000 as a down payment. So he put his $2,000 down on the property and signed a note for the $8,000 that says, "If ever I can't pay the note, the lender has the right to recover his property and sue me for any deficiency." That is *surety*, taking on a personal liability without a certain way to pay.

On the other hand, let us assume that an investor was buying the same $10,000 piece of property. He made a payment of $2,000 and signed a note for the additional $8,000. But the condition of the note reads, "If ever I can't pay, the lender has the right to keep what I have already paid in and to recover his property, but I owe nothing additional." In other words, there is no personal liability for any deficiency. In legal terms, that is called an *exculpatory*, meaning that the contingent liability is limited to the collateral at risk. Thus, surety is avoided because the borrower always has a definite way to pay: surrender of the property. That is the only biblically sound way to borrow.

Key 3: Evaluate risk and return—An important factor in investing is the risk versus return ratio. The guideline is, the higher the rate of return, the higher the degree of risk. The risk can be reduced by education and careful analysis, but cannot be totally eliminated. Any investment paying a high rate of return must do so to attract the needed capital.

For instance, an insured CD or a government note may pay seven percent while an equivalent corporate bond may pay ten to twelve percent. Why does a corporate bond pay a higher interest rate than a government note? Because the risk in corporate bonds is higher than in government notes. Before investing in anything riskier than an insured savings account, a prudent investor needs to ask this fundamental question: "Can I really afford to take this risk?"

The answer to that question normally depends on two factors: age and purpose. The older the investor, the less the risk that should be taken because it is more difficult to replace the money. But if the purpose of the money is for retirement or education and both are still years away, an investor generally can afford to take a higher risk. However, the greater the need for the investment funds, the less risk one should assume—regardless of age.

Investments with relatively low rates of return should carry proportionately low risks. Treasury bills, treasury bonds, certificates of deposit, and the like will yield a relatively low rate of interest, but they also will have a relatively low degree of risk, at least under normal economic circumstances.

An investment that promises a high rate of return but advertises a low degree of risk should be viewed with skepticism. Proverbs 14:18 has a relevant comment: "The naive inherit folly, but the prudent are crowned with knowledge."

Key 4: Keep some assets debt free—As a general rule, a portion of all investments should be maintained debt free. This also assumes investors follow the recommendation of Key 2 and accept no surety. In other words, only the money at risk in the investments can be lost. There is no contingent liability.

The basic idea is to leverage some investments (without personal liability) in order to hedge against inflation. Investment dollars are actually multiplied through leverage, but are also in jeopardy during a deflationary period. Proverbs 22:3 notes that "the prudent sees the evil and hides himself, but the naive go on, and are punished for it."

A wise investor will keep some cash on hand for emergencies to avoid the necessity of borrowing during a bad economic cycle. As a general rule, however, only a small percentage of investments should be in cash, or near cash, type investments. These include bonds, certificates of deposit, treasury bills, and money market funds.

Key 5: Be patient—Patience helps people avoid a great many investment errors. Most investments look good initially, even the bad ones. I have never heard of anyone advertising an investment as a really bad deal. Most salesmen think their deal is the best and sincerely believe in their products.

Wise investors know their goals and objectives and select investments to meet them. Greed and speed often work together, so a key to avoiding greed is patience. Most get-rich-quick schemes rely on greed and quick decisions. Here are the three basic elements associated with most get-rich-quick schemes:

1. To attract people who do not know what they are doing. When people invest in areas they know little or nothing about, it is difficult for them to evaluate a good or bad investment. People are often very gullible and prone to follow the recommendations of friends who do not know what they are doing, either.
2. To encourage people to risk money they cannot afford to lose. Most people are more cautious with money they have earned than with money they borrow. Borrowed money comes so easily that it is more readily risked.
3. To attract people who will make investment decisions on the spot. That is why so many get-rich-quick plans rely on group meetings and a lot of emotional hype. All good investments require thorough evaluation, adequate information, and sincere prayer.

Get-rich-quick schemes always look the best initially. If they did not, nobody would buy them. So be cautious, and above all, be patient: "Rest in the

LORD and wait patiently for Him" (Ps. 37:7). Before you do anything, talk about it, pray about it, and then give God time to answer.

Key 6: Diversify—An old adage says, "Don't put all your eggs in one basket." That certainly applies to investment strategy. Assume, for example's sake, that an investor has a small amount of money to invest, perhaps $1,000, and wants to buy some stock with it. If the entire $1,000 is invested in one company's stock, all of the money rests on that one company's performance. But there is an alternative called a mutual fund. A mutual fund pools investors' moneys and diversifies in various companies. Therefore, diversification can be achieved merely by selecting a mutual fund.

Further diversification can be accomplished by investing in different areas of the economy. For example, one part might be in real estate, some in gold and silver, a percentage in stocks and bonds, and the remainder in CD's. This approach helps to buffer investors from cyclical ups and downs. This principle is described in Ecclesiastes 11:2: "Divide your portion to seven, or even to eight, for you do not know what misfortune may occur on the earth."

Diversification is not a one-time decision. It is not sufficient to diversify and forget it. Changes in the economy often necessitate further diversification.

To properly diversify investments, a multitiered plan is useful. For demonstration purposes, I will describe five tiers.

- Tier 1 is secure income, such as CD's, stocks, government bonds, and notes.
- Tier 2 is long-term income. These investments are higher risks, but have a higher rate of return (mortgages, corporate bonds, and so on).
- Tier 3 is growth investments, such as mutual funds, utility stocks, and gold funds.
- Tier 4 is speculative growth investments, such as development property, limited partnerships, and new businesses.
- Tier 5 is pure speculation investments, such as oil and gas, precious metals, and gemstones.

Depending on age, income, and temperament, an investor may want to omit one or more of these levels. For instance, an older person may not want or need to get into Tier 5, the purely speculative area. A younger person may not want to get into Tier 1, the purely secure income.

Key 7: Follow long-range trends—Invest with an eye to long-range economic trends, especially inflation. Investors often get trapped into following short-range trends. For instance, when the economy is doing well and inflation and interest rates are down, many investors are attracted to the stock market. Some early investors will make money, but many will flee in panic during a short-term downturn and lose most or all of the money they made. In fact, if they chose to speculate, they may lose more than they made, especially if they borrowed to invest. When the market drops and they cannot afford to ride it out, they sell in a downturn. So it is wise to think in terms of long-term economics when deciding where to put investment money. With long-term trends, whatever is going on right now will eventually reverse. As Ecclesiastes 11:6 says, "Sow your seed in the morning, and do not be idle in the evening, for you do not know whether morning or evening sowing will succeed, or whether both of them alike will be good."

Perhaps the most significant economic trend that has affected the area of investments over the last ten years has been inflation, and over the next ten it will be inflation or the threat of depression or perhaps both. One primary weapon in fighting a depression is the expansion of credit, which leads back to inflation again. So for the years 1990–2000, prudent investors who would like their resources to be available in the next decade must hedge both possibilities: inflation and depression.

In a noninflationary economy, investments in treasury bills or certificates of deposit stay even with the economy. But in an inflationary economy, fixed income investments are eroded.

The most inflation-proof investments over the last several decades have been real assets, such as land, metals, apartment buildings, and houses. But during the period when inflation and interest rates abate, many of these assets stagnate, and investors shift to paper assets like stocks and bonds. People tend to forget about inflation—a costly mistake in a debt-run economy. When inflation turns around and interest rates increase to combat it, years of growth can be wiped out in a few months.

Key 8: Focus on what you own—Many erstwhile investors have significant net worths, meaning that, on paper, they look great financially. Unfortunately, most of their assets are tied up in liabilities. In other words, they do not have much ready cash. Often their assets are leveraged and require regular payments. Thus, they are vulnerable to any economic fluctuations.

A classic example occurred in the oil industry during the mid-1980s. Men with net worths in the millions lost everything, including their homes, because they really owned nothing; the lenders did. Proverbs 22:7 promises, "The rich rules over the poor, and the borrower becomes the lender's slave."

The fortunes of the oil industry should be a lesson to all speculators. In the early eighties the price of oil plummeted as the oil cartel fell apart. At the same time the new president, Ronald Reagan, waged a war against inflation through high interest rates. Also at that time, worldwide conservation reduced the demand for oil. The triple blow crippled the oil industry. Even mainline companies such as Shell, Texaco, and Gulf suffered from severely diminished profits and escalating costs. Many new ventures got wiped out, including thousands of leveraged investors.

In a financial crisis, net worth means nothing. It depends on how much is actually owned unencumbered by liabilities. A prudent investor will have a goal to eventually be totally debt free. Proverbs 27:1 admonishes us, "Do not boast about tomorrow, for you do not know what a day may bring forth."

Key 9: Know where to sell—Before buying, know where the investment can be sold. This key is very important when dealing with so-called exotic investments, such as gemstones, silver, gold, or collectibles. Most investors who buy collectibles have no idea how or where to sell them and consequently suffer great losses.

Collectibles, such as figurines, paintings, stamps, and coins, are difficult for a novice to resell profitably. Many investors have said, "The salesman told me if I ever wanted to resell, he would buy the investment back." Only later they discover that the salesman is no longer around. Locating an alternate sales source is often the difference between a profit or a loss. Even companies that have been in business for fifty years can fail in a bad economy. Most investors are better off staying with traditional investments that have multiple markets available. Proverbs 14:15 makes this distinction: "The naive believes everything, but the prudent man considers his steps."

Key 10: Seek good counsel—There is no good substitute for knowledge in the area of investing. The best type of knowledge is what the investor has acquired personally. Second only to personal knowledge is the counsel of other individuals. Proverbs often refers to counsel as an indication of wisdom. However, in great part, that really depends on whether the counsel is wise or ignorant. There are some simple guidelines to follow in seeking counsel in the area of investing that will help avoid many, if not most, losses.

1. Seek the counsel of godly men and women who understand your value system. Follow the advice offered in Psalm 1:1: "How blessed is the man who does not walk in the counsel of the wicked, nor stand in the path of sinners, nor sit in the seat of scoffers!"
2. Look for advisers who have a proven track record with other investors. As Proverbs 13:20 says, "He who walks with wise men will be wise,

but the companion of fools will suffer harm."

The bottom line for any investment counselor is this: Did he make more money for his clients than he cost them? The only way to verify that is to ask those who have dealt with the counselor for several years.

Do not be deceived by seemingly good advisers with short-term track records. Many advisers gain notoriety by guessing a particular event correctly and then subsequently lose all the gains by a succession of bad guesses.

3. Beware of advisers who will cheat on your behalf. An old truism asserts, "If a man will cheat for you, he will eventually cheat you." Proverbs 24:8 makes the point: "He who plans to do evil, men will call him a schemer."

4. A good counselor's advice should be just one input into making good investment decisions. In other words, no one is responsible for the ultimate decision, except the investor. Personal responsibility is a well-established principle in many contexts.

5. No human advice should overrule the advice given in God's Word. If counsel runs contrary to God's Word, avoid it. Listen to Proverbs 3:5-6: "Trust in the LORD with all your heart, and do not lean on your own understanding. In all your ways acknowledge Him, and He will make your paths straight."

Seeking counsel means gathering additional input to help an investor make a more intelligent decision. Ultimately, the final decision about all investments rests with each individual with money at risk. A husband and a wife should discuss all investment decisions together, pray diligently about them, and not risk money they cannot afford to lose.

EDITOR'S PERSPECTIVE

Larry Burkett is right on target when he exhorts us (1) to invest with the goal in mind of being content with a fair return on our investments, not of getting rich, and (2) to invest in a type of investment that we are comfortable with on the basis of our knowledge of and experience with the specific type of investment. For example, people who know nothing about buying undeveloped land for investment purposes should be extremely cautious before investing in such an opportunity. They are open to the stimulus of the seller with little offsetting knowledge with which to balance it.

One investment almost all Christians make—and do so while overlooking some basic biblical principles—is in a home. This is unfortunate, for the home investment is the largest single investment most Christians make. If God's intentions rather than the norms of the world were followed, people would save significant amounts of money that could be used for education, godly ministries, retirement, or other appropriate uses.

To illustrate, if Joe and Mary Mansion decide to take the $10,000 they have saved and purchase a $100,000 home, they will need to secure a $90,000 mortgage. They know that the longer the mortgage runs, the smaller the monthly payments will be, so they will try to borrow $90,000 for thirty years at, let us assume, a fixed rate of ten percent. Their payments of principal and interest (excluding taxes and insurance) will be $789.82 a month for the thirty years.

But if Joe and Mary would heed God's prescription (see Deut. 15:1-5) and limit their purchase to what they could financially manage on a *seven-year mortgage*, they would realize astounding savings. They could own, debt free, a $55,000 home in seven years with a $45,000 mortgage at ten percent and have monthly payments of principal and interest of $747.06 a month. Then at the end of the seven-year period they could sell their $55,000 home (assuming no appreciation) and buy their $100,000 dream home with a new $45,000 mortgage for seven years at $747.06. The financial difference between the two approaches is staggering. The mathematics look like this:

A. $90,000 for 30 years at 10% = $ 789.82 per month
            30 x 12 x $789.82 = 284,335.00 principal and interest paid
                                   – 90,000.00 of principal
                                   _____
                                   $194,335.00 paid in interest

B. $45,000 for *two* 7-year periods at 10%
                                   = $ 747.06 per month
            14 x 12 x $747.06 = 125,506.00 principal and interest paid
                                   – 90,000.00 of principal
                                   _____
                                   $ 35,506.00 paid in interest

If Mary and Joe will follow Plan B, they will save $158,829 of interest ($194,335 minus $35,506); they will own their dream home, free of any debt, in fourteen years instead of thirty years; and in the years fifteen through thirty they will have $789.82 per month not being spent on house payments to use for the education of the children, investments for retirement, and so forth. Our homes are an important part of our investment experience, and we need to be wise and prudent as we make our decisions regarding them.

Mr. Burkett's chapter, by design, was limited to a discussion of personal investments, but it is appropriate to comment on business investments. Specifically, I want to say a few words about corporate managers and directors becoming the owners of the corporations they manage through leveraged buyouts (LBOs) and about the moral issues encountered in the everyday decision-making processes people go through as they develop capital budgets in business.

LBOs have become a popular method of acquiring corporations in the past few years. An interested person or group offers to buy a particular company's common stock and makes arrangements to finance the purchase with the help of investment bankers who agree to underwrite and sell a large quantity of high-interest-rate bonds (high risk, hence, "junk bonds"). The amount of debt used to acquire the company is usually very high compared to the amount of equity put up by the new owners, deriving the name *leveraged* buyouts.

The purchasers' assumptions are that the targeted company's common stock is significantly undervalued in the stock market and that its many divisions and subsidiaries are worth more if spun off and sold individually than if they are kept together as one company. These assumptions are frequently realistic, and because they are, those who engage in this form of buyout also claim that they are rendering a genuine economic service to society by setting into motion market forces that result in the realization of the asset's true value, whether in a liquidated form or as a new privately held entity. These self-justifying rationalizations are widely debated but generally believed.

The deeper motive driving the corporate raiders (persons who initiate LBOs), however, is often greed—acknowledged by some raiders publicly. A few have even stated that greed is good, in a utilitarian sense. But greed is not the focus of this examination. The propriety of the investment bankers might also be examined—the extent to which they are willing to sell questionable risks in the marketplace in exchange for very lucrative rewards for themselves. This is a valid line of inquiry, too, since the investment bankers' personal business risks are generally short term while their products (junk bonds) carry substantial long-term risks. But neither is this our basic concern.

I want to address the issue of managers and directors of publicly held corporations becoming, through a leveraged buyout, the new owners of the corporation they have managed. It is hard to conceive of a more blatant example of conflict of interest. LBOs of this type are inherently unethical. The fact that everyone may be happy with the outcome does not change the moral conclusion one bit, either. (The parties involved in adultery may be "happy," but this does not address the moral issue.) Management LBOs are forms of agreed-upon financial infidelity, and there is nothing to commend them.

If a corporation's stock is selling for $27 a share in the marketplace, but has a restructuring value of $54 a share or a liquidation value of $75 a share, those who manage and direct the company are obligated to represent the owners to the best of their ability without lining their own pockets at the owners' expense once a "raid" on the company has been initiated by others. But the market forces have become so large and manipulative that the fruits of shared corporate piracy and financial infidelity are deemed sufficient to salve moral consciences. The LBO phenomenon is so widely accepted that many managers, and individual investors alike, try to guess where the next LBO is likely to take place so they can get in on the action—a rising stock price—without regard to the ethics of the big players (raiders and managers).

The marketplace allows managers to assume the role of raiders, with impunity, as they cannibalize the very companies they were hired to serve, because everybody makes a *quick* profit. When a stock price moves from $27 a share to $47 in a few weeks, for example, the original owners, who are overwhelmingly institutional investors (mutual funds, pension funds, trust funds, etc.), are generally happy to secure the high return on their investment, which in turn helps them look good in their quarterly reports. Therefore, these investors do not complain that the newest owners may reap an additional high return on the restructured investment by reorganizing, selling off portions of them, or completely liquidating the business. And the small stockholders who were forced out and learned later that the new owners (old managers) pocketed $200 million or more on the transaction have little incentive to complain because of the enormous costs involved in doing so. Furthermore, they have no assurance the courts would sympathize with their injury.

A major recession (with its devastating side effects of bringing about the financial collapse of some previously financially healthy corporations that suddenly become financially anemic through LBOs) may be required before the public pays any attention to the moral implications of the current behavior.

The last issue I want to address in this section is the moral temptation faced by those who develop capital budgets in the corporate world. The problem is subtle and rarely apparent. In fact, it is generally lost in the "income" and "fixed assets" figures of a corporation's financial statements where its stewardship consequences are blurred in the aggregations. It arises more from people's rationalized hopes than from any malicious intent.

In a nutshell, the temptation managers face when they want to have their pet capital project funded—when only thirty-five percent of all capital requests in the company in any year will be authorized, for example—is to look optimistically at sales, revenues, efficiency expectations, and other projected incomes while simultaneously projecting minimal costs and expenses. This two-pronged scenario produces projections showing higher rates of return that will probably never be realized but make one's capital request look better.

God's stewards need to be careful when formulating and presenting requests for capital. We must be on guard against our personal desires, which so easily cloud our thinking. Dr. Rae Mellichamp covered this kind of human behavior and its ethical implications in some detail in chapter 9, particularly in the section "Operations Research" when he discussed biased models. He pointed out that our integrity is on the line when we create figures to be used in evaluating alternatives in making "go" and "no go" decisions. The temptation is to rationalize, "Well, others exaggerate projected return on investment figures so I had better do it, too, if I am to remain on a competitive footing with them." Some people find themselves in a tougher situation when they are part of a team working on a capital proposal and it suddenly becomes apparent that the boss is leading the group to the conclusion he wants, independent of some hard realities. Christians are called on to address situations like this, for Scripture is plain: "Like a trampled spring and a polluted well is a righteous man who gives way before the wicked" (Prov. 25:26).

PART XIII

THE HIGHER AND LOWER·LAWS

Thirty-five years ago when I took a business law course in college, I desperately needed a teacher like John Sparks, the author of this chapter. No other college course frustrated me so much. I was a "deformed" Christian at the time, if I was a Christian at all, but my very nature demanded justice and equity, which seemed obfuscated by the cases and law I was exposed to. My feeble sophomoric efforts to reconcile the gaps I perceived between "what was right" and "what the law said" were simply dismissed with the statement that we were studying the law and not morals. The very idea that there could be a gap between the law and moral reasoning had never before entered my mind and left me reeling, confused, and angry. Was not the law to be equated with justice and fairness?

The chapter before us is the most elucidating work, for a business law layman, that I have ever seen. It sets forth five areas where biblical law speaks directly to the affairs of business: retribution, keeping of agreements, release and rest (matters of bankruptcy), honesty, and property ownership. John Sparks gives us the "essential principles and enduring purposes" of the biblically prescribed civil or judicial laws that continue to our day. He is careful to distinguish these laws from both the ceremonial law that has been fulfilled in the life, death, and resurrection of Christ and the moral law (Ten Commandments).

He notes where God's eternal decrees are not being subscribed to in our contemporary civil business law and shows the consequences of these deviations. But he also points out where there is conformity between God's and man's laws, or where there has been conformity that is now being eroded. We can get a sense of how far-reaching God's common grace was in our heritage and see the decay that has been under way now for some generations.

251

(This latter insight is a byproduct of his work.)

From the editor's perspective, though, one of Mr. Sparks's greatest contributions is his discussion of how he approaches Scripture to seek the mind of Christ. He sets before us two interpretive principles that we should examine carefully and decide on their appropriateness. The first is that "Scripture is its own interpreter." This goes to the heart of one of the three major problems causing divisions in the Bible-believing churches today: Are we to interpret the Scriptures text by text or by seeing what Scripture has to say on the same matter in several places? (The other two areas of trouble are these: What is the relationship between the Old and New Testaments, and what is the role of God's law in the life of a believer?)

Although it was not John Sparks's assignment, or intent, he also addressed the role of God's law in the life of a believer when he set before us the hermeneutical principles he followed—the method of interpreting the Scripture. He walks a carefully balanced line between the extremes of antinomianism (the law of God is not really relevant for the Christian) and theonomism (the moral and civil laws of God should be binding in every regard on the civil authorities of today). He presents his position on these matters in a spirit of informing the reader of the assumptions undergirding his work, not in a spirit of debate, intellectual coercion, or even persuasion. May the Lord help us all to arrive at a clear understanding on these important issues, for they shape our thoughts, motives, and conduct in every area of life in the marketplace.

CHAPTER 13

BUSINESS LAW AND BIBLICAL PRINCIPLES

John A. Sparks

Dr. John A. Sparks is Professor of Business Administration at Grove City College and President of Public Policy Education Fund, Inc. A graduate of Grove City College and the University of Michigan Law School, Sparks has been an Earhart Foundation, Ingersoll Foundation, and R. C. Hoiles Fellow. He is a member of the State Bar of Pennsylvania and the law firm of Bogaty, McEwen, and Sparks where he specializes in education law. Articles by Sparks have appeared in such diverse publications as Private Practice, The University Bookman, The Freeman, Engage/Social Action, Discipleship Journal, Food Policy, *and* Pennsylvania Outlook.

College students have very little difficulty accepting the basic idea of Higher Law as it is perfunctorily presented by most business law or introduction to law texts, for who can disagree with the idea that a manmade law can be in error when compared to a higher standard of right and wrong. Usually, when called upon to give an example of such a human law that is inconsistent with Higher Law, today's students refer to a dictator, usually Hitler or Stalin, who decrees death for a certain innocent group—the Jews or the Kulaks. They correctly say that these "laws" are illegal according to the Higher Law against the murder of innocent people. But beyond that, the business law texts and students view the "primary purpose" of the business law course to be the presentation of concepts of the modern law of contracts, sales, bailments, and other law subjects. In most classrooms the idea of Higher Law and, most certainly, the idea of biblical law are seldom mentioned or even alluded to. One commonly used business law text devotes *one quarter of one page* to a paragraph on natural law, and it is the only reference of its kind in 958 pages of text.[1] This text is no better or worse than most in use in college and university classrooms.

What does such limited reference to Higher Law convey to the student? First, that Higher Law, Divine Law, and God-given Law are relatively unimportant compared with the details of manmade law. Second, that Divine Law is a restraint upon tyrants and not a constant standard to be consulted when studying contracts, sales, bailments, and other "nuts and bolts" subjects. It goes without saying that in such a course the student learns practically nothing about the principles of biblical law as presented in the Ten Commandments, the Mosaic judicials, and numerous New Testament scriptures, and little about principles of interpretation (hermeneutics). For the most part, the American undergraduate business student exists in a wasteland devoid of meaningful academic contact with biblical principles. It is to the task of discovering and discussing some of those principles that this chapter now turns.

GOD'S LAW: INTERPRETIVE APPROACH

The Scriptures affirm that God delivered His perfect law to man in the form of the Decalogue and that this law, often called the moral law, is to be man's norm and guide (see Exod. 20:1-17). God has also ordained the institution of civil government to maintain minimal civic righteousness in the commonwealth by restraining and curbing the effects of sin in the world, to promote peace and tranquility in society, to preserve public honesty, modesty, and civil decency among men, and to protect property and persons from the inevitable ravages of sin.[2] The civil legal foundations of earthly law are to be found in the Divine Law of God. His Higher Law is to be a guide for man's civil law. As the renowned systematic theologian Charles Hodge put it,

> The authority of civil rulers, the rights of property, of marriage, and all other civil rights, do not rest upon abstractions, nor upon general principles of expediency. . . . All human rights are founded upon the ordinance of God. . . . Theism is the basis of jurisprudence as well as of morality.[3]

The biblical lawyer's task is to explain and demonstrate precisely how the Scriptures ought to shape civil law. The analysis in this chapter is based on two *interpretive* principles. The first is the Reformed doctrine "Sacra Scriptural sui interpres" (Sacred Scripture is its own interpreter).[4] This means that the Holy Scriptures are "consistent and coherent."[5] God would not contradict Himself. *Seemingly* contradictory passages should be harmonized. Interpreting scripture by scripture also means that one must examine all passages that mention the same subject to ensure clarity of meaning, and avoid relying on a single verse.

The second interpretive principle that is especially pertinent to the area of law study is the *general equity* approach to the Old Testament codes and judicials found in Exodus, Deuteronomy, Leviticus, and Numbers. The general equity approach is based on the view expressed in the *Westminster Confession of Faith* that organizes the Law of God into three categories—the moral law, the ceremonial law, and the civil law or judicials.[6] The moral law refers to the Ten Commandments and their implications. Of course, the moral law is binding on Christians today in the sense that it is a perfect definition of the relationship of man with God and man with man. The ceremonial law, also given by God in the Old Testament to Israel, was a prefiguring of Christ. The Levitical priesthood, the Mosaic system of ceremonial cleanliness, sacrificial offerings, and redemption are fulfilled and superseded by Christ; therefore, for Christians, these ceremonial laws have been abrogated (see Eph. 2:13; Col. 2:14; Heb. 10:1-10).

The civil laws or judicials were given to Israel to serve that nation as form and substance of their government. The God-given body of laws—the Mosaic judicials—"expired together with the state of that people [Israel], not obliging any other, now, further, than *the general equity thereof may require*"[7] (emphasis added). These words from the *Westminster Confession of Faith* define the interpretive approach of this author to the Old Testament judicials.

It is a view that the judicials should be consulted for *their essential principles and enduring purposes*, but *not* the view that the judicials in their detail and specifics must be imitated by modern civil governments. One writer has well summarized it:

> It is clear that the framers of the [Westminster] Standards felt that there was both continuity and discontinuity in the law of God. God had given to ancient Israel a civil code, which was designed for that people at that time. This code, in the strict sense, was not designed for other nations particularly, and thus expired. . . . At the same time, this civil code was based on eternal moral principles, and these moral principles could clearly be seen in the laws themselves, so that these laws should form the basis of all Christian civil codes, according as the "general equity thereof may require." Thus, these laws could not be ignored or overlooked. Christians are not free to take them or leave them. They *must* be consulted for their "equity."[8]

This approach requires that the biblical lawyer search for the original and lasting purposes of the judicial laws given to the Jewish nation and, by doing so, discover their substance and basic equity.[9]

The general equity approach is different from that used by the theonomic school of Greg Bahnsen, for example. That school takes the position that the moral law and the judicials are binding on the modern civil lawyer in exhaustive detail.[10] By contrast, the general equity approach requires modern law to be consistent with the general equity of Divine Law, but its particular devices and forms need not imitate that law in detail. What are some biblical principles discoverable by this interpretive approach?

PRINCIPLES OF BIBLICAL LAW AND THEIR APPLICATION TO BUSINESS LAW

Retribution or recompense—Retribution is the first fundamental principle of justice and is still best summarized by Cicero's statement: "Justice renders to every man what is due him."[11] Similarly, the Apostle Paul, talking about civic duties, literally says, "Give everyone what is due him" (Rom. 13:7). *Repaying* what is *due* seems to be an irreplaceable principle of doing justice. Injustice is always occurring. Repayment redresses the disorder of injustice. When a criminal is punished, he is said to *pay* for his crime; when the breaching party to a contract *pays* damages to the injured party, he *repays* in order to avoid the perpetuation of injustice. The word *retribution*, despite its unpopularity, captures the idea well because it is composed of two Latin words: *tribuere*, which means "to pay," and "re," which means "back."[12] Therefore, *retribution*, often used to describe criminal punishment, actually means "any paying back or making of recompense, civil or criminal."

When God is specifically described as "doing justice," He is acting retributively. Isaiah says that the Lord looked over the land and was displeased that "there was *no justice*" (Isa. 59:15, emphasis added). And then Isaiah states that the Lord *will do justice*:

> According to what they have done,
>   so will he *repay*
> wrath to his enemies
>   and *retribution* to his foes;
>   he will *repay* the islands their *due*. (Isa. 59:18, emphasis added)

Jeremiah affirms, "For the LORD is a God of *retribution*; he will *repay* in full" (Jer. 51:56, emphasis added). A New Testament writer observed that "God is just: He will *pay back* trouble to those who trouble you and give relief to you who are troubled" (2 Thess. 1:6-7, emphasis added). Numerous scripture references support this view of what constitutes justice (see Deut. 32:35; Ps. 94:2; Isa. 66:6; Heb. 2:2).[13] This, then, is the first principle of biblical law, the principle of proportional repayment or retribution.

The Greek and Roman lawyers also recognized the principle of proportional payment when they recoiled at the harsh code of Athenian lawgiver Draco, which was said to punish both the theft of a cabbage and murder with death. The ancients, outside the Hebrew tradition, discerned that there was no balance in Draco's Code between the crime and the punishment. Nevertheless, the principle of retribution is most clearly set out in Holy Writ.

Modern law's inconsistency with the retributive principle—the criminal law. During the first seventy years of the twentieth century, a psychomedical principle—rehabilitation—rivaled and nearly replaced traditional retribution as the ordering principle for the criminal justice system.[14] Many advocated treatment instead of punishment. C. S. Lewis opposed this new "humanitarian theory of punishment,"[15] and Francis Allen questioned it, labeling it the "rehabilitative ideal."[16] So-called therapeutic justice regarded the offender as sick and in need of care. In his book *The Crime of Punishment*, Karl Menninger even wrote that the real crime in a criminal matter was *not* the wrong done by the offender but the fact that we punished him.

For a time this rehabilitative theory seemed as though it would supplant deserved punishment as the basic rationale for criminal justice. Retribution was discredited as primitive. In recent years the failure of psychological treatment to actually rehabilitate criminals and the basic common-sense demands of ordinary citizens that criminals be punished have dealt blows to the rehabilitative ideal. In summary, the biblical basis for the *criminal* law is retribution. Substituting another alien principle will produce, as it has, only disorder and loss of direction for the criminal law. This topic deserves separate discussion, but it is beyond the purview of this business law paper.

The modern commercial civil law and retribution—consistency and inconsistency. Contract law is central to modern business law. To what extent is the current Anglo-American law of contract consistent or inconsistent with the biblical principle of retribution?

First, the basic rule of contract remedies is the rule of compensatory damages. A party to a contract who is injured by the breach of the other party is entitled to be paid a *recompense* for the loss that the breach has caused him. The rule, one of *repayment*, is an obvious and particular outcropping of the underlying principle of *retribution*.

The compensatory damages rule is retributive, but the rule is not one of unguided recompense. The level of the damages is fixed by the basic idea of compensation, that is, damages are to be measured by actual loss or loss that was reasonably foreseeable by the parties. No more, no less. For example, suppose that Mr. Manufacturer made a valid contract to purchase one thousand bushels of soybeans, with delivery thirty days hence, from Mr. Broker. The contract price agreed upon is $2.00 a bushel. During the intervening month, the market price of soybeans rises to $2.50 a bushel. Mr. Broker defaults, that is, he fails to deliver the soybeans as promised under the contract. To keep his plant going, Mr. Manufacturer must then "cover" by purchasing one thousand bushels at the higher market price. What is Mr. Manufacturer due in damages to right the breach? He is entitled to the difference between the contract price that he was ·expecting to pay ($2.00) and the price he actually had to pay for the soybeans due to the breach ($2.50), that is, he is entitled to $0.50 a bushel in damages. According to the rule of condign recompense, or retribution, he is due these damages. If he were to insist on more, or if he were to receive less, proper repayment would not have been made, and justice would not have been done.

Notice that the compensatory damages rule and all retributive rules *are grounded upon the moral regulative concept of blameworthiness or fault.* Blameworthiness or fault means that a person has inflicted, by omission or commission, undeserved hurt on another. In the criminal law we call blameworthiness *guilt*; in the civil law, *culpability.* The soybean case illustrates this latter species of blameworthiness—culpability. Mr. Broker is blameworthy in that he promised to deliver the soybeans but failed to do so.

Though contract law retains its retributive character, other related areas of business law have followed more and more the concept of liability without fault and departed from blameworthiness as a guide. The *tort law*—the law of private, noncriminal wrongs—has been significantly altered by the idea of "no-fault."[17] How has this occurred, and what does it mean?

The idea of liability without fault (also called by two other names—strict liability or absolute liability) is not unknown to the common law. The common law imposed liability or legal blame upon certain persons *without* a showing of fault if they were engaging in inherently dangerous activities. The two classic examples in which liability was imposed without there being blameworthiness involved blasting companies and the owners of wild animals, such as circus companies. The idea was that these activities—dynamiting and displaying lions—were so potentially dangerous to others that even if the actors took reasonable precautions, they should nevertheless be held responsible if harm came to bystanders as a result of the activities. The common law carved out this exception to the usual requirement of blameworthiness.

However, in American law between 1910 and 1948 a movement extended the strict liability rule to the category of industrial injuries. The workmen's compensation laws from this period to the present have imposed strict liability on the employer for injuries to workers resulting from on-the-job accidents, regardless of fault. The employee's carelessness cannot bar his recovery under such statutes, nor does he have to show negligence (carelessness) on the part of the employer in the arrangement of the workplace. The statutes *abolished* the various defenses that had been available to employers by which they were often able to show that they were not to blame for the injury. The result was a no-fault system. When industrial injuries were cut away from the moorings of tort culpability, American compensation law jettisoned the biblical doctrine of blameworthiness; workers and employers have received in exchange a costly, delay-ridden system that, in most cases, statutorily prohibits an employee from electing an ordinary judicial tort remedy.

A recent expansion of the no-fault idea into areas of the law affecting business is found in no-fault automobile legislation and in strict liability in the sale of manufactured products. The no-fault system for automobile accidents is only a partial no-fault system. For minor accidents, the injured party's insurance company pays for the loss without inquiring into the fault or blameworthiness of the respective parties. The party who was not at fault cannot sue the party at fault but must be content with the insurance proceeds. However, the typical no-fault statutes allow parties to resort to traditional fault-based theories of recovery if the amount of harm exceeds certain limits; the fault system is still in effect for *major* auto accidents. To the extent that the no-fault automobile system ignores blameworthiness, it is in disagreement with the biblical principle of moral responsibility. Most no-fault statutes have been promoted on the basis of reduced total costs to insurers and, therefore, to their premium payers. However, the true effects on costs are far from clear.

The final area of tort law where significant movement has been made away from determining fault and toward strict liability assigned on the basis of some other principle than fault is in products liability law. Once again we can state only the fundamental failing of modern legal developments in this area of the law. Prior to the early 1960s a manufacturer's liability to persons injured while using the manufacturer's product was based on negligence. The injured party had to show negligence on the part of the manufacturer in conceiving and producing the product. Negligence meant a failure to use the degree of care that one would expect a reasonably prudent person to use in like circumstances. Manufacturers could successfully defend themselves under the negligence standard of recovery if they showed they exercised due care in product planning, in production and testing, and in the use of warnings and instructions. If they did those things and a purchaser was harmed despite their efforts, the manufacturers were not liable.[18]

The negligence theory is a fault theory. Culpability is based on the failure of a defendant to exercise the degree of care that *should have been exercised.* Despite this perfectly good and biblical standard, grounded in the requirement of moral culpability, the courts, in the early 1960s, began to allow the negligence standard to be replaced by strict product liability theories of recovery. Beginning with the "creative jurisprudence" of courts like the Supreme Court of California, juridical thought began to insist that a manufacturer be held liable despite his showing that he had used due care in the design, production, and marketing of a product.[19] One well-known formulation of this strict liability rule states, "One who sells any product in a defective condition unreasonably dangerous to the user or consumer . . . is subject to liability [even though] . . . the seller has exercised all possible care in the preparation and sale of his product."[20] This rule means that a manufacturer who has been careful about product development and production may, nevertheless, be judged to owe damages to the user when the product fails in some way that the manufacturer could not have discovered or prevented within the limits of usual and due care.

Richard A. Epstein points out that this strict liability paradigm no longer sees the "major function" of the tort law as "individual redress," but instead "the development of a set of rules that will, among other objectives, enhance the ability of the social system to allocate efficiently 'its' scarce resources."[21] Expressed less guardedly, if the makers of most products are corporations and the persons injured are individual consumers, the manufacturer, despite its care in testing and manufacturing, is in a *better position* to absorb the costs of the loss than is the individual user of the product. Therefore, the law of torts ought to *allocate* the responsibility for payment to the manufacturer. According to this view, when someone is harmed, the tort law is to impose the cost on the one who can best pay, a disregard of the question of fault.

Some courts have become almost indifferent to the need for a causal, which is to say moral, connection between an injured plaintiff and a specific blameworthy defendant. In the now famous case of *Sindell v. Abbott Laboratories* decided by the California Supreme Court in 1980,[22] the court ruled that though the plaintiffs could not actually show which manufacturers made the DES chemical that allegedly produced vaginal cancer, various drug companies known to have produced the drug could be sued. In addition, the court allowed the respective market shares of the companies to determine how they shared the burden of the damages awarded. Once again, no matter how appealing is the need for monetary help for those injured by the products of the modern marketplace, there should still be a connection between particular actions that are blameworthy and damage awards. Embracing principles other than culpability has turned loose unguided and unbridled forces that have thrown the tort system into the confusion from which it suffers today.

We leave now the principle of retribution and moral blameworthiness to look at a second biblical principle, the doctrine that promises must be kept.

Agreements freely entered into must be kept—The principle *that a promise or an agreement, when freely entered into, must be kept* is integral to the formation and maintenance of a scripturally imbued business law. The principle of keeping one's promises is found in the biblical rules and practices concerning vows, oaths, and covenants (pacts) between men. The vow was a promise to devote something to God; "a man was always bound by his vow."[23] The Old Testament rules covering vows are found in Numbers 30, Leviticus 27, and Deuteronomy 23:21-23. The first two verses of Numbers 30 summarize the requirement very well: "Moses said to the heads of the tribes of Israel: 'This is what the LORD commands: When a man makes a vow to the LORD or takes an oath to obligate himself by pledge, he must not break his word but must do everything he said.'" Likewise, taking an oath by which one attested to the truth of something or stated one's solemn intention to keep a promise showed the importance of keeping one's promise.

Biblical figures made covenants with each other, often accompanied by an oath of adherence. The treaty or pact between Abraham and Abimelech over well rights was completed this way, according to Scripture: "So that place was called Beersheba [well of the oath], because the two men swore an oath there" (Gen. 21:31). A similar treaty and oath concluded dealings between Isaac and Abimelech (see Gen. 26:31), and others are found elsewhere in Scripture (see Gen. 31:53; 47:31; 50:25). The author of Hebrews stated that men swear an oath by someone greater than themselves and the oath confirms the reliability of what is said (see Heb. 6:16). Furthermore, the writer pointed out that God condescended to take an oath on Himself in order "to make the unchanging nature of his purpose very clear to the heirs of what was promised" (Heb. 6:17). Paul noted that contracts should be kept (see Gal. 3:17). The principle is that one who makes a contract has a moral obligation to adhere to it making its veracity and sure fulfillment an accomplished fact.

One should not be surprised, then, that the Church canon lawyers of the eleventh and twelfth centuries developed basic ideas of contract law out of their body of regulations having to do with oaths.[24] The canonists went further. They developed and explained the principle "that promises *are in themselves* binding, as a matter of conscience,"[25] regardless of the presence of an oath. According to them, "Every promise is binding, regardless of its form: *pacta sunt servanda* ('agreements must be kept'). . . . An oath and a promise without an oath are equal in the sight of God . . . not to fulfill the obligation of a pact is equivalent to a lie."[26] Of course, this view is in keeping with the New Testament teachings of Christ about oaths and promises when He indicates that one need not take an oath at all in order to be held to honor one's promises: "Simply let your 'Yes' be 'Yes,' and your 'No,' 'No'" (Matt. 5:37).

Other notable jurists have referred to the basic principles of abiding by one's contracts. Hugo Grotius, sixteenth-century Dutch jurist, stated that the principle of honoring agreements is one of four fundamental principles of human law.[27] Similarly, the seventeenth-century German jurist Samuel von Pufendorf wrote,

> Whenever men enter into any agreements the social nature of man
> requires that they must be faithfully observed. It is, therefore, a most
> sacred precept of natural law, and one that governs the grace, manner and
> reasonableness of human life, that every man keep his given word, that is,
> carry out his promises and agreements.[28]

Much of modern contract law is consistent with the fundamental biblical rule that promises, once made, must be kept. It should be obvious to observers that if promises need not be kept, discussion of breaching or breaking a contract (i.e., not fulfilling it) makes no sense whatsoever. Also made more understandable by grasping the underlying principle of contract is the concern about capacity, duress, and undue influence. If a "person" is to have legal significance attached to his act of entering a contract, we ought to be certain that he is not too young and inexperienced to understand the consequences of what he is doing. Thus, rules about capacity of parties actually allow a minor, for example, to treat an "agreement" as voidable and withdraw from it, under the theory that his competence to enter into a binding agreement is absent. Furthermore, since moral culpability for failure to do what one promises is one possible result of entering into a contract, modern contract law will not find blameworthiness in the case where a party is forced into a contract or where another's overpowering will is substituted for one's own. The former case is one of duress, and the latter is undue influence. How can a person who is threatened with a gun into signing a contract be said to be morally culpable when he refuses to perform what is required in the forcibly obtained pact?

The consideration rules of contract law have become overridden with technical requirements often seeming to work against the basic principle that commercial promises, in themselves, ought to be binding. The primary rule of consideration is that each party to a contract must have promised to give something valuable to the other party for the contract to be enforceable. This rule of *mutuality of consideration* is a reasonable requirement. However, as applied in its stricter versions, it may work against the principle that what parties agree to do should be binding.

For example, suppose that Joe agrees to build a marina for Tom for a total price of $16,000. After the work begins, Joe finds that various items are costing somewhat more than he expected. He asks Tom for an extra $1,000, and Tom agrees to pay the extra consideration. At the end of the work, Tom refuses to pay the extra amount. How would a court in a state where the traditional rule of consideration was in effect decide this case? Commonly, the court would see mutuality of consideration in the first promises, that is, when Joe promised a marina to Tom and Tom promised $16,000 to Joe. However, when Tom promised additional or new consideration, the court would ask, "Where is the new consideration promised by Joe?" The answer is that since he is still promising to do only what he *already had agreed* to do, there is no new consideration on his part, and the promise to pay the extra $1,000 is not "supported by consideration." It is, therefore, unenforceable. This technical outcome produces a result that ignores the clear renegotiated agreement of the parties.

The Uniform Commercial Code (UCC), which covers sale of goods transactions (but not sale of services like the case in point), takes a position more in keeping with the view that commercial promises standing alone ought to be binding. Under the UCC, an existing agreement can be modified by the parties *by mere mutual agreement.* No new consideration needs to be given by both parties [UCC sec. 2-209(1)]. Perhaps general contract law will give attention to determining enforceability in the renegotiation cases on the basis of whether the parties agreed to modify the contract and not on the basis of traditional consideration rules. Such a shift would be more in keeping with the principle of the enforceability of promises.

The principle of release and rest—If contracts, agreements, and obligations are meant to be abided by and fulfilled, why does the law allow for a bankrupt to discharge the debts owed to his creditors when the creditors may very well receive little or nothing on the debt? Is bankruptcy inconsistent with the principle that agreements ought to be kept?

Strictly speaking, the discharge of a debtor's obligations by a court of bankruptcy contravenes the preexisting agreement between the debtor and the creditor. However, *biblical law recognizes the principle of the release or cancellation of a debt while at the same time teaching that agreements should be honored and debts paid.*

The principle of release is most obvious in the laws about the Sabbatical Year and the Jubilee Year (see Exod. 23:10-11; Lev. 25; Deut. 15:1-10; 31:10-13). Various commentators have noted that this principle of release and rest from debts is now fulfilled, however imperfectly, by modern bankruptcy laws.[29] The venerable jurist Sir William Blackstone explains that the English law of bankruptcy recognized this tension between the proper interests of the creditor in being paid and the extension of humane release to the debtor:

> The Laws of England . . . have steered in the middle between both
> extremes: providing at once against the inhumanity of the creditor, who is
> not suffered to confine an honest bankrupt after his effects are delivered
> up: and at the same time taking care that all his just debts shall be paid, so
> far as the effects will extend.[30]

As Blackstone states, the English law of bankruptcy as then in force was used by creditors to call debtors who were behind on accounts into bankruptcy to ensure that as far as possible debts were paid. At the same time the English law allowed someone who was hopelessly indebted to be discharged from the burden, even though the debt was paid only in part. This latter feature is the principle of release. According to Berman, from the twelfth century on, Western law of bankruptcy maintained a just tension between debtors and creditors when it "permitted limitation of liability of debtors and at the same time gave preferences to secured creditors."[31]

This is not to say that the current law of bankruptcy properly maintains the dynamic tension between the principles of *obligation* and *release*. But an attempt has been made. When Congress revised the United States bankruptcy laws in 1978 (Bankruptcy Reform Act of 1978, Title 11, U.S. Code Service), the bankrupt debtor received increased protection. Under the 1978 revision, in many states, the bankrupt could retain more of his property after bankruptcy because of increased federal exemptions. Of course, exemptions for some personal property, tools of the trade, and homestead are generally consistent with certain biblical rules between debtors and creditors, namely, exemptions for one's "cloak" (see Exod. 22:26-27; Deut. 24:12-13), that is, for necessary personal property; for one's millstone (see Deut. 24:6), that is, the tools of one's trade; and for one's homestead (see Lev. 25). These exemptions had come into American law from the English common law, which was influenced by Mosaic law.

However, after a few years of operating under the 1978 revised code, Congress determined, among other things, that it had been *too generous* to the *bankrupt debtor* and reduced the amount of exempt property he could retain by passing the Bankruptcy Amendment and Federal Judgeship Act of 1984. The need for adjusting this tension between obligation and release continues today. As with all civil laws, the bankruptcy laws merely enforce a minimal civic rightness and cannot deal with the root problem of indifference to the serious threat to well-being that excessive debt can be.

A brief note on consent—Before leaving the general area of agreement, one distortion of the idea of contract should be noted, and that is what could be called *consentualism.*

A contract begins with two parties *consenting* to an arrangement and promising to see to it that their respective parts of the agreement are carried out. However, not *everything* that one might consent to do with another is enforceable in contract law because the purpose of the contract may be illegal and against public policy. For example, it is black letter law that contracts to commit crimes that are not enforceable. The courts of law cannot on one hand punish murderers or thieves and on the other help them collect their hit money or loot. In other words, consent is not the only consideration or value in contract law. As Hadley Arkes says in his provocative book *First Things*, "Some things cannot be governed solely by consent of parties alone, but are regulated by general moral principles."[32] But one hears recurring arguments today that anything to which "adults consent" should be lawful. Thus, contracts for prostitution, drugs, and pornography ought to be valid, say these proponents, because *consent* is present between the prostitute and "john," addict and dealer, and porn-peddler and buyer.

The view that *consent* is the only valid legal principle should be referred to as consentualism. The sole inquiry under the theory of consentualism is whether persons consent to do something. Arkes properly points out that if we followed such a view to its logical end, "we would be saying, in effect, that there *are no principles* which are valid and binding for an individual unless they accord with his own preferences."[33] To regard consent as *the* determiner of lawfulness is to emasculate the idea of *general principles of law*. When the biblical lawyer speaks of contractual consent, he sees it as an important but *not* an exclusive principle.

Honesty in dealings—The Scriptures stress the necessity of honesty in dealings. The Decalogue and the Old Testament judicial laws warn against dishonesty and falsity. Of course, in the Ten Commandments false testimony and theft are both proscribed. But more specific cases of commercial theft and falsity are prohibited in the judicial laws. "Do not use dishonest standards when measuring length, weight or quantity," says Leviticus 19:35. Others refer to "honest scales" and "accurate and honest weights" (see Lev. 19:36; Deut. 25:13, 15; Prov. 11:1). And the Word proclaims, "The merchant uses dishonest scales; he loves to defraud" (Hos. 12:7).

The general principle of these provisions is to forbid fraudulent and deceitful business dealings. Of course, modern law recognizes this principle in statutory and case law against fraud, misrepresentation, and deceit. The modern rules are sophisticated in that they make distinctions between intentional and unintentional representation of facts that are false and put some responsibility on the buyer to be careful about what he purchases. Basically, the modern law of fraud allows a party who has been defrauded to avoid the contract and be restored to the place he occupied before the contract was made.

Other provisions in modern business law consistent with biblical demand for honesty in legal dealings are warranties, disclosure requirements in agency and trust law, laws against perjury, witnessing requirements in wills and, of course, the statute of frauds, which simply provides that most contracts, to be enforceable, must be evidenced by a *writing* so that no single party can misrepresent the bargain made.

The idea of property ownership—The principle of property is set out in Scripture. All ownership for the Christian is not as an "absolute" owner, but as a vice-regent exercising dominion over the created order as a designee of God Himself (see Gen. 1:28; 9:1; Ps. 8:6-8). Blackstone's rendering of Genesis is one of the plainest and most helpful in this regard:

> In the beginning of the world, we are informed by holy writ, the all-bountiful Creator gave to man "dominion over all the earth: and over the fish of the sea, and over the fowl of the air, and over every living thing that moveth upon the earth." [Blackstone cites Genesis 1:28.] This is the only true and solid foundation of man's dominion over external things . . . the earth, therefore, and all things therein, are the general property of all mankind . . . from the immediate gift of the Creator.[34]

Man's ownership is derivative, not absolute.[35]

The Scriptures specifically protect the claims of real and personal property owners by providing for punishment of those who commit crimes against property. Theft of personal property is condemned by the Decalogue and punished by requiring restitution (the restoring of the good or its value), and the payment of "superrestitution" (an amount that is a multiple of the value of the item stolen [see Exod. 20:15; 22:1-4; Lev. 6:2-7; 19:11; Deut. 5:19; 23:24-25]). Calvin summarizes the Eighth Commandment: "We are forbidden to pant after the possessions of others, and consequently are commanded to strive faithfully to help every man to keep his own possessions."[36] Calvin also says one function of civil government is that "it provides that each man may keep his property safe and sound."[37]

Real estate is also specifically protected by biblical law. The injunctions against moving landmarks (see Deut. 19:14; 27:17) were meant to make inviolate the boundary stones by which the Hebrews, like the Babylonians, marked the limits of their real estate. Moving the stones was a common mode of stealing land,[38] and as can be seen from references in Hosea, Proverbs, and Job,[39] the Almighty hated the abusive practice.

Commentators observe that property in Israel could be acquired by inheritance or sale, much as property is today.[40] From numerous accounts such as Abraham's purchase of the cave of Machpelah (see Gen. 23:16-20) and Jeremiah's transaction concerning the field of Hanamel (see Jer. 32:6-15), we have a picture of the mechanism of transfer of ownership in Hebrew culture.

On the subject of inheritance, clear rules protect descent of property to family members (see Num. 27:1-11; 36:1-12; Deut. 21:15-17; 25:5-6). Moreover, the Old Testament law contains provisions for the restoration of lost property (see Exod. 23:4-5; Deut. 22:1-4), reparation for damage or loss to property (see Exod. 21:28-36; 22:7-15; Lev. 24:18, 21), provisions for governing risk of loss in bailments (see Exod. 22:7, 9-10, 14-15), and redemption regulations (see Lev. 25:24-27, 29-32).

Ownership claims and obligations are well developed in Scripture. Nevertheless, there are ongoing disputes among Christian scholars about the meaning of biblical property. In recent times the communal aspects of the early Jerusalem church (see Acts) and the Jubilee principle (see Lev. 25) have received a great deal of attention. Therefore, they are mentioned briefly.

Does the practice of the Jerusalem church following Pentecost, in which members sold their property and made it available to others, negate private property and endorse communal ownership? Some Christians have thought so. Others, including this writer, have not been convinced that this reference makes a norm of voluntary common ownership. Why? Such a position ignores other scriptures protecting private property claims. Such a position adopts special measures taken in an unusual situation (post-Pentecost) as a rule for all times.[41] Such a position seems to ignore Peter's specific words to Ananias in Acts 5:4; before pledging the property, the piece of land Ananias had sold was his, as were the proceeds of the sale, to dispose of as he thought proper. Though the main point of the "Ananias passage" is to condemn Ananias for deceiving God and others about his giving, the passage also reveals that *not all believers gave their property to the Church nor did Peter expect them to do so*. Therefore, although communalism is arguably practiced, private property was also recognized.

What of the Jubilee of Leviticus 25? One scholar, Ronald J. Sider, has argued that this is a principle for *periodically equalizing* wealth among Christians because Leviticus says that land that had been sold to another was to be returned to the original owner.[42] This same scholar calls Leviticus 25 "one of the most radical texts in all of Scripture."[43] Is this so? What do the verses mean?

First, Leviticus 25 certainly heralds the coming of Jesus Christ as the One who atones for our sins and thus releases us from debt, restores us to the kinship and inheritance with God, and acts as Kinsman-Redeemer to us. The Jubilee is a concrete foreshadowing of what Christ would do and has done. Therefore, in this sense, the Jubilee is ceremonial and fulfilled by Christ.[44]

However, Leviticus 25 may be interpreted to provide guiding principles of the civil law. The Leviticus provisions reinforce the idea of release from obligations similar to what has been mentioned above. Land, especially in a land-based economy, should be able to be redeemed by those who lose it. Modern law recognizes such a principle of redemption. Today, if a bank forecloses on Smith's house, Smith has a redemption period, usually one year, in which to buy back the house.

Second, Leviticus 25 appears to call for a kind of land tenure, based on long-term leases and apparently intended to provide easier access by all to the use of the land.

So, if the detailed provisions of Leviticus 25 were to be enacted into modern law, it would be nothing more radical than ownership taking the form of long-term (fifty-year) leases with the rent adjusted according to the proximity of the beginning of the lease to the Jubilee Year of discharge. Moreover, if one were to follow Leviticus 25:29-30 in detail, *urban* dwellers (walled city dwellers) would be subject only to a one-year redemption period (the period of time in which a foreclosed owner could buy back his property) and not be subject to the Jubilee principle at all. Only rural lands and buildings would be long-term leaseholds. Sider's view that these verses would inaugurate earth-shaking changes, if enacted as civil legislation, is badly overstated. Leviticus 25, the Jubilee, certainly does not proscribe private property.

Many other general principles of biblical law are evident in the Scriptures. Impartiality and certainty stand out. But retribution, blameworthiness, obligation, release, honesty, and ownership are the most important for the specific laws of business.

EDITOR'S PERSPECTIVE

I would really like to duck discussing the Christian's relationship to the law of God, for it is a difficult topic to balance with clarity. Understanding the Christian's relationship to the law involves the balancing of tensions, under the hand of the Holy Spirit, in a manner that creates an inner awareness of the purposes of God as revealed in the law. John Sparks's section "God's Law: Interpretive Approach" contains such a clear delineation of the distinctions of the moral law, the ceremonial law, and the biblical judicials (civil law to be administered by governing authorities) that further elaboration is in order. Few Christians have carefully thought through what their rightful relationship should be to the *law* of God. Most Christians have been subjected to one of two overly simplistic forms of teaching on what that relationship ought to be: We are under grace, not the law; the law is still vital to our Christian walk. What is at stake is our openness to being sanctified, for the Spirit uses the Word of God to help us grow. If we neglect parts of Scripture and immerse ourselves only in certain parts, we resist the Spirit's work.

First, I want to review the scriptural tensions regarding the Christian's relationship to God's law, and then consider the distinction between the law as a standard of judgment and the law as a mirror of love, which only the Holy Spirit can make real and implant in our hearts. The first question to be addressed is, What does the word *law* embody in the Scripture? John Sparks rightfully pointed to the moral law, the ceremonial law, and the civil law or judicials. But Scripture uses ten words in Psalm 119 to describe the breadth of the concepts embodied in the biblical meaning of the law: law, testimonies, ways, precepts, statutes, commandments, judgments, counsel, word, and ordinances. God's law is all of God's Word. We know from this, and throughout Scripture, that the

269

word *law* is not merely confined to the regulations, constraints, or forbidding principles. In fact, David understood that God had also intended the law to be freeing and the provider of true liberty (see Ps. 119:45) and that it was good to make him wiser than his teachers and elders (see Ps. 119:99-100).

A tension between casting the law aside and embracing it arises in the minds of many Christians when they are confronted with this truth from Romans:

> Whatever the Law says, it speaks to those who are *under the Law*, that every mouth may be closed, and all the world may become accountable to God; because *by the works of the Law no flesh will be justified* in His sight; for through the Law comes the knowledge of sin. . . . For we maintain that a *man is justified by faith apart from works of the Law*. (Rom. 3:19-20, 28, emphasis added)

The Church has rightfully emphasized that no one will be *justified* (a judicial term referring to the imputation of Christ's righteousness to us through faith) through the keeping of the law. Persons who would try to be justified by keeping the law are described as being "under" the law or "in" the law (see Rom. 6:14; Gal. 4:21; 5:18), and they are forced to present their own self-righteousness as a basis for justification. This attempt, of course, is doomed to utter failure, for no one can stand in his or her righteousness in the presence of the Holy God of Scripture.

Furthermore, because Scripture uses phrases such as, "You also were made to die to the Law through the body of Christ," and "We have been released from the Law" (Rom. 7:4, 6), many Christians are content to ignore the law and not press on in an effort to discern what else Scripture has to say about their right relationship to it. In truth, Scripture should help us understand "that the Law is good, if one uses it lawfully" (1 Tim. 1:8). Nothing in Scripture would lead us to abandon the appropriate use of the law in our lives.

This statement—"It is written, 'Man shall not live on bread alone, but on every word that proceeds out of the mouth of God'" (Matt. 4:4)—and this one—

> Do not think that I came to abolish the Law or the Prophets; I did not come to abolish, but to fulfill. For truly I say to you, until heaven and earth pass away, not the smallest letter or stroke shall pass away from the law, until all is accomplished. Whoever then annuls one of the least of these commandments, and so teaches others, shall be called least in the kingdom of heaven; but whoever keeps and teaches them, he shall be called great in the kingdom of heaven. (Matt. 5:17-19)

—certainly reveal that Christ thinks all of God's Word is important for us.

David declared, under the inspiration of God's Spirit, that "thy Law is within my heart" (Ps. 40:8). This is exactly what God promised, through the prophet Jeremiah, He would do when He said, "This is the covenant which I will make with the house of Israel after those days. . . . I will put My law within them, and on their heart I will write it" (Jer. 31:33). So the real questions needing answers are these: What law is God going to write on the hearts of His children? And what does it mean to have God's law written on our hearts?

The law that God will write on our hearts is all of His testimonies, ways, precepts, statutes, commandments, judgments, counsel, words, and ordinances. They will be written there by God's Spirit in a manner that transforms them from harsh or "fun-spoiling" restrictions into expressions of love and care accepted by the circumcised and sensitive heart. The old stony self-willed heart gives way to the new heart, which understands that the undisciplined excesses of life produce only momentary pleasures that cannot compare with the long-term freedoms offered by Christ—freedom from guilt, freedom to be truly loved and to love, freedom from the dominion of sin, freedom to realize God's purpose for ourselves, and many other freedoms.

What has just been described is embodied in the Apostle Paul's statement "that we have been released from the Law, having died to that by which we were bound, so that we serve in newness of the Spirit [spirit?] and not in the oldness of the letter" (Rom. 7:6). The release from the law is a release from its ability to enslave us to itself and thereby kill us as we struggle to achieve moral perfection through self-righteousness. Our allegiance to Christ replaces our enslavement to the law. But our faith in Christ does not nullify the law. "On the contrary, we establish the Law" through abiding in Christ and having His Spirit write God's testimonies on our hearts (see Rom. 3:31).

The law of God, which was given because of the extent of the transgressions among His people (see Gal. 3:19), was intended from the beginning to be a tutor to bring people to Him with the realization that they could not be righteous enough in themselves to earn His favor (see Gal. 3:13). King David certainly realized this truth: "How blessed is he whose transgression is forgiven, whose sin is covered! How blessed is the man to whom the LORD does not impute iniquity" (Ps. 32:1-2). The law bears witness to God's righteousness (see Rom. 3:21) but is not intended to make people righteous or call them to self-righteousness.

The law for us continues to reveal, in specific, concrete terms, illustrations of the diversity and complexity of God's love as He calls us to relate to Him and as we are to relate to one another. In addition, the law manifests the specifics of the work that is taking place in us, and will be perfected in us, through faith as the Holy Spirit forms Christ in us (see Gal. 3:1-5; 4:19).

CHAPTER 14

DOING JUSTICE IN THE MARKETPLACE

Richard C. Chewning

With what shall I come to the LORD
And bow myself before the God on high? . . .
Shall I present my first-born for my rebellious acts,
The fruit of my body for the sin of my soul?
He has told you, O man, what is good;
And what does the LORD require of you
But to do justice, to love kindness,
And to walk humbly with your God?
(Mic. 6:6-8)

One of the most frequently quoted Old Testament passages is this: "What does the LORD require of you but to do justice, to love kindness, and to walk humbly with your God?" I had memorized it years before I wrestled with its deeper meaning, especially with what it means to "do justice." I had always thought of justice as something related to making judgments about one's guilt or innocence, or about the appropriate retribution due as a consequence of causing harm. I did not realize that doing justice was usually synonymous with the idea of righteousness in the Scripture—doing what the Lord wants in the manner He wants it done. In fact, justice and righteousness come from the same root word in the Hebrew, $\text{s}^{e}\underline{d}\bar{a}q\hat{a}$. So, the first thing the Lord requires of us is to do what is right (godly) in the marketplace.

Yes, in the marketplace! The prophet Micah is speaking explicitly to people involved in the marketplace. Through Micah, God addressed the injustices He saw as men and women went about their daily commercial tasks. For example,

Woe to those who scheme iniquity,
Who work out evil on their beds!
When morning comes, they do it,
For it is in the power of their hands [financial strength].
They *covet* fields [acquire corporations—unfriendly LBOs, etc.] and then
  seize them,
And houses [HUD scandals], and take them away.
They rob a man and his house,
A man and his inheritance. (Mic. 2:1-2, emphasis added)

The very context of the Micah 6:6-8 passage is concerned with economic justice. God asks, "Can I justify wicked scales and a bag of deceptive weights?" (v. 11). And the seventh chapter begins,

Woe is me! For I am
Like the fruit pickers and the grape gatherers.
There is not a cluster of grapes [for the grape pickers] to eat,
Or a first-ripe fig which I crave.

Malachi also cries out in God's name "against those who oppress the wage earner in his wages" (Mal. 3:5). The reference is not to the unemployed but to those being paid the competitive market rate yet are still in poverty after receiving their wages (while the owners grow wealthy). Amos is burdened with the same concerns when he reports,

Thus says the LORD,
"For three transgressions of Israel and for four
I will not revoke its punishment,
Because they sell the righteous for money
And the needy for a pair of sandals.
These who pant after the very dust of the earth
    on the head of the helpless . . .
Who oppress the poor, who crush the needy,
. . . who turn justice into wormwood
And cast righteousness down to the earth
. . . impose heavy rent on the poor
And exact a tribute of grain from them
. . . trample the needy . . . , saying,
'When will the new moon be over,
So that we may buy grain,

And the sabbath, that we may open the wheat market,
To make the bushel smaller and the shekel bigger,
And to cheat with dishonest scales,
So as to buy the helpless for money
And the needy for a pair of sandals,
And that we may sell the refuse of the wheat?'"
(Amos 2:6-7; 4:1; 5:7, 11; 8:4-6)

Over *four hundred* times Scripture speaks of justice and righteousness and frequently calls for them in the context of the marketplace. The character and behavior embodied in the concepts of justice and righteousness are obviously extremely important to God, and we will explore here what it means to do justice in eight different business relationships. As we do this, though, we should remember that true righteousness (doing justice) will frequently cause those with whom we work to have mixed reactions regarding us. On the one hand, our superiors will frequently admire and respect us for righteous conduct. On the other hand, our peers may come to dislike us because of the very standards we set and uphold through our conduct, which convicts them of their own substandard conduct. This is precisely why Cain slew Abel and is one of the primary reasons the world hates God's children (see 1 John 3:11-13).

DOING JUSTICE TO EMPLOYERS

Work—Most employers would agree that good employees are difficult to find. They typically are referring to employees who work hard and effectively. Working hard, or the work ethic, has its genesis in the biblical ethic our forefathers brought to this country. Max Weber dubbed it the Protestant Ethic. The Apostle Paul espoused it when he wrote to the Colossians, "Whatever you do, *do your work heartily*, as for the Lord rather than for men" (Col. 3:23, emphasis added; also see Rom. 14:6-9; 1 Cor. 10:31; Col. 3:17).

One of my earliest memories of work involves being encouraged by a fellow worker to follow him around so he could teach me how to look busy and generate the impression I was working hard while not really doing much. (I neither followed him nor practiced his deception.) But we do not have to go this far to cheat our employers out of our wages. Halfhearted work qualifies as theft; habitual tardiness and early departures are no better than stealing; taking advantage of sick-leave policies to go hunting or to just rest when one is not "up to par" are dishonest behaviors; and wasting time talking with others (two or more people are now taken from their work) is a violation of the Eighth Commandment regarding stealing. This point even applies to evangelizing on the job during business hours when both persons should be doing what they were employed to do. Doing justice means we will give a full day's work for a full day's pay.

Stewarding resources—Employees have many opportunities to practice responsible stewardship over the assets entrusted to them—from the selection of hotel accommodations and food on a business trip to the careful preparation of a capital budget that will eventually compete with similar requests for a company's limited resources. Another everyday example is the perception that there is nothing wrong with taking business supplies home for personal use. However, it is absolutely unethical to use business materials at home without explicit permission. We must be faithful in small things before Christ will trust us with larger responsibilities (see Matt. 25:21). The possible illustrations are many, but if we are aware that we have such stewardship responsibilities, it is not too hard to figure out what is just and right with regard to the use of business property.

Obeying policies—A general biblical principle regarding submission tells us we are to take seriously our obligation to do what those in authority over us ask of us, so long as the request does not contradict God's expressed will (see Eph. 5:21; 6:5-9; Col. 3:22; 1 Tim. 6:1-2; 1 Pet. 2:13-17). An owner or a manager has the responsibility to determine which policies will help the business reach its goals most effectively. Persons placed in positions of responsibility may, therefore, establish policies regarding everything from outlining dress codes (for reasons of safety or the projection of a business image) to prohibiting employees from accepting invitations to sporting events as guests of suppliers and customers. (Christ gave directions to us for combing our hair and washing our face to guard what may be communicated when we fast [see Matt. 6:16-18].)

Loyalty—Biblically, loyalty and faithfulness are closely related. So long as we choose to work for people in an organization, we are obligated to respect and protect their good name and to avoid all conduct that might undermine their or the business's reputation in the marketplace. Bad-mouthing an employer—whether off duty or on duty—is unrighteous conduct. Or accepting employment with an organization that has a quality training program, with the intention of leaving after garnering the benefits of the training, is deceitful and disloyal. Being careless with proprietary information in the marketplace or intentionally using it to secure employment with a competitor is also absolutely unethical. Doing justice to employers covers these and many more concerns.

DOING JUSTICE TO EMPLOYEES

Compensation—Although the free market system has over time enhanced the physical standard of living for a larger proportion of society's population than any other economic system, the free market is still not devoid of rather wide-spread compensation injustices. Israel enjoyed a predominantly free market during its biblical days, but the prophet Malachi was moved by God to pronounce His imminent judgment on persons "who oppress the wage earner in his wages" (Mal. 3:5).

In our country, the gap between the incomes of those in the top fifteen percent of the income scale and those in the bottom fifteen percent continues to widen. Executives in the United States, for example, earn approximately ten times what the average employee earns, while in Japan the ratio is about four to one. These differences reflect pervasive ethical values that influence the market, and not some natural economic law.

Compensation discrimination occurring along sex and race lines reflects entrenched and perverted values. The same can be said for the compensation packages frequently offered to top executives but not generally to those in lower echelons. Profit sharing and stock option plans, for example, should be as readily available for one class of workers as another. Economic laws alone do not determine equity in the marketplace.

Stewardship of ideas—Our economic system rewards managers and monetarily discriminates against laborers on the grounds that managers are the innovators and risk bearers while laborers contribute little besides their physical and technical skills. This position is not realistic when examined in the light of the experiences of organizations that encourage and reward employees for creative ideas and stewardly conduct. The lower ranks seem as capable of innovative thinking as managers. Supervisors who want to glorify God should search for ways to encourage and release the creative abilities of their subordinates so that their greatest possible contribution can be achieved and their highest potential developed. It is incumbent upon every steward to provide opportunities for others to grow and assume meaningful responsibility.

Health and safety—God's precepts assert that "when you build a new house, you shall make a parapet for your roof, that you may not bring bloodguilt on your house if anyone falls from it" (Deut. 22:8). From that statement and similar ones, we can rightly conclude that health and safety are equated with bloodguiltiness in the mind of God and should therefore be extremely important to us. It is no violation of the intent of God's Word to carry this interest in health and safety to the point of being concerned about stress in the workplace and its effect on the health and well-being of workers' family life. For example, too much overtime work, though financially rewarding in the short run, can be detrimental to health and family needs in the long run. Justice demands that we have a sincere concern for the health and safety of our employees on the job.

Discrimination—Discrimination is an inherent part of the natural order and an essential component of choice. We all must make decisions involving some process of selection that automatically results in discrimination. Moral judgments are essentially discriminatory. Unjust discrimination, however, is the result of improper judgments, and that is at the center of our society's historic concern regarding this entire issue. At the very core of unjust discrimination lies the use of inappropriate criteria for making moral judgments. Unjust discrimination reveals an ungodly form of favoritism and rejection that violates biblical norms. God is not a respecter of persons, and unjust discrimination is an abomination to Him (see Deut. 10:17; Acts 10:34; Rom. 2:11; Eph. 6:9; Col. 3:25; James 2:1-9; 1 Pet. 1:17). The first line of defense against unjust discrimination must be constructed in our thinking as we realize that our "old nature" will automatically become protective and defensive when our psychological comfort is threatened. This perverted reflex is at the root of discrimination and generally reveals personal insecurities or false pride.

DOING JUSTICE TO PEERS

Building up, tearing down—The apostles gave Joseph of Cyprus the name of Barnabas, which means Son of Encouragement, because of his propensity to build up his fellow workers (see Acts 4:36). He enhanced life and elevated people's worth by encouraging their good while simultaneously covering their sin and deficiencies with love. Barnabas, as you remember, did not abandon John Mark when Paul refused to let him go on the second missionary journey (see Acts 15:36-41). Love covers a multitude of transgressions and problems (see Ps. 32:1; Prov. 10:12; James 5:20; 1 Pet. 4:8). Love encourages the best, even in the face of inadequacies. Personal insecurities, bitterness, jealousy, and an unforgiving spirit frequently generate gossip, sow seeds of distrust, find fault in others, and impugn the reputation of others. God hates all these things. Justice cries for the spirit of Barnabas and repudiates the spirit that tears others down. We are to build up our peers in an honest, constructive manner.

Crediting others—Plagiarism is not confined to the academic world or the profession of writing. Taking personal credit for good ideas or results for which others deserve recognition is rampant in the world of business, too. For example, a group leader can easily report to a superior and imply (if not overtly claim) that the positive results coming from the group ought to be credited to the leader rather than group members who actually made the specific contributions. The biblical standard calls us to look out for the interests of others, not just our own (see Rom. 15:1-2; 1 Cor. 10:24; Phil. 2:4). Stealing credit is just that—stealing! Justice demands that credit be accurately awarded as surely as it requires the careful placement of blame.

Helping—Bearing one another's burdens fulfills a vital aspect of the law of love (see Gal. 6:2), that of helping our peers (and others) who may be overwhelmed with their work at a time when we are free to assist them. Being of help (bearing their burdens) can run the gamut from stuffing envelopes to performing computer tasks at our work station that can be reintegrated into their work at a later point. Righteousness expressed in this form does two things: It lightens the load while reducing the pressure, and it expresses an interest in and concern for the individual being helped. This is doing justice in the marketplace.

DOING JUSTICE TO CUSTOMERS

Truth telling—At the point of sale, when the seller and the buyer meet face to face, the seller has opportunities to be "less than candid" to make the sales offer appealing. Stretching the truth, exaggerating performance expectations, being silent when less than positive facts ought to be shared, answering questions with half-truths, and making promises that cannot be kept are all ethical temptations. The inevitable rationalizations accompanying such behavior are generally grounded in the belief that statements "smoothing the way" are insignificant. If people truly believed such behavior was insignificant, though, they would avoid it and build their reputation on impeccable integrity, which God desires. God cannot ignore such self-promoting behavior. He hates lying in any form, and broken promises violate His will. David once asked and noted,

> O LORD, who may abide in Thy tent?
> Who may dwell on Thy holy hill?
> He who walks with integrity, and works righteousness,
> And speaks truth in his heart . . .
> [And] swears to his own hurt, and does not change. (Ps. 15:1-2, 4)

Quality/price—Tampering with a product's quality while maintaining the price, or even raising it (without disclosing the intended change), is likened to harlotry by God (see Isa. 1:21-22). In a world of material abundance, the opportunities to adversely alter quality yet maintain existing price structures in highly competitive markets facing rising costs are temptations many succumb to. If the product can be reengineered to reduce costs without adversely affecting the quality, that is good stewardship. But reducing a product's quality while maintaining its price is deceitful. The intentions of the heart are always open before God, and we must avoid self-serving rationalizations in such matters and carry out justice in the marketplace for our customers. God's requirements for behavior and standards are clearly devoid of even the appearance of deception or dishonesty, and ours ought to be, too.

Service—Because the United States economy is rapidly becoming service oriented, doing justice in service areas is going to become much more ethically significant. It is important to meet the expectations for service we generate at the time of the original sale. To do less is to perpetuate injustice. For example, the quality of replacement parts used in servicing products should be a major concern of persons offering the service. Customers need to be made aware of their choices as to quality of replacement parts and the extent of the service made available. To illustrate, if a new fully warranted (three years) electric motor costing $785 is available as a replacement, and a rebuilt motor with a ninety-day warranty is also available for $350, the customer needs to be fully informed of these options and allowed to choose accordingly. Otherwise, potential problems and the appearance of deception cannot be avoided in the future. If the owner assumed a new motor was installed, but the cheaper motor was used and it broke down in 250 days, a misunderstanding is obviously at hand. Although customers can bring disappointments on themselves by "sharp bargaining" and the self-generation of false expectations, Christians should make every effort not to create those situations or allow them to develop. Clarifying actions should be taken up front to minimize this possibility.

DOING JUSTICE TO COMPETITORS

Pirating—Efforts to secure proprietary information from competitors, which are widespread in many industries, are simply forms of stealing. Such activity can occur intentionally by hiring personnel from a competitor, by attempting to purchase inside information from willing informants, by collecting a competitor's trash and searching it for revealing information, or by taking the competitor's product and making just enough minor alterations to it to claim that the differences are significant and not an encroachment on a patent or copyright. Competing in this manner is really an admission that the perpetrator is incapable, for whatever reason, of being a genuine leader on individual merits and must therefore cheat to gain an advantage. It is a form of stealing that is as wrong as robbing a bank.

Intentional attacks—Does the Bible ever encourage or permit the intentional hurting of someone? Can God delight in one human trying to tear another one down? No! We are told, "Do not rejoice when your enemy falls, and do not let your heart be glad when he stumbles; lest the LORD see it and be displeased" (Prov. 24:17-18). Efforts such as employing "disinformation" and the intentional fanning of harmful rumors are ungodly behaviors. The Scripture warns us not to delight in another's troubles; any form of acrimonious competition between people in the marketplace is called "vanity and striving after wind" (Eccles. 4:4). Scripture never urges us to focus on our neighbors in an effort to get ahead of them. Instead, we are to use our imagination, creativity, resources, and abilities so that we can glorify God as we serve others. Competition is a fact of life and a part of the natural law operating in a fallen world, but it is not the purpose behind business or the motivating force for Christians.

Respect—We are commanded to love our enemies (make a commitment to act in a godly way for their best interest), so it is not asking too much of us to love those who work beside us in the marketplace, offering alternatives to our products and services. These people are surely not our enemies but fellow sojourners who are also attempting to exercise dominion over the created order. We are to respect them and avoid all demeaning and disrespectful conduct that could reflect adversely on them. We are to be kind and build up their self-worth when it is in our power to do so. Acknowledging another's success, complimenting (encouraging) the other's integrity, and gracefully handling our own successes in the presence of our competitors are all part of doing justice in the marketplace. Christ would have us do no less.

DOING JUSTICE TO OWNERS

Financial fidelity—In the "Editor's Perspective" following Larry Burkett's chapter (pages 248-250), I discussed the "business investment" subject of corporate directors and managers becoming owners of the very corporations they had been managing through leveraged buyouts (LBOs). The inherent conflict of interest in those particular circumstances was described and the practice denounced. For an agent who represents a body of owners to profit at the owners' expense is simply unethical. The same conflict of interest issues are present when managers and directors take actions to provide themselves with special monetary benefits (extraordinary severance pay known as "golden parachutes," for example) should an unwelcomed corporate raider buy the business and then dismiss them. This practice is self-serving and seldom in the best interest of the owners, even though it is widespread today. Still other directors and managers create what have been called "poison pills," which are designed to set in motion, at the conclusion of a takeover, specific disruptive policies that would create adverse financial conditions in the acquired firm. They do this to discourage potential uninvited buyers from trying to take over the business. Behavior of this kind is also highly unethical, for it drives away legitimate buyers who might benefit the existing owners. LBOs, "poison pills," and "golden parachutes" are all unethical practices.

Compensation—In a free market economy, one would hope to see some correlation between the salaries executives earn and the level of efficiency and productivity of the organizations they manage. Such a correlation does not exist. There is a correlation, however, between the size of the corporations (dollars of sales) and the salaries of the chief executive officers. There is a great deal more interest in corporate mergers and acquisitions that create larger economic units than there is in pursuing relationships that might result in greater efficiency and productivity. That size represents financial power has proven more valuable to the personal interests of the executives than has the rate of return on equity or the return on a dollar of sales. Doing justice for the owners would mean that efficiency and productivity play a more significant role in the evaluation of officers and their financial rewards than they do. This compensation issue raises a fundamental question about the accountability (and ultimately the legitimacy) of corporate management in larger corporations where the owners are numerous, scattered, and unable to monitor the directors and managers. Directors and managers in the largest corporations have ascended to their seats of power through means other than ownership and are able to self-perpetuate themselves with little accountability apart from the internal standards they established. This does not create the best climate for doing justice to the owners.

DOING JUSTICE TO GOVERNMENT

Obedience—A careful reading of Romans 13:1-7, Titus 3:1-2, and 1 Peter 2:13-17 makes it abundantly clear that God is the establisher of governments; He has established governments to be His ministers for good; we are to obey and live in submission to the governing authorities; and we are to pay taxes, observe governing customs, honor those in authority, and fear their authority. Therefore, we are to obey the laws in the marketplace, even when we disagree with them. In the 1970s, as federal regulations multiplied, there was an enormous increase in the reporting of businesses breaking the law. The two major reasons offered by businesses at the time for their behavior were that (1) business leaders resented the regulations and chose to ignore them and (2) the economics of breaking the law were better than the economics of obeying the law (that is, the penalties were not severe enough). Such illegal conduct, on both accounts, was wrong. The law, however, should be a minimum (not a maximum) standard for business conduct. While there are certainly some unreasonable and counterproductive government regulations (we must obey these, too), the majority of the concerns embodied in the law are legitimate. Christian businesspeople should, in most cases, exceed the government's standards. Christians should see that God's standards of justice are being met, and if they are, it is unlikely that the government's standards will be higher than those they have voluntarily selected.

DOING JUSTICE TO SOCIETY

Community responsibilities—A major disappointment with modern business is that corporations are often silent and fail to act responsibly on behalf of the larger community interests. As the most powerful economic entities in our communities, they ought to assume responsibility for seeking social justice and economic justice—the two are often inseparable. Business leaders will complain bitterly when local, state, and federal governments pass regulations requiring them to do what they ought to do voluntarily, but they rarely act for social righteousness. For example, no one seriously doubts that automobile emissions and industry pollutants are the principal culprits in the creation of acid rain. Yet industry has done little to seek a solution or to encourage self-regulation in an effort to eliminate the problem. In fact, much lobbying has been conducted to stop or slow the development of emissions regulations. How sad!

Christians in the marketplace should lead efforts encouraging self-regulation, and if this fails, they should be prepared to seek public assistance in bringing about justice in the marketplace through incentives (first) and, if necessary, through legal mandate. Someone must look out for the general public's interest. I would like to see business leaders in the forefront of such concerns so that those who govern have less reason to further regulate business.

Companies generally avoid public involvement in social issues, such as public housing or voter registration matters, but the leaders of our largest corporations should speak out as community leaders for social justice or economic justice whenever they discern its absence. Christians must learn to take seriously the reality that "like a trampled spring and a polluted well is a righteous man who gives way before the wicked" (Prov. 25:26). Christians must call for justice and righteousness wherever they are perverted.

LOOKING BACK

The following statement was made in the Preface (page 9) of the first book in this series, *Biblical Principles and Business: The Foundations*:

> The three overarching objectives of the series are (1) to encourage the development of a mature Christian world view . . . that encompasses bus-iness, economics, and public policy; (2) to demonstrate the application and integration of Scripture with the concerns of business, economics, and public policy in order to assist the development of a Christian world view; and (3) to encourage a *response* to God's revealed will regarding business, economics, and public policy, so that *justice* will be done in the

marketplace. The first two are means to this end: doing justice. God has called us (hundreds of times in Scripture) to *do* justice, and many of these calls come in the context of the marketplace. The prophet Micah's call "to do justice, to love kindness, and to walk humbly with your God" (6:8) was in such a context (see 2:1-2, 9; 6:9-13; 7:1-6). This series of books is devoted to stimulating a response to God's active call.

The examples just given of doing justice to employers, employees, peers, customers, competitors, owners, government, and society barely scratch the surface of what is embodied in Micah's call to do justice in the marketplace, but they are a start. Christians in the marketplace must explore, with God's help (biblical study, prayer, and fellowship in a Christian accountability group), how to realize God's call to do justice where they work.

Being salt and light in the marketplace depends on our attitudes, motives, and actions, which ought to manifest a loving concern for the accomplishment of justice. Our love needs to be expressed "in such a way" (Matt. 5:16) that it truly reflects God's means and ends, so that those who see it are affected by it. They will ultimately have to acknowledge to God that they were without excuse when they resisted justice. To do this requires a good deal of wisdom, but we lack such wisdom only when we fail to ask God for it, because He delights in providing it (see James 1:5).

It is also fair to ask at this juncture if the biblical principles we have been endeavoring to discover and apply in the first three books of this series have been exhausted or are still unfathomed. I believe the answer is yes in both cases—exhausted and unfathomed.

We are to take Christ literally when He tells us that all the Law and the Prophets depend on and are embodied in the two great commandments calling us to love the Lord our God with all our heart, soul, mind, and strength, and to love our neighbors as ourselves. There is really nothing more to be added to these two statutes; they exhaust the intent of God's revelation.

But we all need a great deal more understanding of the commandments. In His mercy and kindness, God has helped us with this by revealing His mind to us from many perspectives and in many situations. He is unchanging, but the insights we gain from the amplified view of His administration of the law of love are incredibly important to our comprehension of the breadth and depth of what is involved in loving God and loving our neighbor. So it can be truthfully said that the principles are still unfathomed. The intent of the law, however, is made much clearer to our spiritual eyes through the many biblical illustrations.

Only modest repetition has appeared in the work of the scholars who participated in the creation of the forty-two chapters in these first three volumes.

Words like *integrity* and *honesty* are repeated, but by and large the principles continue to be fresh as to their content (although love is at the heart of each) and their application. We should expect the application of the unchanging eternal verities to remain fresh over the centuries, though, as systems, structures, technology, and procedures change. The unchanging eternal verities, which reflect the unchanging character of God, their Author, are being applied.

LOOKING FORWARD

All of the biblical principles identified during the work on this series will be reviewed at the conclusion of the fourth volume, *Biblical Principles and Economics: A Just Society*. This volume will also add new principles (new to this series) and examine the application of biblical principles to a national policy on income distribution, unemployment, health care, resource/environment policy, education, public welfare, national security, monetary/banking policy, government regulation of business, taxation, foreign trade, and agriculture. These are the toughest issues to deal with because they pull us away from the application of biblical principles in the realm of personal ethics and carry us into the arena of public policy where Scripture is less explicit. This changes the dynamics and confronts the scholars with tough challenges of application. Dr. Carl F.H. Henry leads the way by establishing the clear link between the Bible and public policy. The other twelve scholars follow with the identification of the biblical principles that apply to the respective public policy areas. It is an exciting book with which to conclude the series.

NOTES

PREFACE

1. Material of this type (what the Bible says to Christians in the marketplace about power, fairness, accountability, etc.) is covered in considerable detail in *Business Through the Eyes of Faith*, by Richard Chewning, John Eby, and Shirley Roels (San Francisco: Harper & Row, 1990).

CHAPTER 2

1. Philip Thomas, "Environmental Analysis for Corporate Planning," *Business Horizons*, October 1974, pages 27-38.
2. Edgar Schein, *Organizational Culture and Leadership* (San Francisco: Jossey-Bass Publishers, 1985), pages 233-243.

CHAPTER 4

1. James F. Engel, *Contemporary Christian Communications* (Nashville: Thomas Nelson, 1979), and James F. Engel and H. Wilbert Norton, *What's Gone Wrong With The Harvest?* (Grand Rapids, Mich.: Zondervan, 1975).
2. Richard T. DeGeorge, *Business Ethics*, 2d ed. (New York: Macmillan, 1986).
3. Gene R. Laczniak and Patrick E. Murphy, *Marketing Ethics* (Lexington, Mass.: Lexington Books, 1985).
4. Peter Dickson, *Survival of the Fit* (Columbus: Merrill Publishing, forthcoming).

5. Robert Bartels, "A Model for Ethics in Marketing," *Journal of Marketing* (January 1967), pages 20-26.
6. Patrick E. Murphy and Gene R. Laczniak, "Marketing Ethics: A Review with Implications for Managers, Educators and Researchers," *Review of Marketing–1981*, pages 251-266.
7. Shelby D. Hunt and Scott Vitell, "A General Theory of Marketing Ethics," *Journal of Macromarketing* (Spring 1986), pages 5-16.
8. Geoffrey P. Lantos, "An Ethical Best for Marketing Decision Making," *Journal of Consumer Marketing* (Fall 1986), pages 5-10, and "Ethics Has Its Roots in Judeo-Christian Morality," *Marketing News*, July 18, 1986, pages 41ff.
9. Jack D. Sparks, "W. Arthur Cullman Executive Award Acceptance Speech," in "Edited Proceedings from the Fourth Bi-Annual W. Arthur Cullman Symposium—Fostering Corporate Citizenship: Governments—Universities—Corporations," ed. W. Wayne Talarzyk (Columbus: Ohio State University Press, 1988).
10. Dennis McCallum, "Toward an Approach to Christian Ethics," *The Xenos Journal* (Fall 1987), pages 77-90.

CHAPTER 8

1. Herbert G. Heneman, III, Daniel P. Schwab, John A. Fossum, and Lee D. Dyer, *Personnel/Human Resource Management*, fourth edition (Homewood, Ill.: Irwin, 1986), Figure 1-1, page 8. Used by permission.
2. This is similar to Cornelius Van Til's Creator/creature distinction.
3. For this discussion, I have relied heavily on G.C. Berkouwer's book *Man: The Image of God* (Grand Rapids, Mich.: Eerdmans, 1962).
4. Edward Henry Bickersteth, *The Trinity* (Grand Rapids, Mich.: Kregel Publications, 1959).

CHAPTER 9

1. Barry Shore, *Introduction to Computer Information Systems* (New York: Holt, Rinehart & Winston, 1988), page 4.
2. Harvey M. Wagner, *Principles of Management Science* (Englewood Cliffs, N. J.: Prentice-Hall, 1975), page 2.
3. Joseph Weizenbaum, "The Last Dream," *Across the Board*, vol. 14, no. 7 (July 1977), pages 34-46.
4. Ronald A. Howard, "An Assessment of Decision Analysis," *Operations Research*, vol. 28, no. 1 (January-February 1980), pages 4-26.

5. Howard, "An Assessment of Decision Analysis," page 6.
6. Milton Friedman, *Capitalism and Freedom* (Chicago: University of Chicago Press, 1962), page 136.
7. John Naisbitt, *Megatrends* (New York: Warner Books, 1984), page 1.
8. Rod Willis, "White Collar Crime," *Management Review*, vol. 75, no. 1 (January 1986), page 26.
9. Irving Howe, *Nineteen Eighty Four Text, Sources, Criticism* (New York: Harcourt, Brace & World, 1963).
10. Joseph M. Mellichamp, "Designing Spacelab's Data Management System with Simulation," *Interfaces*, vol. 9, no. 3 (May 1979), pages 87-93.
11. Chris Wloszczyna, "IBM Settlement," *USA Today*, November 30, 1988, Money Line, Sec. B.
12. Friedman, *Capitalism and Freedom*, page 136.
13. Harold Joseph Highland, "Random Bits and Bytes," *Computers and Security*, vol. 7, no. 2 (1988), pages 117-127.
14. Philip Elmer-DeWitt, "The Kid Put Us Out of Action," *Time*, November 14, 1988, page 76.
15. Christopher Evans, *The Micro Millennium* (New York: Washington Square Press, 1979), and Edward A. Feigenbaum and Pamela McCorduck, *The Fifth Generation* (Reading, Mass.: Addison-Wesley, 1983).
16. Stanley Letovsky, "Ecclesiastes: A Report From the Battlefields of the Mind-Body Problem," *AI Magazine* (Fall 1987), pages 63- 67.
17. Jerome Kagan, "Reflections: On Love and Violence," *Science*, March 1985, pages 28-32.
18. Kagan, "Reflections," page 32.
19. Letovsky, "Ecclesiastes," page 67.
20. Joseph M. Mellichamp, "The 'Artificial' in Artificial Intelligence Is Real," (Artificial Intelligence and the Human Mind: An International Interdisciplinary Symposium, New Haven, Conn., Yale University, March 1-3, 1986).
21. Howard, "An Assessment of Decision Analysis," page 19.
22. Harvey M. Wagner, "Operations Research: A Global Language for Business Strategy," *Operations Research*, vol. 36, no. 5 (September-October 1988), pages 797-803.
23. Wagner, "Operations Research," page 800.
24. Wagner, "Operations Research," page 801.
25. Howard, "An Assessment of Decision Analysis," page 14.
26. Howard, "An Assessment of Decision Analysis," page 8.
27. Howard, "An Assessment of Decision Analysis," page 19.
28. Wagner, "Operations Research," page 802.
29. Weizenbaum, "The Last Dream," page 44.

CHAPTER 10

1. Richard C. Chewning, John Eby, and Shirley Roels, *Business Through the Eyes of Faith* (San Francisco: Harper & Row, 1990), chapter 18.

CHAPTER 13

1. Kenneth Clarkson, Roger L. Miller, and Gaylord A. Jentz, *West's Business Law*, 3d ed. (St. Paul, Minn.: West Publishing Co., 1986), page 4.
2. Romans 13:1-5; Titus 3:1; 1 Peter 2:13-14; see also John Calvin, *Institutes of the Christian Religion*, 4.20.3, "On Civil Government" (Philadelphia: Westminster, 1975).
3. Charles Hodge, *Systematic Theology* (New York: Charles Scribner's Sons, 1893), vol. 3, page 260.
4. "Of the Holy Scriptures," *The Westminster Confession of Faith*, 1.9. See also R. C. Sproul, *Knowing Scripture* (Downers Grove, Ill.: InterVarsity, 1977), page 46.
5. Sproul, *Knowing Scripture*, page 46.
6. "Of the Law of God," *The Westminster Confession of Faith*, 19.3-5.
7. *The Westminster Confession of Faith*, 19.4.
8. James B. Jordan, "Calvinism and 'The Judicial Law of Moses,'" *Journal of Christian Reconstruction*, vol. 5, no. 2 (Winter 1978–1979), page 41.
9. Jordan, "Calvinism and 'The Judicial Law of Moses,'" page 30.
10. Greg L. Bahnsen, *Theonomy In Christian Ethics* (Nutley, N.J.: Craig Press, 1977), page 34.
11. Marcus Tullius Cicero, *De Legibus*, 1.15, in *Hoyt's New Cyclopedia of Practical Quotations*, Kate Louise Roberts ed. (New York: Funk & Wagnalls Co., 1922), page 413.
12. *Black's Law Dictionary*, 4th ed. (St. Paul, Minn.: West Publishing Co., 1951), page 1480.
13. It should be noted that *recompense* is also used in the sense of reward for doing good.
14. John A. Sparks, "The Reconstruction of the Criminal Law: Retribution Revived," *Journal of Christian Reconstruction* (Winter 1976–1977), pages 128-138.
15. C. S. Lewis, "The Humanitarian Theory of Punishment," *The Twentieth Century: An Australian Quarterly Review*, vol. 3, no. 3 (1949), pages 5-12, reprinted in *God in the Dock*, Walter Hooper ed. (Grand Rapids, Mich.: Eerdmans, 1970).
16. Francis A. Allen, *The Borderland of Criminal Justice* (Chicago: University

Chicago Press, 1964); also see his "Criminal Justice, Legal Values and the Rehabilitative Ideal," *Journal of Criminal Law, Criminology, and Police Science* (1959), page 226, "Law and the Future: Criminal Law and Administration," *Northwestern University Law Review* (1956), page 207, and "The Borderland of the Criminal Law: Problems of Socializing Criminal Justice," *Social Service Review* (1958), page 107.

17. Arthur L. Harding, ed., *Responsibility In Law and In Morals* (Dallas, Tex.: Southern Methodist University Press, 1960), page 62.

18. For a generally good discussion of negligence in a product case see *Libby-Owens Ford Glass Co. v. L. & M. Paper Co.*, 189 Neb. 792; 205 N. W. 2d 523 (1973).

19. See *Greenman v. Yuba Power Products, Inc.*, 59 Cal. 2d 57; 27 Cal. Rptr. 697; 377 P. 2d 897.

20. *Restatement* (Second) of Torts, section 402A.

21. Richard A. Epstein, *Medical Malpractice, The Case for Contract* (New York: Center for Libertarian Studies, 1979), page 12.

22. Peter H. Schuck, "The New Ideology of Tort Law," *The Public Interest* (Summer 1988), pages 99-100.

23. Rousas John Rushdooney, *The Institutes of Biblical Law* (Nutley, N.J.: Craig Press, 1973), page 86.

24. Harold J. Berman, *Law and Revolution, The Formation of the Western Legal Tradition* (Cambridge, Mass.: Harvard University Press, 1983), page 225.

25. Berman, *Law and Revolution*, pages 246-247 (emphasis added).

26. Berman, *Law and Revolution*, page 247.

27. See Jan Dengerink, "The Idea of Justice in Christian Perspective," *Westminster Theological Journal* (Fall 1976), page 16. The other three principles according to Grotius were (1) the principle of mine and thine, which states that we should refrain from taking what belongs to someone else; (2) the principle that we must compensate others for injury that we have caused them by our fault; and (3) the principle that violations of natural and positive laws must be punished (pages 15-16).

28. Samuel von Pufendorf, "On Keeping Faith and on the Divisions of Obligations," in *On the Law of Nature and Nations*, quoted in George C. Christie, *Jurisprudence* (St. Paul, Minn.: West Publishing Co., 1973), page 210.

29. H. B. Clark, *Biblical Law*, page 179, as quoted in Rushdooney, *Institutes*, pages 145, 380.

30. St. George Tucker, ed., *Blackstone's Commentaries* (1803; reprint, New York: Augustus M. Keeley Publishers, 1969), vol. 3, page 472.

31. Berman, *Law and Revolution*, page 352.

32. Hadley Arkes, *First Things, An Inquiry Into the First Principles of Morals and Justice* (Princeton, N.J.: Princeton University Press, 1986), page 18.
33. Arkes, *First Things*, page 18 (emphasis added).
34. Tucker, ed., *Blackstone's Commentaries*, vol. 3, page 2.
35. Gary North, "From Covenant to Contract: Pietism and Secularism in Puritan New England, 1691–1720," *Journal of Christian Reconstruction*, vol. 6, no. 2 (Winter 1979–1980), page 156.
36. Calvin, *Institutes*, 2.8.45, page 408.
37. Calvin, *Institutes*, 4.20.3, page 1488.
38. Charles Foster Kent, *Israel's Laws and Legal Precedents* (New York: Charles Scribner's Sons, 1907), pages 120ff.
39. Kent, *Israel's Laws and Legal Precedents*, pages 120ff., and Job 24:2; Proverbs 22:28; 23:10; Hosea 5:10.
40. Madeleine S. Miller and J. Lane Miller, eds., *Harper's Bible Dictionary* (New York: Harper & Row, 1973), pages 281, 512-513.
41. David Chilton, *Productive Christians In An Age of Guilt Manipulators* (Tyler, Tex.: Institute for Christian Economics, 1981), page 138.
42. Ronald J. Sider, *Rich Christians In An Age of Hunger* (Downers Grove, Ill.: InterVarsity, 1977), pages 88-90.
43. Sider, *Rich Christians In An Age of Hunger*, page 88.
44. See Luke 4:17-20 in which Christ quotes the language of release and Jubilee of Isaiah 61 and says the references are to Him.